ILLUSTRATED GUIDE TO FOOD PREPARATION

ILLUSTRATED GUIDE TO FOOD PREPARATION

Eighth Edition

by
Margaret McWilliams, Ph.D., R.D.
Professor Emeritus
California State University, Los Angeles

Published by Plycon Press

Other Books by the Author

Foods: Experimental Perspectives, 3rd ed.
Merrill, 1997

Experimental Foods Laboratory Manual, 4th ed.
Plycon Press, 1994

Food Fundamentals, 7th ed.
Plycon Press, 1998

Nutrition for the Growing Years, 5th ed.
Plycon Press, 1993

Fundamentals of Meal Management, 3rd ed.
Plycon Press, 1997

Meatless Cookbook
Plycon Press, 1974

Living Nutrition, 4th ed.
(with Frederick Stare, Ph.D., M.D.)
Macmillan, 1984

Nutrition for Good Health, 2nd ed.
Stickley, 1982

Modern Food Preservation
(with Harriett Paine)
Plycon Press, 1977

Understanding Food
(with Lendal Kotschevar)
Wiley, 1969

Food For You, 2nd ed.
(with Linda Davis)
Ginn, 1976

World of Nutrition
(with Holly Heller)
Ginn, 1988

Main Office Enquiries:	Book Orders:
Plycon Press	**Plycon Press**
c/o Main Office	c/o Orders/Billing
P.O. Box 220	2487 Duraznitos Rd.
Redondo Beach, CA 90277	Ramona, CA 92065
Phone: (310)379-9725	Phone: (760)788-9455
FAX: (310)798-2834	FAX: (760)788-4627

PREFACE

Who would have thought that learning could have such immediate and satisfying rewards as you will experience while you work your way through this book! Granted, the study of food with its technical and scientific foundations certainly presents academic challenges, but you also will encounter great food that illustrates the principles you are studying. I am sure you will find your work in the foods laboratory will not only help you build a strong foundation in this field, but also will stimulate you to develop an adventurous and enthusiastic attitude toward food preparation.

Remember, the satisfaction that food provides is determined by the quality of its preparation. This manual is designed to illustrate the scientific principles underlying food preparation while also emphasizing the techniques that are essential to assure production of tempting, pleasing food. In short, this manual will help you develop the foundation needed for a lifetime of good eating. New recipes have been added and some others have been modified in this edition to reflect some of the evolving trends in the nation's food tastes and the increasing variety of ingredients.

This revision of *Illustrated Guide to Food Preparation* has focused on recipes that incorporate the U.S. Dietary Guidelines while also including those recipes that are needed to illustrate key scientific principles. Wherever feasible, the levels of fat and the amount of salt often have been reduced to conform to current nutrition practice. If you are seeking other ways of reducing fat, substitution of nonfat milk for whole milk in recipes may prove useful.

Each chapter is complete individually and may be studied at any point in the term, according to the sequence chosen by your professor. When this book is integrated with *Food Fundamentals* (by **Plycon Press**) or other basic food preparation text, you will have the complete system needed for studying foods. The emphasis in this book is placed on interrelating principles with practice to achieve functional laboratory skills and to develop the knowledge needed to evaluate food accurately.

Special recognition goes to Paul F. Peterson, whose photographs throughout this manual serve as invaluable illustrations to clarify numerous steps in the preparation of selected foods.

My hope is that you will gain a deeper appreciation for and interest in food as a science and an art as you pursue your study of food and its preparation. May you have many years of pleasure and success in your career and in your own kitchen!

Margaret McWilliams
Redondo Beach, California
June, 1998

Photograph Acknowledgments

California Milk Advisory Board
American Egg Board
National Presto Industries
Pineapple Growers Association of Hawaii
CA Fresh Market Tomato Advisory Board
CA Iceberg Lettuce Commission
CA Prune Board
CA Table Grape Commission
CA Tree Fruit Agreement
CA Department of Health Services
Sunkist Growers, Inc.
Durum Wheat Institute
California Egg Advisory Board
American Egg Board
Coffee Development Group
Processed Meats Committee of the National Livestock and Meat Board
American Egg Board
Betty Crocker, Division of General Mills, Inc.
Pet Incorporated
The Sugar Association
The Coffee Development Group
Sunkist Growers, Inc.
Sunkist Growers, Inc.
National Presto Industries, Inc.

TABLE OF CONTENTS

Chapter 1
Laboratory Basics

Welcome to the foods laboratory! Here you will have exciting moments as you begin to develop your laboratory skills and knowledge of food and how to prepare it to allow you to produce tempting and satisfying products. There is much to learn about both the preparation and the evaluation of the foods you have prepared. Be sure to let your head, as well as your appetite, participate throughout each lab.

SAFE FOOD HANDLING

Food safety (definitely an unglamorous topic) is essential to your work in the foods lab and anytime you are preparing food. A lapse in your attention to this subject can result in a variety of illnesses that can lead to considerable discomfort and even death (yours or those who have eaten your food). Because of the importance of good safety practices whenever food is involved, you will want to establish good personal habits when handling food. Be sure to develop the following habits so that you always will:

1. Cover hair or tie it back before entering the lab.
2. Wash hands thoroughly with hot water and soap before handling food.
3. Be sure to turn away from food and cover your mouth and nose when sneezing and/or coughing.
4. Wash hands with hot water and soap anytime you have blown your nose, coughed, sneezed, touched your hair or mouth, or have been to the bathroom.
5. Use only clean spoons for tasting. Drop tasting spoons in the sink or other designated area and do not reuse them. Never use your fingers for tasting food.
6. Maintain a clean kitchen and avoid contaminating food while preparing it.
7. Keep protein-containing foods chilled or sufficiently hot to minimize risk from bacteria.
8. Always use the serving silver to transfer samples from the serving table to your taste plate. Never use your personal silver to obtain samples from the display or serving table.
9. Be sure to always have very, very hot water and plenty of soap in the water being used to wash dishes. Rinse thoroughly with scalding water.

KEY CONCEPTS — SAFE FOOD HANDLING

1. Food has the potential for making people ill unless it is handled with careful attention to sanitation and temperature control.

2. Each person preparing or otherwise handling food must assume individual responsibility for personal habits to avoid contaminating the food.

The equivalent measures in the table below are often utilized in altering recipes. Be sure to make them part of your working tools in the laboratory. You can memorize them quickly, which will help you save time and avoid possible mistakes in your work.

EQUIVALENT MEASURES	
1 tbsp (tablespoon)	= 3 tsp (teaspoon)
2 tbsp	= 1 fl oz (fluid ounce)
4 tbsp	= 1/4 c (cup)
5 1/3 tbsp	= 1/3 c
8 tbsp	= 1/2 c
16 tbsp	= 1 c
8 fl oz	= 1 c
2 c	= 1 pt (pint)
4 c	= 2 pt = 1 qt (quart)
4 qt	= 1 gal (gallon)
16 oz	= 1 lb (pound)

DRY INGREDIENTS

FLOUR

To measure flour (either cake or all purpose), the flour should be sifted once prior to measuring. The sifting process helps to lighten the flour enough to allow sufficiently accurate measurement by volume. This sifting can be done with a sifter or a strainer directly onto waxed paper. Let the flour fall lightly on the paper. Sift only *once* before measuring. Recipes are developed for measures of sifted flour.

Lightly spoon the flour into the appropriate graduated measuring cup. Be careful not to pack flour at this point, and avoid bumping the cup or jarring it in any way that would cause the flour to become more compact. The graduated measuring cups (also called Mary Ann cups) are appropriate for measuring all ingredients except liquids. These cups are designed so that the ingredients can be scraped off to give a level measure. This provides important accuracy in food preparation. Remember, this technique is used to help standardize flour measurements. The goal is *not* to see how much flour can be packed into the cup.

Without packing the flour, use a spatula to scrape off the extra flour which extends above the top of the cup. Be sure to use the straight portion of the metal blade of the spatula. Avoid the area of the blade which angles in toward the handle. Also avoid the curved area at the end of the blade.

BROWN SUGAR

Brown sugar presents a slightly different problem in measuring than is posed by other dry ingredients. A graduated measuring cup still is the utensil of choice. However, the sugar is *packed lightly* into the cup until the cup is overflowing. A spatula is used to level the measure. When properly measured, brown sugar will be packed just firmly enough to hold the shape of the container when it is turned out after measurement is completed. This packing technique is needed because brown sugar packs very non-uniformly without pressure. Only light pressure, rather than heavy pressure, is expected when brown sugar measurements are being made.

OTHER DRY INGREDIENTS

Sugar, cornmeal, rice, and other dry ingredients can be measured simply by spooning them directly into the appropriate graduated measuring cup. For greatest accuracy in measuring, use as few of the cups as possible. For example, greater accuracy probably will be achieved by measuring 3/4 cup of rice using a 1/2 cup and a 1/4 cup measure rather than by simply filling the 1/4 cup measure 3 times.

Measuring of dry ingredients always is completed by leveling the heaping cup with the straight portion of the blade of a metal spatula.

SMALLER AMOUNTS

When dry ingredients are needed in amounts less than 1/4 cup, graduated measuring spoons are used in place of the graduated measuring cups. Most measuring spoon sets consist of a tablespoon, a teaspoon, a half teaspoon, and a quarter teaspoon. Amounts smaller than these can only be estimated. The appropriate spoon is heaped more than full with the ingredient to be measured, and then a spatula is used to level the measure.

SOLID FATS

Solid shortenings, butter, margarine, and lard also are measured in graduated measuring cups. For accuracy, the fat should be pressed firmly into the cup so that any air pockets are eliminated. This step is necessary because of the inability of the hard fat to flow at all.

After the appropriate graduated measuring cup has been packed full of fat, a spatula is used to level the measure. Care should be taken to be certain that only the straight portion of the blade is being used to level the fat.

LIQUIDS

A glass measuring cup is the appropriate device for measuring liquids. The cup should be placed on a flat, level surface to help promote accurate measurement. The ingredient should be poured in the cup only to the appropriate mark. The reading should be made by bending over so that the eye is even with the desired level in the cup. This avoids the distortion which occurs when the measure is taken by looking down on the cup. Glass measuring cups are suitable only for measuring liquids because it is not possible to level other types of ingredients accurately in the cup. The extra space above the cup measure in a glass cup is designed to prevent spills while lifting the cup from the counter to the mixing bowl.

Liquid ingredients in amounts less than a fourth of a cup are measured with graduated measuring spoons. Ingredients should be measured over an empty bowl or over the container holding the ingredient. Measurements are not made over a bowl containing other ingredients because of the possibility of spilling extra amounts into the product. Liquids should be poured slowly to avoid overflowing the measure.

THE METRIC SYSTEM

KEY CONCEPTS — METRIC SYSTEM

1. The metric system is the common system for expressing volume, weight, and temperature in most countries today.

2. Knowledge of a few basic equivalencies and terminology will make conversion between metric and household units comparatively easy.

The metric system has been the means of weighing and measuring in Europe and most other parts of the world for a very long time. However, the United States has based its recipes (and must of its industry) on cups and pounds, not liters and kilograms. Length is stated in inches and yards, not in meters; temperature is in Fahrenheit, not in Celsius.

These differences in weighing and measuring systems sound rather insignifcant, yet they are the source of many problems in international trade. Because of the economic and trade difficulties arising from these differences, the United States several years ago legislated to convert to the metric system over a 10-year period. Large investments were made in industry and in education to prepare for this crucial change. However, the momentum for making the change gradually was lost during the transition period.

Despite the fact that consumers in the United States may not be converting to metrics, professionals still need to be able to interpret units of weights and measures in the metric system, for the technical and industrial world exists today in an international setting, and the language of that setting is the metric system.

The language of technical laboratories where research and development are done in food companies also is metric. Food technologists and other scientists working in these competitive laboratories must be totally familiar with the metric system and be able to work with it. They also must be able to convert recipes into consumer language, our present system of weights and measures.

Although the metric system is not a fact of life in the American home, the ability to convert to and from the metric system is essential to food professionals. They also will need to be functional in the metric system itself. Although the metric system includes a logical organization based on units of ten, it still is necessary to be familiar with the prefixes and the basic measures of weights, volumes, and lengths of the metric system. The key information for application to the food industry, including temperature conversion, is presented below.

The prefixes for the units which are used commonly in food preparation are:

$$kilo \ = 1,000 \ = 10^3$$
$$centi = 1/100 \ = 10^{-2}$$
$$milli = 1/1000 = 10^{-3}$$

Conversions can be made readily if the following equivalencies are known:

Weights:
    1 kilogram (kg) = 2.2 pounds (lb)
    1 lb = 454 grams (g)

Volumes:
    1 liter (l) = 1.06 quarts
    1 cup = 236 milliliters (ml)

Lengths:
    1 meter (m) = 39.37 inches (in)
    1 inch = 2.54 centimeters (cm)

The formulae for converting temperature are:

$$^\circ C \ = 5/9(^\circ F - 32)$$
$$^\circ F \ = (9/5 \times {}^\circ C) + 32$$

Calculate the following equivalencies:

    1 1/2 c   = _____ ml
    472 ml   = _____ c
    3.3 lb   = _____ kg

```
5 kg    = _____ lb
9 in    = _____ cm
25 cm   = _____ in
300° F  = _____ ° C
400° F  = _____ ° C
220° C  = _____ ° F
100° C  = _____ ° F
190° C  = _____ ° F
```

Examples of a recipe for coffee cake in both the metric and standard systems are presented on the next page. Note particularly the use of the *temperature scales* in the two versions, the *pan sizes*, and the designations of *ingredient amounts*.

BLUEBERRY COFFEE CAKE

Metric:		Standard:	
125 ml	*sugar*	1/2 c	sugar
125 ml	*shortening*	1/2 c	shortening
1	*large egg*	1	medium egg
500 ml	*sifted flour*	2 c	flour
10 ml	*baking powder*	2 tsp	baking powder
1 ml	*salt*	1/4 tsp	salt
125 ml	*milk*	1/2 c	milk
500 ml	*blueberries, well drained*	2 c	blueberries, well-drained
125 ml	*brown sugar*	1/2 c	brown sugar
125 ml	*flour*	1/2 c	flour
3 ml	*cinnamon*	1/2 tsp	cinnamon
30 ml	*margarine, melted*	2 tbsp	margarine, melted

Oven: 175° C

1. Preheat oven.
2. Cream the shortening and sugar until light and fluffy.
3. Beat in the well-beaten egg.
4. Sift the dry ingredients together. Add a third of the dry ingredients to the creamed mixture, and stir.
5. Add half the milk, and stir.
6. Repeat with the remaining thirds of dry ingredients alternately with the other half of the milk.
7. Pour into a well-greased pan. Metric: 20 cm x 30 cm.
8. Put blueberries over surface of the batter.
9. Combine brown sugar, flour, cinnamon, and melted margarine, and sprinkle over the blueberries.
10. Bake at 175° C for 35–45 minutes until a toothpick inserted in the center comes out clean.

Oven: 350° F

1. Same as metric.
2. Same as metric.
3. Same as metric.
4. Same as metric.
5. Same as metric.
6. Same as metric.
7. Pour into a well-greased pan. Standard: 8 in x 12 in.
8. Same as metric.
9. Same as metric.
10. Bake at 350° F for 35–45 minutes until a toothpick inserted in the center comes out clean.

TEMPERATURES USED IN COOKING

KEY CONCEPTS — COOKING TEMPERATURES

1. Various temperatures can be used in cooking foods, depending upon the food being heated, the results desired, and the cooking medium.

   a. Water may be heated to lukewarm, scalding, simmering, or boiling to cook foods.

   b. The addition of sugar or salt to cooking water has the potential for altering the temperature at which boiling takes place, but foods that do not ionize or dissolve as very small molecules do not have a significant effect.

   c. Oil can be heated to very high temperatures when frying foods because oil does not boil at frying temperatures.

LABORATORY DEMONSTRATION

1. Place a thermometer in a 1-quart saucepan containing 2 cups water. Heat the water to a boil. In the table, record the appearance of the water at each temperature.

TEMPERATURE	APPEARANCE
104° F or 40° C (Lukewarm)	
149° F or 65 ° C (Scalding)	
180–211° F or 82–99° C (Simmering)	
212° F or 100° C (Boiling)	

2. Place 1 cup water in the bottom of a *double boiler* and 1 cup water in the top portion. Heat until the water in the top of the double boiler comes to a constant temperature. Note the highest temperature reached in the upper unit.

   _____ ° F or _____° C

   Place 1 cup water in a *steamer*. Put the steamer basket in position and cover the assembled unit. Heat the water until it boils and the steamer is well filled with steam. Barely lift the cover enough to insert a thermometer into the steam-filled upper chamber. Quickly note the temperature.

   _____ ° F or _____° C

3. In a 1-quart sauce pan, place 2 cups water. Mark the water level with a wax marking pencil. Heat the water to boiling. When the water boils actively throughout the pan, note the temperature. By tablespoons, add the ingredient assigned, as indicated in the table. After each addition, be sure that the liquid has

returned to an active boil before reading the temperature. As the water level drops below the mark in the pan, add water to maintain the original volume. Record results in the table.

AMOUNT	INGREDIENT ADDED			
	SALT	SUGAR	CORN MEAL	GELATIN[1]
1 tbsp				
2 tbsp				
3 tbsp				
4 tbsp				

[1]Hydrate gelatin (1 envelope in 1/4 c water) before using.

4. Heat 1 cup salad oil in a 1-quart saucepan and complete the table. Place the pan and oil on a cool surface unit of the range to cool.

TEMPERATURE	APPEARANCE OF OIL
212° F or 100° C	
375° F or 190 ° C	

LABORATORY FUNDAMENTALS

PRECAUTIONS WITH HEAT

Hot pads adequate for protecting the hands from any hot pans or hot food should always be available for instant use near the range. To avoid steam burns, which can result when a lid is removed from a pan containing steam and boiling water, always tilt the lid to direct the escaping steam away from the body. This is an important precaution because steam burns can be serious. If a burn does happen, immediately put ice wrapped in paper towel or cloth on the burned area for several minutes, but do not freeze the skin.

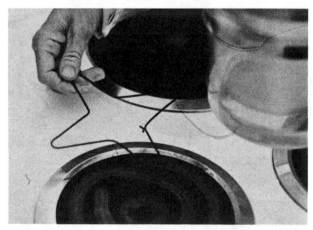

When using Pyrex pans on electric surface units, be sure to first position a wire trivet on the heating element before turning on the unit. Then place the pan on the trivet. The wire trivet helps to distribute the heat without concentrating the energy in a limited area and stressing the material. Be sure to let the wire trivet cool before touching it or removing it from the range.

Hot pans require particular attention if kitchen counters are to remain undamaged over a period of time. Any pan that has been used for frying, deep-fat frying, or pan broiling will be much hotter than the boiling point of water. These pans and skillets should remain on the range, be placed on special metal trivets, or be moved to a metal surface for cooling. Under no circumstance should they be placed immediately on vinyl or formica-covered countertops. The heat will scar the counter surface badly. On the other hand, pans that have been used to boil vegetables or to cook other water-containing items can be put safely on any type of surface commonly used for kitchen counters. The temperature of pans containing water will not cause scarring of the counter.

Pans should always have something in them when they are being heated on the range. Empty pans will be become dangerously hot very quickly, causing warping and possibly creating a fire hazard, too. When using a double boiler, always be certain that there is water remaining in the lower unit. For prolonged heating, it will be necessary to check the level and to add more water if the level has dropped greatly. Proper water level in a double boiler is usually about an inch, but the actual level recommended will vary with the design of the unit. The upper pan should *not* be in contact with the water in the lower pan. Usually, the water should be maintained at a gentle boil, but stirred custard can be prepared better by maintaining the water at simmering.

Be sure pan handles do not extend over another burner or over the edge of the range. For safety, form the habit of holding the handle of a pan with a hot pad whenever the food is being stirred. This practice helps to avoid the possibility of tipping the pan off the burner or of being burned by a hot handle.

A wooden spoon is a useful utensil for stirring foods while they are cooking. The spoon feels comfortable in the hand, and the handle does not get hot as the food heats.

Before beginning to heat an oven, always pull out the rack to its extended position and press down to be sure the rack is locked properly into its slides so that it will not tip down when food is placed on it. This should be done as the first step in preparing any baked item. This is also the time to change the location of the rack if it is not in the correct position. Be sure to check the locking of the rack when the rack is in the desired position.

Broiler pans for oven broiling will vary in design, but they basically will be made to provide some means of protecting the fat and drippings from the very intense heat of the broiler unit. The pans should be used in the manner specified by the manufacturer. This will keep the fat from igniting when meat is being broiled. Aluminum foil should *not* be used to line the rack because it will allow pockets of fat to accumulate on the rack. Since the rack is so close to the heat, there is a likelihood that the fat will ignite and start a broiler fire.

DEEP FAT FRYING

For deep-fat frying, oil should be heated just long enough to bring the oil to 190° C (375° F), the temperature best suited to frying doughnuts. Vegetable oils, such as corn or cottonseed oil, are suitable choices for deep fat frying because of their high smoke points. The oil used in a deep fat fryer can be used several times if suitable precautions are observed. The oil should be heated just long enough to bring it to frying temperature and held at the desired temperature only until the frying is completed. Long heating periods cause the fat molecules to begin to break down to release free fatty acids, glycerol, and eventually, acrolein. This breakdown will cause the smoke point of the oil to begin to drop toward the temperature needed for frying. These breakdown products are detrimental to the flavor of fried foods, and acrolein is irritating to the eyes.

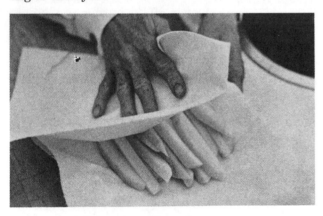

One of the concerns in deep-fat frying is the splattering that can occur. Temperatures used in deep-fat frying are considerably hotter than the temperature of boiling water. If water happens to come in contact with the hot fat, the water will cause an apparent boiling and splattering. To avoid the potential of burns and kitchen cleanup that can result from contact between hot fat and water, dry foods thoroughly before they are placed in the

hot fat. Paper towels are ideal for drying potatoes before they are French-fried or for preparing chicken and other foods for frying.

Use a deep-fat frying thermometer or a heat-controlled element to aid in regulating the temperature used for deep-fat frying. When the fat has reached the correct temperature and the food has been prepared appropriately for frying, use a slotted spoon or a pair of tongs to

place the food in the hot fat. This makes it possible to lower the food into the fat without the risk of the fingers coming in contact with the hot fat. It also minimizes the likelihood of dropping the food into the fat with a splash.

For maximum useful life of fats used for frying, the fat should be strained through cheesecloth after each use. The cheesecloth removes extraneous particles of food that may have remained in the fat after the food was removed. This straining should be done *after* the fat is *cool*. Since oils are the preferred choice for deep-fat frying, there is not a problem with the fat becoming too hard to pour before it is cool enough to handle safely. An empty coffee can or other can with a tightly-fitting plastic lid is ideal for storing the strained fat.

CUTTING TECHNIQUES

Attention needs to be directed in the laboratory at all times toward personal safety as well as toward achievement of high standards of food prepration. Selection of the proper equipment can make many operations easier and faster. Chopping can be done with the aid of a French chef's knife. This type of knife is identified by its large blade, the recessed handle (which permits the fingers to grasp the handle without hitting the knuckles on the chopping board) and the linear, rather than curved cutting edge. The tip of the blade is held in contact with the chopping board continually by gentle pressure from the left hand. The right hand moves the handle up and down to accomplish the chopping motion. For safety and maintenance of good cutting edges, store knives in a rack or sheath.

A utility knife can be used for numerous small cutting operations in the kitchen. Always cut on a cutting board. Avoid holding food in the hand while cutting, and be sure not to cut toward the thumb. The regular use of a cutting board will do much to reduce accidents caused by improper use of knives. The cutting board needs to be scrubbed thoroughly after each use. This practice avoids the possibility of spreading food-borne illnesses when foods come in contact with unclean surfaces.

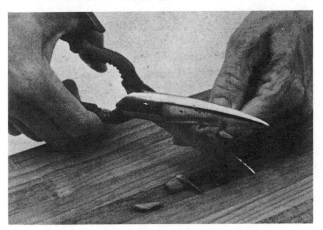

Kitchen shears are useful for a wide number of purposes, ranging from cutting up poultry to snipping the green tops of scallions and parsley. These shears need to be washed thoroughly after each use. They can be washed well in a dishwasher or by hand.

A vegetable peeler provides a quick means of paring potatoes, carrots, and other vegetables. Operate by using long strokes directed away from the body. This device can be used to prepare thin slices of potatoes for potato chips and for making the thin, center slices needed for making carrot curls.

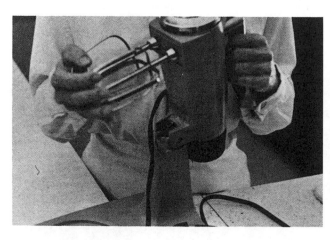

MIXERS

For best results with electric mixers, *read the manufacturer's directions carefully before using*. The beater blades should be inserted with the mixer *unplugged*, and the switch turned to *OFF*. This dual insurance will certainly avoid the possibility of having the blades begin to spin while they are still in the hand. Although seemingly redundant, both measures provide increased protection against the possibility of kitchen accidents.

The best results on a mixer are achieved when the mixer is set on the right bowl adjustment (small or large bowl). Check this before starting the mixer. Also check to be sure that the blades have been locked securely in the correct position. Use only the bowls designed for the mixer.

When conventional mixers are in operation, nothing more substantial than a rubber spatula should be used to scrape the bowl. Absolutely *nothing metallic* should be in the bowl. Even a rubber spatula cannot be used to scrape the bowl when a mixer with hypocycloidal action is used; the irregular path of the beaters makes it impossible to avoid having the spatula being caught in the mixer. For absolutely the safest operation with any type of mixer, *turn off the mixer* before scraping the sides of the bowl.

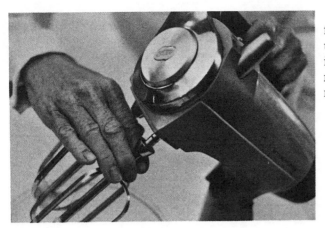

Remove the beater blades according to the manufacturer's directions after turning off the mixer and unplugging it. In removing blades from the type of mixer illustrated, twist the handle at the top of the mixer to release the blades from the locked position. After they are released, they will slide easily from the mixer head.

VOCABULARY

Lukewarm

Scalding

Simmering

Boiling

Atmospheric pressure

Vapor pressure

True solution

Ionize

Colloidal dispersion

Coarse suspension

Chapter 2
Vegetables

Vegetables are gaining considerable prestige as their nutritional merits and health benefits, such as possibly helping to prevent cancer, are being touted. They are so important that a national campaign urging everyone to eat "5 a day" (servings of vegetables and fruits) is being trumpeted. This chapter is designed to help you learn how to prepare vegetables in a variety of ways to make them colorful and tempting parts of meals and snacks.

Obviously, the range of suitable recipes is very wide. The ones appearing in this chapter are merely an introduction to what you might wish to try on your own at home. Examples of boiling, steaming, broiling, baking, stir-frying, and deep-fat frying are included. Try such simple ideas as boiling or steaming a vegetable and then serving it with one of the sauces in this chapter. You also may wish to experiment with different combinations of vegetables, in addition to some of the recipes presented here. Also, consider using vegetables, either raw or cooked, in salads (see Chapter 4 for some ideas). Have fun letting your creativity with vegetables take over!

KEY CONCEPTS — VEGETABLES

1. The principal pigment groups in vegetables are: 1) chlorophyll, 2) carotenoids, and 3) flavonoids (anthocyanins and anthoxanthins).

2. Cooking conditions can influence the color of cooked vegetables.

    a. *Acid* in the cooking medium promotes 1) an unpleasant olive-drab color in green (chlorophyll-containing) vegetables, 2) limited bleaching in orange (carotenoid-containing) vegetables and white in anthoxanthin-containing vegetables, and 3) reddish hue in anthocyanin-containing vegetables.

    b. Alkali in the cooking medium promotes 1) a bright green color in green vegetables, 2) little if any color change in orange-colored vegetables, 3) a yellowish hue in anthoxanthin-pigmented vegetables, and 4) a blue tone in anthocyanin-containing vegetables.

    c. Cooking time influences the color of chlorophyll: 1) a very brief time in boiling water intensifies the green color of chlorophyll-containing vegetables and 2) green vegetables cooked more than 5 minutes gradually begin to develop an olive-drab color.

---

3. Cooking conditions can influence the texture of cooked vegetables.

   a. An acidic cooking medium seriously retards softening of vegetable tissues.

   b. An alkaline medium quickly promotes softening of tissues to the point of becoming mushy.

4. Selection of the method of preparing cooked vegetables (boiling, steaming, sautéing, stir-frying, deep-fat frying, microwaving, broiling, or baking) is determined by considering such factors as the type of vegetable being prepared, time and equipment that are available, and dietary requirements or preferences.

5. Vegetables always need to be washed and cleaned thoroughly.

PIGMENTS

Although there are many specific compounds which contribute to the pigmentation of fruits and vegetables, these substances can be categorized into *chlorophyll*, *carotenoids*, and *flavonoids*. The chlorophylls include chlorophyll a and chlorophyll b; the carotenoids are the compounds contributing various bright colors in the yellow, orange, and red range; the flavonoids range from white to reds and blues. These pigments are modified in some cases by the medium to which they are exposed. Thus, there is a need to know what the pigment change may be in an acid versus an alkaline medium.

Chlorophyll a is a rather strong blue green color, as can be seen in the flowers of brocolli. *Chlorphyll b* is also green, but it has a bit of yellow overtone to the color. Most green vegetables contain both of these forms of chlorophyll. In an alkaline medium, such as is provided by adding some soda to the cooking water, the green color will be intensified. However, on the acid side of neutral, as can be illustrated by adding lemon juice or vinegar to water, the green color of chlorophyll changes to the olive green color of pheophytin. This color generally is considered to be less desirable than the green of chlorophyll. Thus, it can be concluded that it is wise to cook green vegetables in an uncovered pan to aid in the escape of volatile acids which might otherwise promote the development of pheophytin during cooking. The other factor which can cause the formation of pheophytin is prolonged cooking. This can be minimized by placing the vegetables in boiling water to begin cooking and by cutting them into relatively small pieces that will tenderize quickly.

Carotenoids include a range of compounds in the color range from yellow through orange and red. The carotenes, which are nutritionally significant as being precursors of vitamin A, range from yellow through orange. Lycopene represents the red color found in tomatoes; the xanthophylls provide still different shades of yellow and orange, such as can be found in corn. All members of the carotenoids are stable pigments, remaining the same color in either an acid or an alkaline medium. The use of a cover to trap volatile organic acids is not a necessary consideration when planning the cookery of vegetables pigmented by carotenoids.

The *flavonoids* include *anthoxanthins* and *anthocyanins*, two chemically related types of pigments with very different colors. The *anthoxanthins* are bleached or colorless in an acid medium. A good example of anthoxanthins is provided by cauliflower. In an acid medium, this pigment bleaches to a desirable white. In an alkaline medium, anthoxanthins become an unappealing yellow, as illustrated in the cooking of cauliflower in an alkaline medium created by the addition of soda.

Anthocyanins are the reds and purples found in a few fruits and red cabbage and beets. Red cabbage provides the most useful illustration of the pigment changes that develop when anthocyanins are subjected to acidic and alklaine media. In acid, the anthocyanin will become a reddish color reminiscent of the color reaction of litmus paper. In an alkaline medium the anthocyanins become blue, a reaction also paralleling litmus paper. It is common to see the color develop to amost a deep green, a reaction in alkali which is caused by the change of anthocyanin to blue coupled with the change of anthoxanthins also present in the cabbage. The yellow of the anthoxanthins in alkali, when superimposed on the blue of anthocyanins, gives the overall impression of green.

To summarize the changes caused by the use of an acidic cooking medium, such as may be caused by using a lid or adding lemon juice, the green color of chlorophyll will be changed to an undesirable olive green, the flavonoids (both anthoxanthins and anthocyanins) will be satisfactory, and the carotenoids will not be influenced by acid.

The pigments also are influenced by the use of soda. This alkaline medium develops a yellow color in anthoxanthins and a blue color in anthocyanins. Besides the changes noted in the flavonoid family, alkali causes a bright green color in chlorophyll and presents no change in the carotenoids. Thus, the changes in the flavonoids are detrimental, while the change in chlorophyll is acceptable from an aesthetic, if not from a nutritional standpoint.

TEXTURE

The addition of lemon juice or vinegar greatly retards the softening of cellulose, making it extremely difficult to cook vegetables to the correct degree of doneness. If lemon juice or other flavoring substance of

---

ACIDIC AND ALKALINE COOKING MEDIA

Method Directions:
1. Wash each of the vegetables; pare the carrot, and cut each vegetable in half.
2. Prepare 4 1-quart saucepans, each containing 2 cups boiling water and 4 tablespoons vinegar.
3. Place half a carrot in one of the pans and note the time. Place half the red cabbage in another of the pans and note the time. Similarly, place half the cauliflower and half the broccoli in the remaining two pans, *noting the time* when each is started.
4. Prepare 4 1-quart saucepans, each containing 2 cups boiling water and 2 tablespoons baking soda.
5. Place each of the remaining vegetables in one of these pans, noting the time when each is started.
6. Boil each of the vegetables without a cover on the pan until the vegetable tests tender when pierced with a fork. Note the elapsed time required to reach this point, and record in the table.
7. Remove the vegetable and place on a serving plate.

Complete the evaluation table.

1	stalk broccoli
1/4	head cauliflower
1/4	red cabbage
1	large carrot

Vegetable Pigments Table Directions:
Mark an asterisk (*) beside each acid and alkaline color reaction that is pleasing to the eye. (Ignore the texture and look only at color for this decision.) For vegetables having the best color in an alklaine medium, it is preferable to cook them without using a lid on the pan so that volatile organic acids can escape. If a vegetable looks best in an acid medium, it is wise to consider cooking it with the cover on the pan.

Note: What generalization can be drawn about the rate of cooking in acid versus the rate in alkali?

_____

_____

VEGETABLE PIGMENTS

PIGMENT	VEGETABLE USED	COLOR		COOKING TIME/TEXTURE	
		ACID	ALKALI	ACID	ALKALI
Chlorophyll					
Carotinoid					
Anthoxanthin					
Anthocyanin					

acidic reaction is to be used, this needs to be done after the vegetable is tender. In an alkaline medium, the cellulose will soften very rapidly, leading quickly to a very mushy texture. In addition, there will be excessive loss of thiamin in an alkaline cooking medium. This nutritional note is of special concern when cooking dried legumes because these vegetables are excellent sources of this B vitamin when properly prepared.

The influence of acidic and alkaline cooking media on vegetable pigments and on texture can be demonstrated by cooking vegetables, selected to represent the various types of pigments, in a vinegar-containing solution and in a soda-containing solution, as described on page 17.

PREPARATION FOR COOKING

Prior to cooking, vegetables should be washed thoroughly. In the case of leafy vegetables, such as spinach, this task is done most easily by immersing them in a sinkful of water and changing the rinse water as many times as necessary. A firm scrubbing with a vegetable brush is useful in preparing potatoes and other vegetables with dirt-retaining skins. A stream of cold water from the faucet is the most efficient way of removing dirt from fresh vegetables.

The final form in which the vegetable is to be served should be considered at this time. If a head of cauliflower is to be served whole with a cheese sauce over it, the only preparation remaining to be done prior to cooking is the removal of any leaves or blemishes and a trimming of the core to remove the woody center portion. On the other hand, if cabbage wedges are the plan, the head of cabbage should be cut into wedges prior to cooking to help reduce cooking time and improve color and flavor. Carrots, parsnips, and other vegetables with an outer skin ordinarily are pared before being cooked. An exception to this is beets, which are boiled with their skins on to help retain their highly soluble pigment. Extraneous parts of the vegetable, including the ends of string beans and the woody lower stalk of broccoli, are removed with a sharp knife. Then the vegetable is cut into the desired pieces.

BOILING

Boiling is a method suitable for preparing almost all vegetables. This method is done most efficiently by placing a saucepan containing the desired amount of salted water on the range, covering it with a tightly-fitted lid, and preheating the water to a boil while quickly preparing the vegetable. By *having the water boiling* when the vegetable is added, the actual cooking time for the vegetable will be shortened. This helps to retain optimum color and flavor in the vegetable. Long cooking is detrimental to green colors, nutritive value, and sulfur-containing flavoring compounds in vegetables.

The two main concerns in boiling vegetables are the *amount of water* and the *use of a lid*. For vegetables with *mild flavors*, the flavor will be retained at its maximum by using just enough water to boil over the vegetables and using a lid on the pan. Vegetables with *strong flavors* can be made more palatable by using an additional half inch of water to dilute the flavor and avoiding the use of a lid so that the volatile flavor compounds can escape into the air. *Green vegetables* will have a more pleasing color if they are cooked without a lid since the lid traps volatile organic acids in the pan and increases the likelihood of changing chlorophyll to the less desirable compound, pheophytin. Obviously, some vegetables present a conflict in logic. Peas, for example, are mild flavored, thus suggesting that a lid should be used; the chlorophyll would be harmed by the use of the lid. The recommendation in such cases is to boil without using a lid. If there is no reason for boiling the vegetable uncovered, a lid should be used.

In all cases, vegetables should be boiled just until they are tender enough to be cut with a fork. A very tender vegetable has less interesting texture, and the color and flavor will be less appealing.

A guide for boiling a number of fresh vegetables is presented in the table. Canned vegetables require only reheating until they are hot throughout. Frozen vegetables should be cooked according to directions on the package. Specific suggestions for boiling spinach, artichokes, boiling onion, cabbage, carrots, and broccoli follow.

SPINACH

Fresh spinach affords an excellent illustration of the need for careful washing. Its deep veins in the leaves afford shelter to the sand and dirt which cling to the spinach as it comes from the field. The easiest and most efficient way to assure thorough washing is to immerse the leaves in a sinkful of water, dousing them up

GUIDE FOR BOILING FRESH VEGETABLES

VEGETABLE	SIZE	AMOUNT OF WATER	USE OF LID	TIME (MIN.)
Artichokes, globe	Whole	1 inch	Yes	40–60
Artichokes, Jerusalem	Whole	To cover	Yes	25–35
Asparagus	Spears	To base of tips	No	15
Beans, green	1 inch	To cover	No	20
Beans, lima	Shelled	To cover	No	30
Beets	Whole	To cover	Yes	35–60
Beets, greens	Leaves	Clinging to leaves	Until Wilted	10
Broccoli stalks	Split	To base of flower	No	15
Brussels sprouts	Whole	1/2 inch above vegetable	No	15
Cabbage	Wedges	1/2 inch above vegetable	No	15
Carrots	Strips	To cover	Yes	12
Cauliflower	Whole	1/2 inch above vegetable	No	20–30
Cauliflower	Flowerets	1/2 inch above vegetable	No	10
Corn	On cob	To cover	Yes	6
Okra	Sliced	To cover	No	12
Onions, boiling	Whole	1/2 inch above vegetable	No	15–20
Parsnips	Quartered strips	1/2 inch above vegetable	No	10–15
Peas	Shelled	To cover	No	10
Potatoes	Halves	To cover	Yes	20
Rutabagas	Diced	1/2 inch above vegetable	No	25
Spinach	Leaves	Clinging to leaves	Until wilted	5–8
Squash, summer	Sliced	1 inch	No	5
Squash, winter	2-inch cubes	1 inch	Yes	20
Sweet potatoes	Quarters	To cover	Yes	20
Turnips	Sliced	1/2 inch above vegetable	No	18
Zucchini	1 inch slice	1 inch	No	5

and down in the water several times. While holding the leaves to one side, drain the water from the sink, and rinse the sand and other sediment from the sink. Replace the sink stopper, and fill the sink with water again in preparation for another thorough rinsing of the leaves. Again the leaves are agitated in the water to help loosen clinging dirt and sand. Again the water is drained from the sink. This process is repeated until there is no sediment remaining in the sink when the water is drained out. At this point, the leaves are examined, and the roots and longer stems are broken from the leaves.

For boiled spinach, the washed leaves are placed in a large pan. No water is added to the pan because there will be enough moisture present from the water clinging to the leaves to prevent burning. The lid is placed on the pan at first to help trap steam in the pan and wilt the leaves to a smaller volume in the bottom of the pan. The lid remains on the pan until the leaves have wilted in the pan. When the leaves have wilted down into the cooking water which has collected from the leaves, the lid is removed. Boiling is continued just until the spinach is tender, usually in a matter of only about 3–5 minutes after the spinach wilts. Since there is a limited amount of water in the bottom of the pan, more uniform cooking is achieved by using a spoon or cooking fork to turn the spinach in the pan so that all of the spinach is in

the water during part of the cooking period. To serve spinach, drain it thoroughly in a colander before adding desired seasonings.

GLOBE ARTICHOKES

Globe artichokes are dramatic to serve and are well suited to a menu when last minute touches would be a burden. Preparation again begins with a careful washing. Since dirt may get trapped between the leaves, the most effective washing is done by allowing a stream of water to run hard between the petals. Turn the artichoke upside down to allow the rinse water to run out. Repeat the washing and draining process several times to insure all dirt and sand have been removed. With a sharp knife, cut the stem off at the base of the flower, being careful to make a straight cut. The cut needs to be straight so that the artichoke will sit up straight on the plate when it is served. As is true with all cutting, a cutting board should be used to cut against. This reduces the hazard to the cook and prevents dulling the knife on a hard surface.

The ends of the petals are tipped with a sharp point. Artichokes will be easier to eat and will be more attractive when these points are cut off. This can be done quickly with the aid of a pair of kitchen shears. Simply cut straight across the upper portion of each petal.

Artichokes require a long cooking period, often as long as 45 minutes to an hour, to tenderize the heart (base) of the vegetable. The most practical way to cook this vegetable is to place it in a pan containing approximately 3/4 inch of salted water. If desired, garlic and a teaspoon of olive oil may be added to the water to brighten the flavor. A lid is placed on the pan to trap the steam and help in cooking the petals which extend above the water level. Artichokes are boiled gently until the base of the vegetable can be pricked easily with a cooking fork.

The artichoke petals will trap cooking water which will drain onto the serving plate unless the artichoke is inverted to drain out the water before the vegetable is served. This vegetable can be served either hot or cold. It is eaten by removing a petal, dipping the base of the petal in melted butter or other sauce, and then scraping the small amount of meat at the base from the petal with one's teeth. There is only a small amount of meat on each petal. This process is repeated until the center of the artichoke if reached. Then the choke is removed and set aside. Additional butter or sauce may be added to the heart which is revealed. The heart is the principal edible part of this vegetable.

BOILING ONIONS

Boiling onions are an example of a strong-flavored vegetable whose acceptance can be promoted by good preparation techniques. The strong flavor can be minimized by using enough water to cover the onions a half inch above the top. This extra water helps to dilute the onion flavor. Volatile flavoring compounds can be reduced by cooking the onions without a lid, thus allowing these substances to escape from the pan. While the salted cooking water is being brought to a boil, the onions are prepared by cutting off the root and stem ends and removing the husk-like outer skins of the onions. The washed onions then are boiled uncovered until the center can be penetrated easily with a fork. As is true with other vegetables, onions should be drained well before serving.

CABBAGE

Cabbage is a vegetable which can be very attractive when properly prepared. One good way of cooking it is to prepare wedges and then boil them. Wedges are cut from the washed head with the aid of a sharp knife. Care should be taken to insure that the wedge contains a portion of the core. This core is essential if the wedge is to be held intact during boiling. Since the core is somewhat woody and resistant to softening during the time required to cook the leaves to the desired end point, the core can be trimmed so that it is only about a quarter of an inch thick along its length. This trimming should be done on a cutting board, being careful to avoid releasing any of the cabbage leaves from the core.

For both optimum color and flavor, it is important to cook cabbage as short a time as possible. This is accomplished by dropping the wedges into salted water that is boiling actively and maintaining the active boil

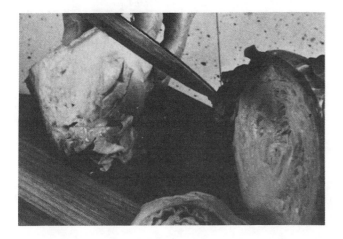

until the cabbage is done. Cabbage and related vegetables have a strong flavor which can be improved by the use of an excess of water to dilute the flavor. The flavor is reduced also by avoiding the use of a cover on the pan. To minimize cabbage-like flavors, cook cabbage and other sulfur-containing vegetables just until they are tender enough to be cut easily with a fork. The longer they are cooked, the stronger will be the flavor. Therefore, it is better to cook cabbage just until barely tender rather than until it is quite limp. A short cooking time is important for the color as well as the flavor of cabbage. Chlorophyll will change to pheophytin when it is heated more than seven minutes. This change to an olive green color will make the color less inviting to diners. Thus, cabbage and related vegetables will be most palatable when cooked a very short time in an uncovered pan containing an excess of water.

CARROTS

Carrots can add great variety to menus while also contributing a potential source of vitamin A. Whether they are to be served raw or cooked, carrots require thorough scrubbing. Their appearance will be enhanced by paring, too. This can be done quickly and economically with the aid of a vegetable peeler. After

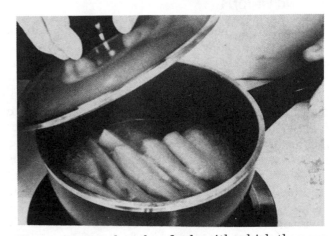

paring, carrots may be left whole or cut into shapes that will complement the other foods with which they are to be served. If they are to be cut, use a sharp knife and a cutting board to cut them into strips or slices, being careful to make the pieces uniform in size.

Carrots are mild-flavored vegetables which need to be cooked carefully to retain as much of their flavor as possible. This goal is achieved by boiling them just until they are tender in a covered pan with just enough salted, boiling water to barely cover the carrots. By having the water boiling when the carrots are added, the actual cooking time will be kept to a minimum. This is useful in promoting optimum retention of the nutrients in carrots as well as in other vegetables.

Carrots are cooked with a cover on because they have a mild flavor, and their color will not be impaired by trapping volatile acids in the pan. If either the flavor or color of a vegetable will be harmed by the use of a cover, it is recommended that the lid not be used. The most important single concern in vegetable preparation is palatability. When vegetables are tempting, enough of them will be consumed to provide the nutrients available from them. Highly nourishing, but unappetizing vegetables probably will not be consumed and, therefore, are wasted.

BROCCOLI

Broccoli requires thorough washing and some trimming and cutting before cooking. The best broccoli will have a bluish green color to the flowers. The stalk of broccoli is somewhat woody and resistant to softening during cooking. The tenderizing can be hastened by cutting off the more woody portions of the stalk and then slitting the remaining stalk almost to the point where the flowers begin. The stalk may be split in halves or quarters, depending on the size of the stalk. The splitting

reduces the cooking time required to tenderize the stalk, thus helping to finish cooking the vegetable before the green chlorophyll has been converted to the less attractive olive-green color of pheophytin.

BROILING

Broil vegetables, such as tomato slices, mushroom caps, eggplant slices, or zucchini slices by arranging them on a broiler pan, sprinkling them liberally with buttered crumbs, and broiling them about 3 inches from the heat source until pleasingly browned and heated throughout. Thick slices may need to be broiled at a distance of 4 inches or more to allow time for the vegetable to cook before the surface becomes too brown. If a vegetable, such as boiling onions or green peppers, is to be broiled, the vegetable should be parboiled (boiled until amost fork tender) before being placed in the broiler for the broiling and final browning process.

A few vegetables have a tender enough structure so that they will be appetizing and appealing when they are broiled. Fresh tomatoes or mushrooms are vegetables which often are broiled. Broiling, like stir-frying, avoids the loss of water-soluble vitamins. To prepare vegetables for broiling, wash them well. Tomatoes ordinarily are cut in half. A coating of buttered bread crumbs or Parmesan cheese is optional, but will add to the eye appeal of the finished vegetable. The tomatoes are arranged on the broiler pan and then placed in the broiler with the upper surface of the tomatoes approximately three inches from the heat source.

The tomatoes are broiled with the door ajar so that the heat is coming continuously directly onto the food. It is not necessary to turn vegetables when they are being broiled, but it is important to watch them carefully to avoid burning them. The intense heat will brown them quite quickly. Since vegetables do brown quickly when broiled, it is wise to parboil vegetables such as onions if they are to be broiled. The parboiling softens the vegetable, and the broiling simply finishes the cooking process and adds a pleasing appearance. Vegetables should be removed from the broiler as soon as they are attractive in appearance and have been heated through.

BAKING

Winter squash and potatoes, both sweet and Irish, are the vegetable smost commonly baked. The well-scrubbed vegetables are placed on a rack in the middle of the oven and baked at 375–425° F until a fork can be inserted easily. If desired, the vegetable may be placed on aluminum foil or in a shallow pan to protect the oven.

SAUTÉING

Sautéing is a suitable method for very tender or thinly sliced vegetables, such as thin slices of raw potato. To sauté, melt enough butter or margarine or use enough salad oil to cover the bottom of a skillet. Add the sliced vegetable and fry at medium heat until pleasingly browned on the bottom of the vegetable slices. Turn with a spatula and brown the other side. If the vegetable is still raw in the center, the vegetable may need to be turned more than once. Continue frying until the interior of the vegetable is tender. The heat should be controlled throughout the cooking period to avoid excessive splattering or any smoking of the fat. When the vegetable is tender and pleasing in appearance, remove from this skillet, salt, and serve.

STIR-FRYING

Vegetables to be stir-fried are cut into very thin strips unless they are a vegetable, such as zucchini, which will become tender very quickly. Stir-frying is a method of cookery developed in Oriental cuisines. A wok is the preferred utensil for stir-frying because it has a small portion which is very hot. The vegetable is added to the wok which contains a very shallow layer of fat in the bottom. The vegetable pieces are stirred frequently to slide the browned, fried portions up the sides and bring uncooked portions down into the fat. This is a very rapid cooking process, one which requires careful attention and stirring to be successful. As soon as all of the vegetable has been fried just to the point of tenderness, the vegetable is served. If a less tender vegetable is being stir-fried, the heat may be reduced a bit after the initial browning of the vegetable, a very small amount of water may be added, and the vegetable steamed with a cover just long enough to finish tenderizing the food. This method of vegetable cookery is excellent because it is so quick that flavor, color, and nutritive value are retained at maximum levels.

STEAMING

Vegetables can be cooked in a device known as a *steamer*. In this method, water is boiled actively in a lower container, and the vegetable is placed on a rack suspended in the steam above the water. The entire device is covered with a lid to trap the steam. Any vegetables that are suited to boiling can also be steamed. Preparation is begun by bringing the water to a boil in the lower portion of the steamer. The vegetable then is placed on the rack, and the lid is replaced on the steamer. A large volume of steam should be maintained in the steamer throughout the steaming period. Steaming will take approximately 15 minutes longer than boiling. This method is good for retaining water soluble vitamins despite the fact that the cooking period is lengthened. Chlorophyll, however, will undergo an undesirable color change with this method unless the pieces of vegetable are small enough to steam quickly.

DEEP-FAT FRYING

Vegetables sometimes are deep-fat fried. This cooking method affords additional variety in the preparation of vegetables, but its use probably should be kept to a minimum because of the higher fat content of vegetables prepared in this way. For optimum quality of deep-fat fried vegetables, the pieces should be approximately 1/4 to 1/2 inch thick. While the pieces of vegetable are being cut, oil should be pre-heated in a deep fat fryer or in a saucepan on a controlled heat unit to a temperature of 375° F. The vegetable pieces should be dried thoroughly on paper towels before being transferred to the hot fat. If desired, the vegetables can be dipped in flour or in a batter before frying. This use of a batter is demonstrated in the making of the Japanese dish called *tempura*. Vegetables are fried until golden brown and tender. They should be drained well on paper towels, salted, and then served quickly.

MICROWAVING

Vegetables to be cooked in a microwave oven are heated more quickly when cut into small pieces than when prepared whole. Place the washed vegetables in a glass dish, with the slower-cooking portions (stalks or cores) arranged toward the edge of the container. For most vegetables, the addition of about half a cup of water improves the quality of the finished product. The dish of vegetables should be covered, either with its own lid or with plastic wrap to trap steam around the vegetables. During the heating period, the pieces should be stirred occasionally to facilitate uniform heating. Since vegetables will continue to soften during the standing time after they are removed from the oven, a slightly crisp end product is the recommended degree of doneness when the vegetables are removed from the microwave oven. The time required to reach this state varies with the type of vegetable and the amount being prepared. A standing time of three minutes, with the vegetable covered, is recommended to aid in distributing the heat. Suggested guidelines for microwaving vegetables are presented in the table.

MICROWAVE COOKERY OF VEGETABLES[1]

VEGETABLE	PIECE SIZE	AMOUNT	WATER ADDED (C)	TIME (MIN.) (HIGH)	PRODEDURE
Artichokes	whole	1	1/4	8	Cover; rotate after 8 min.
		4	1	15	Cover; rotate after 8 min.
Asparagus	spears	8	1/4	7	Cover; tips toward center of dish
	2"	1/2 lb	1/4	7	Cover; stir after 3 min.
frozen	spears	10 oz	0	9	Cover; rearrange after 5 min.
Beans, green	1–2"	1 lb	3/4	15	Cover; stir after 8 min.
frozen		10 oz	1/4	9	Cover; stir after 5 min.
Beets	whole	4 med	To cover	20	Cover; rearrange after 10 min.
Broccoli	split stalks	1 bunch	1/4	12	Cover; flowerets in center
	1"	1 lb	1/2	9	Cover; stir after 5 min.
frozen	chopped	10 oz	1/8	9	Cover; stir after 5 min.
Brussels sprouts	whole	1/2 lb	1/4	5	Cover; stir after 3 min.
frozen	whole	10 oz	1/8	8	Cover; stir after 4 min.
Cabbage	shredded	1 small	1/4	9	Cover; stir after 5 min.
Carrots	thin slices	4 med	1/2	12	Cover; stir after 6 min.
Cauliflower	floweret	1 small head	1/2	13	Cover; stir after 7 min.
	whole	1 small head	1/2	14	Cover; turn over after 7 min.
frozen	floweret	10 oz	1/8	8	Cover; stir after 4 min.
Corn	cob	2 ears	1/4	7	Cover; rearrange after 4 min.
	kernels	1 c	1/2	5	Cover; stir after 3 min.
frozen	kernels	10 oz	1/8	5	Cover; stir after 3 min.
Eggplant	1" cubes (peeled)	3 c	1/8	6	Cover; stir after 3 min.
Onions	quartered	4 med	1/2	11	Cover; rearrange after 6 min.
Parsnips	sticks	2	1/4	7	Cover; stir after 4 min.
Peas	shelled	1 lb	1/4	10	Cover; stir after 5 min.
frozen	shelled	10 oz	1/8	6	Cover; stir after 3 min.
Potatoes	whole	1	0	5	Pierce before cooking; turn after 3 min.
Spinach	leaves	1 lb	0	7	Cover to trap water clinging to leaves, stir after 4 min.
frozen	leaves	10 oz	1/8	8	Cover; stir after 4 min.
Squash					
summer	sliced	1 lb	1/8	10	Cover; stir after 5 min.
winter	half	1	0	8	Scrape out seeds, place cut side down; cover with wax paper
frozen	puree	10 oz	0	6	Cover; stir after 3 min.
Turnips	1" cubes	2 med	1/4	10	Cover; stir after 5 min.

[1]Times are approximate. Glass casserole dishes or plates and plastic wrap are recommended. Plastic wrap or bag should be slightly loose or slit.

RECIPES

ARTICHOKE WITH GARLIC BUTTER

Time: 1 hour

1. Cut off stem at base so that artichoke sits up straight.
2. Use kitchen shears to trim off the sharp point on each petal.
3. Place artichokes in deep pan containing 1" water, oil, and garlic salt.
4. Cover and bring to a boil before reducing heat to maintain simmering until the bottom(s) of the artichoke(s) are moderately tender when tested with a fork.
5. Melt butter and stir in garlic salt shortly before serving.
6. Drain by inverting each artichoke and serve with individual small bowls of garlic butter for dipping (and a plate to hold the stripped petals and the choke).

(Serves two)

2	*artichokes*
1 tsp	*olive oil*
1/2 tsp	*garlic salt*
1 tbsp	*butter*
1/8 tsp	*garlic salt*

(Serves four)

4	artichokes
1 tsp	olive oil
1/2 tsp	garlic salt
2 tbsp	butter
1/4 tsp	garlic salt

CARNIVAL GREEN BEANS

Total Time: 20 minutes

1. Bring water to boil; add beans and boil until just tender (about 15 minutes).
2. While beans are boiling, melt margarine in saucepan; stir in mustard, flour, salt, and pepper.
3. Blend egg yolks and milk; add to roux (a cooking mixture of flour and fat), stirring constantly.
4. Heat mixture (while stirring constantly) until mixture thickens slightly. Be careful to avoid boiling the mixture.
5. Stir in lemon juice.
6. Drain beans well. Pour sauce over beans, and garnish with pimiento.

(Serves two)

1/2 lb	*green beans*
1 1/2 tsp	*margarine or butter*
1/4 tsp	*dry mustard*
1/2 tsp	*flour*
	pinch of salt
	pinch of black pepper
1	*egg yolk, beaten*
6 tbsp	*milk*
1 tsp	*lemon juice*
2 tsp	*chopped pimiento*

(Serves four)

1 lb	green beans
1 tbsp	margarine or butter
1/2 tsp	dry mustard
1 tsp	flour
1/4 tsp	salt
1/4 tsp	black pepper
2	egg yolks, beaten
2/3 c	milk
1 1/2 tsp	lemon juice
1 tbsp	chopped pimiento

GREEN BEAN CASSEROLE DELUXE

Total Time: 25 minutes
Baking: 375° F oven for 15 min.

1. Preheat oven.
2. Boil beans according to package directions and drain well.
3. In a skillet, sauté onion and mushrooms in margarine to golden brown. Remove from heat.
4. Stir flour into onions and mushrooms until blended.
5. Add milk while stirring.
6. Return sauce to heat and stir constantly until mixture boils.
7. Remove from heat and add cheese, soy sauce, Worcestershire sauce, and water chestnuts.
8. Mix the drained beans with the sauce and place in casserole.
9. Garnish with almonds.
10. Bake at 15 minutes at 375° F.

(Serves two)	
1/2	package frozen green beans
1 tbsp	margarine or butter
1 tbsp	chopped onion
2 tbsp	canned mushrooms, drained
1 tsp	flour
1/3 c	milk
2 tbsp	grated cheddar cheese
1/4 tsp	soy sauce
1/4 tsp	Worcestershire sauce
1/4 c	water chestnuts, drained and sliced
1 tbsp	slivered almonds

(Serves four)	
1	package frozen green beans
2 tbsp	margarine or butter
2 tbsp	chopped onion
1/4 c	canned mushrooms, drained
2 tsp	flour
2/3 c	milk
1/4 c	grated cheddar cheese
1/2 tsp	soy sauce
1/2 tsp	Worcestershire sauce
1/2 c	water chestnuts, drained and sliced
2 tbsp	slivered almonds

POLISH BEETS IN SOUR CREAM (BY MARY KRAMER)

Total Time: 10 minutes

1. Grate beets on coarse grater.
2. Melt margarine.
3. Add flour and stir.
4. Remove from heat; add vinegar, salt, and sugar, and stir in grated beets.
5. Stir while simmering mixture for 5 minutes.
6. Remove from heat.
7. Stir in sour cream quickly, and serve immediately to avoid curdling sour cream.

(Serves two)	
3	cooked beets
1 tbsp	margarine or butter
1 1/2 tsp	flour
1 1/2 tsp	vinegar
	pinch of salt
1 1/2 tsp	sugar
1/4 c	sour cream

(Serves four)	
6	cooked beets
2 tbsp	margarine or butter
1 tbsp	flour
1 tbsp	vinegar
1/8 tsp	salt
1 tbsp	sugar
1/2 c	sour cream

BROCCOLI BROIL

Total Time: 15 minutes

1. Boil broccoli.
2. While broccoli is boiling, lightly sauté onion in margarine in a 1-quart saucepan.
3. Remove saucepan from heat and stir flour and seasonings into onion and margarine.
4. Add bouillon cube and milk gradually, stirring constantly.
5. Return to heat and bring to a boil, stirring constantly. Remove from heat and add all but 2 tablespoons of cheese.
6. Drain broccoli and arrange in casserole.
7. Pour sauce over broccoli. Sprinkle remaining cheese and paprika over top.
8. Broil until lightly browned.

(Serves two)	
1 c	broccoli flowerets
1 1/2 tsp	chopped onion
2 tsp	margarine or butter
1 1/2 tsp	flour
1/4 tsp	dry mustard
1/8 tsp	marjoram
	pinch of pepper
1/2	chicken bouillon cube
1/2 c	milk
3 tbsp	grated Parmesan cheese
	paprika to garnish

BROCCOLI BROIL (CONTINUED)

(Serves four)

2 c	broccoli flowerets
1 tbsp	chopped onion
1 1/2 tbsp	margarine or butter
1 tbsp	flour
1/2 tsp	dry mustard
1/4 tsp	marjoram
	dash of pepper
1	chicken bouillon cube
1 c	milk
1/3 c	grated Parmesan cheese
	paprika to garnish

BROCCOLI SALAD CHINOISE

Total Time: 30 minutes

1. Combine garlic, oils, soy sauce, salt, lime juice, vinegar, and ginger root to make marinade.
2. Clean mushrooms, slice in 1/4" slices, and add to marinade (stirring to coat). Chill.
3. Wash broccoli, cut into bite-sized flowerets, and steam until barely tender. Chill broccoli.
4. Combine broccoli with mushrooms to coat the broccoli and mushrooms with the marinade.
5. Spoon broccoli and mushrooms from marinade. Serve topped with a garnish of toasted, slivered almonds. (Serve on greens or in a serving bowl.)

(Serves two)

1/2 clove	*garlic, crushed*
1 1/3 tbsp	*walnut oil*
1 tsp	*sesame oil*
1 tsp	*soy sauce*
1/4 tsp	*salt*
2 tsp	*lime juice*
1 1/3 tbsp	*rice vinegar*
1/2 tsp	*minced ginger root*
1/2 bunch	*broccoli*
3	*mushrooms, medium*
1 tbsp	*almonds, slivered, toasted*
	salad greens (optional)

(Serves four)

1 clove	garlic, crushed
2 2/3 tbsp	walnut oil
2 tsp	sesame oil
2 tsp	soy sauce
1/2 tsp	salt
1 1/3 tbsp	lime juice
2 2/3 tbsp	rice vinegar
1 tsp	minced ginger root
1 bunch	broccoli
6	mushrooms, medium
2 tbsp	almonds, slivered, toasted
	salad greens (optional)

BROCCOLI SOUP

Total Time: 15 minutes

1. In a large saucepan, melt margarine. Sauté green pepper and onion just until translucent.
2. Add broccoli and water and boil until broccoli is tender.
3. Place in blender and whirl until smooth.
4. Add cream; stir in just enough milk to thin to consistency of a cream soup.
5. Add curry powder, and salt and pepper to taste.
6. Reheat quickly to serving temperature and serve with dollop of sour cream and chopped parsley as garnish.

(Serves two)

1 tbsp	*margarine or butter*
1 tbsp	*chopped green pepper*
1 1/2 tbsp	*chopped onion*
1 c	*chopped broccoli*
1/3 c	*water*
1/3 c	*light cream*
~1/4 c	*milk*
1/4 tsp	*curry powder*
	salt and pepper to taste
2 tbsp	*sour cream*
1 tsp	*chopped parlsey*

(Serves four)

2 tbsp	margarine or butter
2 tbsp	chopped green pepper
3 tbsp	chopped onion
2 c	chopped broccoli
2/3 c	water
2/3 c	light cream
~1/2 c	milk
1/2 tsp	curry powder
	salt and pepper to taste
1/4 c	sour cream
2 tsp	chopped parlsey

SWEET-SOUR RED CABBAGE

Total Time: 15–25 minutes

1. Wash, pare, core, and slice the apples into thin slices.
2. Combine the ingredients in a skillet or wok.
3. Cover and simmer over low heat, stirring occasionally. Continue to cook until desired tenderness is reached (approximately 15 minutes for crisp cabbage and 25 minutes for more tender cabbage).

(Serves two)	
1 tbsp	salad oil
2 c	shredded red cabbage
1	medium Pippin (or other tart apple)
2 tbsp	brown sugar
2 tbsp	vinegar
3/4 tsp	salt
2 tbsp	water

(Serves four)	
2 tbsp	salad oil
4 c	shredded red cabbage
2	medium Pippins (or other tart apple)
1/4 c	brown sugar
1/4 c	vinegar
1 1/2 tsp	salt
1/4 c	water

VEGETARIAN CABBAGE ROLLS

Total Time: 35 minutes
Baking Time: 350° F oven for 25 minutes

1. Preheat oven.
2. Boil cabbage leaves 3 minutes; drain.
3. Sauté bean sprouts and mushrooms in margarine until golden brown, stirring frequently.
4. Remove from heat and stir in remaining ingredients, except half the cheese and the tomato sauce.
5. Divide mixture onto cabbage leaves; roll and secure with toothpicks.
6. Place in casserole; top with tomato sauce and then sprinkle remaining cheese on top.
7. Bake at 350° F for 25 minutes.
8. Remove toothpicks and serve.

(Serves two)	
4	cabbage leaves
1/4 lb	chopped bean sprouts
1/8 lb	mushrooms, chopped
1 1/2 tbsp	margarine or butter
6 tbsp	wheat germ
2 tbsp	water chestnuts, drained and chopped
1/4 c	almonds, slivered
2 1/2 tbsp	minced parsley
1/2 tsp	crumbled marjoram leaves
1/8 tsp	salt
6 tbsp	grated Parmesan cheese
1/2 c	tomato sauce

(Serves four)	
8	cabbage leaves
1/2 lb	chopped bean sprouts
1/4 lb	mushrooms, chopped
3 tbsp	margarine or butter
3/4 c	wheat germ
1/4 c	water chestnuts, drained and chopped
1/2 c	almonds, slivered
1/3 c tbsp	minced parsley
1 tsp	crumbled marjoram leaves
1/4 tsp	salt
3/4 c	grated Parmesan cheese
1 c	tomato sauce

DUTCHED CABBAGE

Total Time: 10 minutes

1. Fry bacon. Drain on paper towels, saving drippings in frying pan.
2. In a saucepan, combine flour, sugar, and salt. While stirring, slowly add water, followed by vinegar and egg. Stir until smooth.
3. Heat over a low heat, stirring constantly; continue heating until thick enough to coat spoon. Set aside.
4. Add cabbage and celery to frying pan containing bacon drippings; stir fry until cabbage is just tender.
5. Add crumbled bacon, pepper, and sauce; toss and serve.

(Serves two)	
1	slice bacon
1 tbsp	flour
2 tbsp	sugar
1/8 tsp	salt
1 c	water
1/2	egg
1/4 c	vinegar
1/2	cabbage, small head, shredded
1/4 c	celery, diced
	pinch of pepper

(Serves four)	
2	slices bacon
2 tbsp	flour
1/4 c	sugar
1/2 tsp	salt
1 c	water
1	egg
1/4 c	vinegar
1	cabbage, small head, shredded
1/2 c	celery, diced
1/8 tsp	pepper

KALDOMAR

Total Time: 1 hour and 20 minutes
Baking: 375° F oven for 1 hour

1. Preheat oven.
2. Boil cabbage for 10 minutes.
3. While cabbage is boiling, combine the meat, rice, egg, onion, salt, allspice, and milk.
4. Form meat mixture into balls and wrap in cabbage leaf, securing with toothpick.
5. Melt margarine in frying pan and brown each cabbage roll.
6. Place browned rolls in casserole.
7. Add water and onion soup mix to drippings; pour over cabbage rolls.
8. Bake at 375° F for 1 hour.
9. Remove toothpicks and serve.

(Serves two)

4	*large cabbage leaves*
1/2 lb	*ground beef*
3/4 c	*boiled rice (barely tender)*
1/2	*egg*
1/2	*onion, minced*
1/4 tsp	*salt*
1/2 tsp	*allspice*
1/4 c	*milk*
1 tbsp	*margarine or butter*
1/4 c	*water*
1 tbsp	*dry onion soup mix*

(Serves four)

8	large cabbage leaves
1 lb	ground beef
1 1/2 c	boiled rice (barely tender)
1	egg
1	onion, minced
1/2 tsp	salt
1 tsp	allspice
1/2 c	milk
2 tbsp	margarine or butter
1/2 c	water
2 tbsp	dry onion soup mix

CABBAGE SUPREME

Total Time: 15 minutes

1. Melt margarine in skillet.
2. Stir in garlic powder, water, and cabbage.
3. Cover and steam gently for 10 minutes.
4. In a small bowl, stir together sour cream, sugar, vinegar, and salt.
5. Stir into the cabbage and continue to heat just until the added ingredients are heated through.
6. Serve immediately, garnished with the sesame seeds.

(Serves two)

1 1/2 tsp	*margarine or butter*
2 c	*cabbage, finely shredded*
2 tbsp	*water*
1/8 tsp	*garlic powder*
2 tbsp	*sour cream*
1/2 tsp	*sugar*
1 1/2 tsp	*vinegar*
1/4 tsp	*salt*
1/8 tsp	*sesame seeds, toasted*

(Serves four)

1 tbsp	margarine or butter
4 c	cabbage, finely shredded
3 tbsp	water
1/4 tsp	garlic powder
1/4 c	sour cream
1 tsp	sugar
1 tbsp	vinegar
1/2 tsp	salt
1/4 tsp	sesame seeds, toasted

GINGER CARROTS

Total Time: 12 minutes

1. Wash and pare carrots. Cut in sticks (approximately 2" long and 1/3" in diameter).
2. Bring enough salted water to a boil to just cover the carrots.
3. Add the carrots to the boiling water, cover the pan, and boil until just fork tender (approximately 10 minutes.
4. While carrots are boiling, stir together the sugar, cornstarch, and salt.
5. Gradually stir in the orange juice.
6. In a saucepan, heat the sauce, while stirring continuously. Bring the sauce to a boil and continue to boil 1 minute.
7. Remove from the heat, and stir in the margarine, ginger, and lemon rind.
8. Drain the carrots thoroughly before pouring the sauce over them.
9. Toss in the sauce until carrots are coated with the sauce.
10. Serve immediately.

(Serves two)

3	*small carrots*
1 tsp	*sugar*
1/2 tsp	*cornstarch*
1/8 tsp	*salt*
1/8 tsp	*grated fresh ginger*
2 tbsp	*orange juice*
1/8 tsp	*grated lemon rind*
1 tsp	*margarine or butter*

(Serves four)

6	small carrots
2 tsp	sugar
1 tsp	cornstarch
1/4 tsp	salt
1/4 tsp	grated fresh ginger
1/4 c	orange juice
1/4 tsp	grated lemon rind
2 tsp	margarine or butter

CARROT PUFF

Total Time: 75 minutes
Baking: 350° F for 40 minutes and then 10 minutes

1. Preheat oven.
2. Peel carrots, cut in half, and cook in boiling water until tender.
3. Drain; cool in ice water; drain.
4. Place cooled carrots, flour, vanilla, eggs, nutmeg, cayenne, curry powder, and butter (melted, but not hot) in blender.
5. Puree in blender until completely smooth, scraping sides as needed.
6. Bake in preheated oven at 350° F for 40 minutes before sprinkling nuts on top. Then bake 10 more minutes

(Serves two)

1/2 lb	*carrots (4 medium)*
1 1/2 tbsp	*flour*
1/2 tsp	*vanilla*
2	*eggs*
1/4 c	*butter, melted*
	pinch of nutmeg
	dash of cayenne
1/8 tsp	*curry powder*
2 tbsp	*coarsely chopped pecans*

(Serves four)

1 lb	carrots (4 medium)
3 tbsp	flour
1 tsp	vanilla
3	eggs
1/3 c	butter, melted
	dash of nutmeg
1/8 tsp	cayenne
1/4 tsp	curry powder
1/4 c	coarsely chopped pecans

FROSTED CAULIFLOWER

Total Time: 20 minutes (small); 25 minutes (large)
Baking: 375° F oven for 10 minutes

1. Preheat oven.
2. Trim off the leaves and stalk of the head.
3. Wash thoroughly under cold, running water.
4. Bring the salted water to a boil, and add the cauliflower.
5. Boil actively, uncovered, until the cauliflower is barely able to be penetrated with a fork (approximately 12–15 minutes).
6. Drain thoroughly before placing on a sheet of foil in a shallow baking dish.
7. Thoroughly mix the mayonnaise and mustard before spreading over the upper surface of the cauliflower.
8. Sprinkle the grated cheese on top.
9. Bake at 375° F until cheese melts and topping bubbles (about 10 minutes).

(Serves two)
1/2	*head cauliflower*
1/2 tsp	*salt*
	Water to cover cauliflower
1/4 c	*mayonnaise or creamy salad dressing*
1 tsp	*prepared mustard*
1/3 c	*grated, sharp cheddar cheese*

(Serves four)
1	head cauliflower
1 tsp	salt
	Water to cover cauliflower
1/2 c	mayonnaise or creamy salad dressing
2 tsp	prepared mustard
2/3 c	grated, sharp cheddar cheese

CELERY ORIENTALE

Total Time: 5 minutes

1. Wash celery thoroughly; cut diagonal slices 1/4" thick. Wash, drain, and slice mushrooms.
2. In a wok or frying pan, melt the margarine.
3. Add the celery, and stir-fry with constant stirring just until celery is slightly tender.
4. Add the mushrooms and almonds.
5. Continue to stir-fry, stirring constantly until the mushrooms are somewhat transparent and the almonds begin to brown.

(Serves two)
3	*large outer stalks of celery*
1/2 c	*sliced fresh mushrooms*
1 tbsp	*margarine or butter*
2 tbsp	*chopped, blanched almonds*

(Serves four)
6	large outer stalks of celery
1 c	sliced fresh mushrooms
2 tbsp	margarine or butter
1/4 c	chopped, blanched almonds

CHILES RELLENOS

Total Time: 30 minutes
Frying Temperature: 375° F

1. Begin preheating oil to 375° F.
2. Place tomato sauce and seasonings in 1-quart, covered saucepan and simmer 10 minutes.
3. Stuff chiles with cheese.
4. Beat egg yolks to foam and set aside.
5. Beat egg whites until peaks just bend over.
6. Fold egg yolks (which have been sprinkled with the flour) into the egg whites.
7. Dip chiles individually into the foam to coat thoroughly.
8. Carefully slip individual chiles into the hot fat and fry until golden brown.
9. Drain on paper towels before serving, topped with tomato sauce.

(Serves two)
	Oil for deep fat frying
1/2 c	*tomato sauce*
1 tbsp	*diced onion*
1/8 tsp	*oregano*
	salt and pepper to taste
1/2 can	*small ortega chiles, drained*
1/4 c	*grated Monterey Jack cheese*
2	*eggs, separated*
1/2 tbsp	*flour*

(Serves four)
	Oil for deep fat frying
1 c	tomato sauce
2 tbsp	diced onion
1/4 tsp	oregano
	salt and pepper to taste
1 can	small ortega chiles, drained
1/2 c	grated Monterey Jack cheese
4	eggs, separated
1 tbsp	flour

EGGPLANT ITALIANATE

Total Time: 15 minutes (small); 17 minutes (large)
Baking: 450° F oven for 10–12 minutes

1. Preheat oven.
2. Dip eggplant in margarine and then in cracker crumbs.
3. Place on jelly roll pan lined with aluminum foil.
4. Salt lightly.
5. Spoon tomato sauce over each slice; sprinkle lightly with oregano and top with mushrooms and cheese.
6. Bake at 450° F until tender (approximately 10–12 minutes).

(Serves two)

1/2	*medium eggplant, pared and cut in 1/2" slices*
1/4 c	*melted margarine or butter*
1/3 c	*fine cracker crumbs*
	dash of salt
1/2 c	*tomato sauce*
1 tbsp	*canned, sliced mushrooms*
1/8 tsp	*powdered oregano*
1/2 c	*grated Mozzarella cheese*

(Serves four)

1	medium eggplant, pared and cut in 1/2" slices
1/2 c	melted margarine or butter
2/3 c	fine cracker crumbs
1/8 tsp	salt
1 c	tomato sauce
2 tbsp	canned, sliced mushrooms
1/4 tsp	powdered oregano
1 c	grated Mozzarella cheese

MUSHROOM APPETIZER

Total Time: 30 minutes
Baking: 350° F oven for 15–20 minutes

1. Preheat oven.
2. Boil onion in 1/2 cup water until tender; drain.
3. Combine all ingredients thoroughly and spread in baking dish (loaf pan for small recipe; 9x9" pan for large recipe).
4. Bake at 350° F until set (about 15 minutes for small and 20 minutes for large recipe).
5. Cut in 1" squares; serve hot.

(Serves two)

1/4	*chopped onion*
2	*eggs, well beaten*
2 tbsp	*dry bread crumbs*
1/4 tsp	*salt*
	dash of pepper
	dash of paprika
	dash of oregano
1	*drop of Tabasco sauce*
4 oz	*grated sharp cheddar cheese*
6 oz	*jar marinated mushrooms, drained, finely chopped*

(Serves four)

1/2	chopped onion
4	eggs, well beaten
1/4 c	dry bread crumbs
1/2 tsp	salt
1/8 tsp	pepper
1/8 tsp	paprika
1/8 tsp	oregano
3	drops of Tabasco sauce
8 oz	grated sharp cheddar cheese
12 oz	two 6-oz jars marinated mushrooms, drained, finely chopped

PIÑON-STUFFED MUSHROOMS

Total Time: 20 minutes
Baking: 425° F oven for 10–12 minutes

1. Preheat oven.
2. Thaw spinach in microwave oven and drain thoroughly.
3. Clean mushrooms, removing stems.
4. Chop stems; sauté stems with onion and garlic for 2 minutes.
5. Add spinach to stems and heat to evaporate the liquid.
6. Stir in crumbs, nuts, and seasonings.
7. Fill top of each mushroom with mixture; dust with Parmesan cheese.
8. Bake at 425° F about 10 minutes until mushrooms are tender.

(Serves two)

1/4	*package frozen chopped spinach*
2	*large mushrooms*
1 tbsp	*chopped onion*
1/2	*clove garlic, minced*
2 tsp	*olive oil*
1 tbsp	*grated Parmesan cheese*
1 tbsp	*dry bread crumbs*
2 tbsp	*piñon nuts*
1/8 tsp	*dry oregano*
1/8 tsp	*dry basil*

(Serves four)

1/2	package frozen chopped spinach
4	large mushrooms
2 tbsp	chopped onion
1	clove garlic, minced
1 1/2 tbsp	olive oil
2 tbsp	grated Parmesan cheese
2 tbsp	dry bread crumbs
1/4 c	piñon nuts
1/4 tsp	dry oregano
1/4 tsp	dry basil

QUICHÉ FLORENTINE

Total Time: 40 minutes
Baking: 350° F oven for 25 minutes

1. Preheat oven.
2. Cook spinach and squeeze out water thoroughly.
3. Beat eggs until light; add milk, cream, and cheese.
4. Puree spinach and add to above mixture. Add salt and pepper.
5. Pour into quiché pan lined with baked pastry.
6. Bake at 350° F until filling no longer shakes when moved (approximately 25 minutes).
7. Serve while hot.

(Serves two)

2	*baked tart shells (see Pastry)*
1/2 lb	*fresh spinach*
1 1/2	*eggs*
1/2 c	*cream*
2 tbsp	*milk*
1/6 lb	*gruyere cheese, grated*
1/4 tsp	*salt*
	dash of pepper

(Serves four)

1	baked 10" shell in quiché pan (see Pastry)
1 lb	fresh spinach
3	eggs
1 c	cream
1/4 c	milk
1/3 lb	gruyere cheese, grated
1/2 tsp	salt
1/8 tsp	pepper

SPANISH SPINACH

Total Time: 10 minutes

1. Wash spinach thoroughly and drain well.
2. In a skillet, cook bacon until crisp; remove and crumble.
3. Pour off all but 1 tbsp drippings.
4. Add remaining ingredients.
5. Stir constantly while sautéing over medium heat until spinach is wilted and hot.
6. Sprinkle with crumbled bacon.

(Serves two)

2	*slices bacon*
2 tbsp	*sliced pimiento-stuffed olives*
1/8 tsp	*garlic powder*
1/2 tsp	*grated lemon peel*
1	*bunch fresh spinach*
1 1/2 tsp	*lemon juice*

(Serves four)

4	slices bacon
1/4 c	sliced pimiento-stuffed olives
1/4 tsp	garlic powder
1 tsp	grated lemon peel
2	bunch fresh spinach
3 tsp	lemon juice

SPINACH SAUTÉ (BY MARY KRAMER)

Total Time: 10 minutes

1. Break off stems and any blemished leaves.
2. Rinse leaves thoroughly in several changes of water until clean; drain well.
3. In a skillet melt the margarine, and add the oil.
4. Sauté onion and garlic for 5 minutes.
5. Add the spinach, a handful at a time, and stir-fry until wilted.
6. In a bowl, combine lemon juice, sour cream, salt, and pepper.
7. Drain off any liquid in the skillet.
8. Stir the sour cream mixture throughout the spinach.
9. Heat just to serving temperature and serve immediately. Avoid boiling the sour cream.

(Serves two)

1	*bunch spinach*
1 tbsp	*margarine or butter*
1 tbsp	*salad oil*
1/4 c	*chopped onion*
1/2	*clove garlic, minced*
1 1/2 tsp	*lemon juice*
1/4 c	*sour cream*
1/8 tsp	*salt*
1/8 tsp	*pepper*

(Serves four)

2	bunches spinach
2 tbsp	margarine or butter
2 tbsp	salad oil
1/2 c	chopped onion
1	clove garlic, minced
1 tbsp	lemon juice
1/2 c	sour cream
1/4 tsp	salt
1/4 tsp	pepper

Spanakopita (Spinach Pie)

Total Time: 1 hour 15 minutes
Baking: 300° F oven for 1 hour

1. Preheat oven.
2. Clean, chop, and blanch spinach; drain very thoroughly.
3. Sauté onion until tender.
4. Combine all ingredients except filo dough and margarine.
5. Melt margarine.
6. In a greased baking dish (8x8" for small recipe; 13x9" for large recipe), layer 8 filo sheets, brushing each with melted margarine.
7. Spread spinach mixture over dough.
8. Layer another 8 sheets of filo dough, brushing each with melted margarine.
9. Score with parallel diagonal lines at 2" intervals.
10. Bake one hour at 300° F until golden brown.
11. Cut in squares to serve.

(Serves four)
1 lb	spinach	
1 tbsp	margarine or butter	
1/3 c	chopped green onion	
1 tbsp	chopped parsley	
1 tsp	dill weed	
1/4 lb	feta cheese, crumbled	
1/8 lb	Romano cheese, grated	
3	eggs, beaten	
16	half-sheets filo dough	
1/8 lb	margarine or butter	

(Serves eight)
2 lb	spinach
2 tbsp	margarine or butter
2/3 c	chopped green onion
2 tbsp	chopped parsley
2 tsp	dill weed
1/2 lb	feta cheese, crumbled
1/4 lb	Romano cheese, grated
7	eggs, beaten
16	sheets filo dough
1/4 lb	margarine or butter

Okra Delight

Total Time: 35 minutes

1. Sauté onions in olive oil until golden.
2. Stir in okra (uncut), tomatoes, salt, and pepper. Cover and simmer 25 minutes.
3. Microwave bacon until crisp; crumble into coarse pieces.
4. Add shrimp and bacon to tomato mixture.
5. Simmer 4 minutes.
6. Serve over rice.

(Serves two)
1/2	Spanish onion, sliced and halved
1/2 tbsp	olive oil
5	small okra (leave whole)
1 c	stewed tomatoes
1/8 tsp	salt
1/4 tsp	coarse grind pepper
2	strips bacon
1/4 lb	raw shrimp, shelled
1 c	cooked rice

(Serves four)
1	Spanish onion, sliced and halved
1 tbsp	olive oil
10	small okra (leave whole)
2 c	stewed tomatoes
1/4 tsp	salt
1/2 tsp	coarse grind pepper
4	strips bacon
1/2 lb	raw shrimp, shelled
2 c	cooked rice

HERBED PEARL ONIONS

Total Time: 40 minutes
Baking: 350° F for 30 minutes

1. Preheat oven.
2. Blanch unpeeled onions 3 minutes.
3. Cut stem end and peel.
4. Melt butter in small saucepan and remove from heat. Stir in flour and milk. Heat with constant stirring until sauce thickens and comes to boil.
5. Add seasonings and onions and stir just to mix.
6. Put in shallow baking dish and sprinkle cheese on top.
7. Bake at 350° F until lightly browned and very hot.

(Serves two)	
9 oz	(1/2 package) pearl onions
1 tbsp	butter
1 tbsp	flour
1/2 c	milk
1/4 tsp	salt
1/4 tsp	dry thyme
1/4 tsp	garlic powder
	Freshly ground pepper to taste (optional)
1 tbsp	grated Parmesan cheese

(Serves four)
18 oz	(1 package) pearl onions
2 tbsp	butter
2 tbsp	flour
1 c	milk
1/2 tsp	salt
1/2 tsp	dry thyme
1/2 tsp	garlic powder
	Freshly ground pepper to taste (optional)
2 tbsp	grated Parmesan cheese

RATATOUILLE

Total Time: 70 minutes
Baking: 350° F for 50 minutes

1. Preheat oven.
2. Sauté onions, peppers, and garlic in oil 4 minutes. Set aside.
3. In a bowl, combine cheese, basil, oregano, salt, and pepper. Set aside.
4. Arrange 1/2 of vegetables in a layer in a shallow baking pan.
5. Arrange 1/2 of onion mixture on the vegetables; add a layer of 1/2 of the cheese mixture.
6. Repeat layering.
7. Bake (covered) at 350° F for 40 minutes and then 10 minutes uncovered.

(Serves two)	
1/2 c	sliced onion
1/2 c	red bell pepper strips
1/2 c	yellow bell pepper strips
1	garlic clove, minced
1 tbsp	olive oil
1/4 c	grated Parmesan cheese
2 tsp	dry basil
2 tsp	dry oregano
	dash of salt
1/8 tsp	pepper
1 c	sliced zucchini
3/4 lb	tomatoes, sliced
1/2	small eggplant cut in 1/4" slices

(Serves four)
1 c	sliced onion
1 c	red bell pepper strips
1 c	yellow bell pepper strips
2	garlic clove, minced
2 tbsp	olive oil
1/2 c	grated Parmesan cheese
4 tsp	dry basil
4 tsp	dry oregano
1/4 tsp	salt
1/4 tsp	pepper
2 c	sliced zucchini
1 1/2 lb	tomatoes, sliced
1	small eggplant cut in 1/4" slices

CHINESE SNOW PEA SAUTÉ

Total Time: 15 minutes

1. Wash snow peas and cut away stems and tails.
2. Clean mushrooms, and slice into vertical pieces 1/8" thick
3. Heat olive oil slightly in a shallow skillet before adding the pea pods, mushrooms, and drained water chestnuts.
4. Sauté quickly while stirring frequently until mushrooms are somewhat translucent.
5. Quickly stir in soy sauce and serve.

(Serves two)
1/8 lb	*snow peas*
1/8 lb	*mushrooms*
1 tbsp	*sliced canned water chestnuts*
2 tsp	*soy sauce*

(Serves four)
1/4 lb	snow peas
1/4 lb	mushrooms
2 tbsp	canned sliced water chestnuts
4 tsp	soy sauce

SPAGHETTI SQUASH SALAD

Total Time: 30 minutes

1. Halve squash lengthwise; remove seeds and microwave in 1/4 cup water until tender (10–15 minutes).
2. Scrape strands from shell; chill.
3. Slice radishes, basil, and onions thinly; cube tomatoes; cut cheese and salami in julienne strips.
4. Combine all ingredients and toss.

(Serves two)
1/2	*small spaghetti squash*
2	*radishes*
2	*leaves fresh basil*
2	*green onions*
1	*Roma tomato*
1 oz	*Provolone cheese*
1 oz	*salami*
1 oz	*crumbled feta cheese with herbs*
2 tbsp	*green bell pepper, diced*
2 tbsp	*red pepper, diced*
1/4 c	*alfalfa sprouts*
1 tbsp	*Italian dressing*
	salt and pepper to taste

(Serves four)
1	small spaghetti squash
4	radishes
4	leaves fresh basil
4	green onions
2	Roma tomatoes
2 oz	Provolone cheese
2 oz	salami
2 oz	crumbled feta cheese with herbs
1/4 c	green bell pepper, diced
1/4 c	red pepper, diced
1/2 c	alfalfa sprouts
2 tbsp	Italian dressing
	salt and pepper to taste

STUFFED TOMATOES PROVENCALE

Total Time: 1 hour
Baking: 375° F 30–40 minutes

1. Preheat oven.
2. Prepare rice according to package directions.
3. Remove a thin slice from the top of each tomato.
4. Carefully remove interior to leave shell 1/2" thick.
5. Chop flesh of tomato and drain off the liquid.
6. Sauté onion and garlic in oil.
7. Combine rice, onion mixture, vinegar, olives, salt, and pepper.
8. Stuff tomato shells with mixture and top with basil leaf and tomato slice.
9. Place on foil on baking sheet and bake in 375° F about 30 minutes until tomato is very hot, but not mushy.

(Serves two)

1/2 c	*uncooked rice*
2	*large tomatoes*
1/4 c	*red onion, diced*
1/2	*clove garlic, minced*
2 tsp	*olive oil*
2	*Kalamata olives*
1/2 tsp	*balsamic vinegar*
2	*basil leaves*

(Serves four)

1 c	uncooked rice
4	large tomatoes
1/2 c	red onion, diced
1	clove garlic, minced
1 tbsp	olive oil
4	Kalamata olives
1 tsp	balsamic vinegar
4	basil leaves

ZUCCHINI SAUTÉ (BY MARY KRAMER)

Total Time: 7 minutes

1. Wash zucchini thoroughly, and cut off stem.
2. Grate zucchini coarsely.
3. In a skillet, sauté onion and garlic in the oil for 5 minutes.
4. Add tomatoes and heat to boiling.
5. Stir in the zucchini, salt, and pper.
6. Heat quickly just to boiling point. (Cooking beyond this point will cause zucchini to be very watery.)
7. Serve, garnished with Parmesan cheese.

(Serves two)

2	*zucchini, coarsely grated*
1 tbsp	*salad oil*
1/2	*onion, chopped*
1/2	*clove garlic, minced*
1	*fresh tomato, peeled and diced*
1/4 tsp	*seasoned salt*
1/4 tsp	*seasoned pepper*
	Parmesan cheese

(Serves four)

4	zucchini, coarsely grated
2 tbsp	salad oil
1	onion, chopped
1	clove garlic, minced
2	fresh tomato, peeled and diced
1/2 tsp	seasoned salt
1/2 tsp	seasoned pepper
	Parmesan cheese

ZESTY ZUCCHINI

Total Time: 7 minutes

1. Stir-fry zucchini and onions in oil until just tender.
2. Stir in remaining ingredients.
3. Serve immediately.

(Serves two)
2	*medium zucchini squash, cut in 1/8" slices*
1 tbsp	*onion, minced*
1 tbsp	*olive oil*
1/4 c	*chopped parsley*
1/8 tsp	*grated lemon peel*
1 tsp	*lemon juice*

(Serves four)
4	medium zucchini squash, cut in 1/8" slices
2 tbsp	onion, minced
2 tbsp	olive oil
1/2 c	chopped parsley
1/4 tsp	grated lemon peel
2 tsp	lemon juice

SAUCES FOR VEGETABLES

LEMON SAUCE

Total Time: 1 minute

1. Melt margarine or butter.
2. Stir in lemon juice; serve over well-drained, boiled vegetables, such as carrots or broccoli.

(Serves two)
1 tbsp	*margarine or butter*
2 tsp	*lemon juice*

(Serves four)
3 tbsp	margarine or butter
2 tbsp	lemon juice

CREAM SAUCE

Total Time: 5 minutes

1. Melt margarine or butter.
2. Remove from heat and stir in flour and salt.
3. Gradually add milk while stirring constantly to avoid lumps.
4. Return to heat. Heat to a rolling boil, stirring constantly.

(Serves two)
1 tsp	*margarine or butter*
1 tsp	*flour*
	pinch salt
1/4 c	*milk*

(Serves four)
2 tsp	margarine or butter
2 tsp	flour
1/8 tsp	salt
1/2 c	milk

CHEESE SAUCE

Total Time: 7 minutes

1. Make the cream sauce as described above.
2. Add grated cheese.
3. Reheat sauce over low heat, if necessary, to melt the cheese.
4. Serve immediately over well-drained, boiled vegetables or use in casserole recipes. Avoid heating sauce to boiling or holding at serving temperature for more than 5 minutes. Excessive heat will toughen the cheese and may cause fat separation.
5. If fat does separate, stir in just enough milk to reunite the sauce.

(Serves two)
1/4 c   cream sauce (see previous recipe)
3 tbsp grated sharp cheddar cheese

(Serves four)
1/2 c   cream sauce (see previous recipe)
1/3 c   grated sharp cheddar cheese

SWEET-SOUR SAUCE

Total Time: 5 minutes

1. Melt margarine or butter.
2. Remove from heat and stir in cornstarch, sugar, and salt. Gradually stir in white vinegar.
3. Return to heat. Heat to boiling, while stirring constantly.
4. When sauce becomes clear and thick, pour over well-drained, boiled vegetables.

(Serves two)
*   1 tsp   margarine or butter*
1/2 tsp cornstarch
1/2 tsp sugar
*   pinch salt*
1/4 c   white vinegar

(Serves four)
  1 tbsp margarine or butter
1-1/2 tsp cornstarch
1-1/2 tsp sugar
           pinch salt
  1/2 c   white vinegar

HOLLANDAISE SAUCE

Total Time: 10 minutes

1. Cream margarine or butter until soft.
2. Carefully stir in well-beaten egg yolk.
3. Slowly add hot water, while stirring.
4. Cook over hot, but not boiling water, and stir constantly until sauce thickens.
5. Remove from heat and gradually stir in lemon juice.
6. Serve over well-drained, boiled vegetables.

(Serves two)
2 tbsp margarine or butter
1   egg yolk
2 tbsp hot water
1 tsp lemon juice

(Serves four)
1/4 c   margarine or butter
2   egg yolks
1/4 c   hot water
2 tsp   lemon juice

JIFFY HOLLANDAISE SAUCE

Total Time: 5 minutes

1. Combine sour cream, mayonnaise, mustard, and lemon juice.
2. Stir while heating to serving temperature over low heat.

(Serves two)
2 tbsp dairy sour cream
2 tbsp mayonnaise
1/4 tsp prepared mustard
1/2 tsp lemon juice

(Serves four)
1/4 c   dairy sour cream
1/4 c   mayonnaise
1/2 tsp prepared mustard
1 tsp   lemon juice

ROQUEFORT VEGETABLE DIP

Total Time: 5 minutes

(To accompany a tray of raw vegetables as an appetizer.)

1. In a bowl, mash cheese with fork.
2. Add mayonnaise and sour cream gradually, blending until smooth.
3. Add remaining ingredients and blend completely.
4. Store in refrigerator in tightly covered container.
5. Serve in a bowl on an attractive tray, surrounded by carrot sticks, radish roses, turnip slices, cauliflowerets, celery curls, zucchini slices, or other crisp, raw vegetables.

(Serves two)

1/8 lb	*Roquefort, Bleu, or Gorgonzola cheese*
1/4 c	*mayonnaise*
1/4 c	*sour cream*
1 tbsp	*lemon juice*
1 tbsp	*chopped parsley*
1 tbsp	*chopped green onion tops*
	dash of curry powder
	dash of Worcestershire sauce
	dash of season salt
	dash of garlic powder
1/8 tsp	*coarse grind black pepper*
	dash of cayenne
	assorted raw vegetables for dipping

(Serves four)

1/4 lb	Roquefort, Bleu, or Gorgonzola cheese
1/2 c	mayonnaise
1/2 c	sour cream
2 tbsp	lemon juice
2 tbsp	chopped parsley
2 tbsp	chopped green onion tops
1/8 tsp	curry powder
1/8 tsp	Worcestershire sauce
1/8 tsp	season salt
1/8 tsp	garlic powder
1/4 tsp	coarse grind black pepper
1/8 tsp	cayenne
	assorted raw vegetables for dipping

POTATOES

Potatoes of different varieties are available in various parts of the country. Basically, potatoes may be classified as waxy or nonwaxy. Usually potatoes that are round in shape will tend to be waxy, whereas the long flat ones tend to be nonwaxy. A waxy potato is one that is comparatively high in sugar and low in starch. A nonwaxy (mealy) potato is just the reverse, that is, it is high in starch and low in sugar.

The storage temperature as well as the variety will influence the waxy nature of a potato. Storage temperatures close to room temperature promote starch content, while temperatures below 45° F promote more sugar formation. Optimum storage is approximately 60° F. At this temperature, the basic starch to sugar ratio of a variety will be maintained. Russet potatoes provide a classic example of nonwaxy potatoes, and Red Triumphs are a familiar example of waxy potatoes.

SPECIFIC GRAVITY

The cooking quality of different potatoes within a variety and even different varieties can be determined by placing

The potato at the bottom of the container has a high solids content and is good for baking; the one at the top has a low solids content which is well suited to boiling and use in salads. The middle potato has qualities of both types.

1) Potatoes vary in their cooking properties according to their comparative sugar and starch content.

   a) *Waxy* potatoes are relatively high in sugar and low in starch.

   b) *Nonwaxy* (mealy) potatoes are higher in starch and lower in sugar than waxy potatoes.

2) Waxy potatoes are well-suited to preparing boiled potatoes and potato salad because they hold their shape well during preparation.

3) Nonwaxy (mealy) potatoes are a good choice for making baked, fried (including French fries), and mashed potatoes.

   a) Because of their high starch content, nonwaxy potatoes swell during boiling to give a light texture to baked and a fluffy texture to mashed potatoes.

   b) The low sugar content of nonwaxy potatoes results in rather slow browning, which allows time for frying potatoes to soften appropriately in the center without burning on the surface.

the potatoes in a brine solution made by dissolving 1/2 cup of salt in 5 1/2 cups of water. (Dr. Andrea Mackey, Oregon State University, developed this technique for testing potatoes.) If a potato has a high solids content, it will sink to the bottom of the container. Such potatoes are classified as non-waxy or mealy potatoes. Potatoes which float on the surface are low in solids and are waxy potatoes. The higher starch content of the nonwaxy potatoes makes them desirable for mashed potatoes, French fries, and baked potatoes. The best choice for making boiled potatoes, potato salads, and scalloped potatoes is the waxy potato with the low solids content. Make up the above brine solution and test each of the potatoes used in the potato lesson to determine the solids content.

BOILING POTATOES

Boiled potatoes should retain a distinct outline even after cooking is completed. A waxy potato will be the better choice for boiling and for use in any potato recipe in which distinct pieces of potato are desired. Scalloped potatoes, potato salad, and au gratin potatoes are examples of potato preparations in which the distinct outline of the waxy potato is preferred to the less distinct and sloughed off exterior that develops when nonwaxy potatoes are used. The nonwaxy (mealy) potato is on the left; the waxy potato is on the right (see photo below).

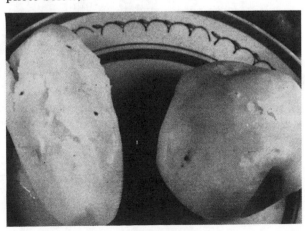

FRYING POTATOES

French fried potatoes should be tender in the center without being too dark on the exterior. The browning on the exterior of frying potatoes is the result of chemical change in the sugar. A potato that is high in sugar, specifically a waxy potato (right side of dish), will brown so readily that it may become almost burned on the outside before the interior is cooked. A nonwaxy potato (left side of dish) is a better choice for frying because its lower sugar content means that it will take a longer time for the potato to become the desired brown on the exterior. This slower browning allows time for the potato to be cooked on the inside.

MASHING POTATOES

For mashing, a light and fluffy character is considered to be best. The fluffiness is provided by having a high starch content because the starch will swell during the gelatinization process. The preferred type of potato for mashing is the nonwaxy potato (left side of plate) because it has a higher starch content than does the waxy potato (right side of plate). Waxy potatoes will become rather gummy, pasty, and often darker in color than will nonwaxy potatoes when they are mashed.

BAKING POTATOES

Nonwaxy potatoes (left side of plate) are best suited to baking because the finished product should have a somewhat fluffy character. This texture is provided by a potato which is high in starch. Waxy potatoes (right side of plate) will be rather gummy and soggy when baked.

SUMMARY ON POTATO SELECTION

Russets or nonwaxy potatoes are preferred for mashing, baking, and frying because of their higher starch content. Red Triumphs or other varieties of waxy potatoes are the potato type of choice for boiling or for use in recipes requiring a potato that will hold its shape well. When practical, it is wise to stock the type of potato needed for specific preparations. When only a few pota-

toes will be consumed, it may be more practical to purchase an all purpose potato such as a White Rose. All purpose potatoes are not as desirable as the correct type of potato, but they can be used satisfactorily for any recipe.

RECIPES

To determine the best type of potato to use for each of the following preparations, prepare each recipe using waxy and nonwaxy potatoes. Identify and record the characteristics of each in the table in this chapter and indicate the preferred type of potato for each recipe. Compare your findings with the preceding discussion.

BOILED POTATOES

Total Time: 22 minutes

1. Pare potatoes.
2. Place them in a pan containing enough boiling water to just cover the potatoes. Add salt.
3. Cover and boil until easily penetrated with fork.
4. Drain and serve.

> *(Serves two)*
> 2   potatoes
> 1/2 tsp   salt

(Serves four)
4   potatoes
1 tsp   salt

FRENCH-FRIED POTATOES

Total Time: 20 minutes
Frying Temperature: 375° F

1. Begin preheating fat to 375° F.
2. Pare potatoes. Cut lengthwise into strips.
3. Blot dry with paper towels.
4. Place in wire basket and fry in deep fat that has been preheated to 375° F.
5. Fry until golden brown and tender in the middle.
6. Drain on paper towels.
7. Salt and serve.

> *(Serves two)*
> 2   potatoes
>   salad oil

(Serves four)
4   potatoes
    salad oil

MASHED POTATOES

Total Time: 25 minutes

1. Pare potatoes, cut in quarters, and boil in salted water (to cover the potatoes) until tender.
2. Drain the potatoes.
3. With a potato masher or electric mixer (on low speed), mash the potatoes.
4. After adding margarine or butter and sufficient warm milk, whip the potatoes until light and fluffy.
5. Add more salt and pepper, if desired.
6 Serve immediately.

> *(Serves two)*
> 2   potatoes
>   nonfat milk
> 2 tsp   margarine or butter

(Serves four)
4   potatoes
    nonfat milk
4 tsp   margarine or butter

BAKED POTATOES

Total Time: 1 minutes
Baking: 425° F oven for 1 hour

1. Preheat oven.
2. Under running water, scrub potato vigorously with a vegetable brush.
3. Grease potatoes with margarine or butter, place on a sheet of aluminum foil, and bake in a 425° F oven for about 1 hour.
4. After 30 minutes, perforate skins with a fork to release steam.
5. When done, cut an X in the potato and squeeze potato partially open, using both hands.
6. Drop a dollop of margarine or butter or sour cream in the X on each potato.

> *(Serves two)*
>   potatoes
>   margarine or butter or sour cream

(Serves four)
4   potatoes
    margarine or butter or sour cream

EVALUATION OF TYPES OF POTATOES IN RECIPES[1]

RECIPE	TYPE PREFERRED	APPEARANCE AND PALATABILITY	
		WAXY	NONWAXY
Boiled			
French-fried			
Mashed			
Baked			

[1]The Red Triumph is a typical example of a waxy potato; the Russet is an example of a mealy or nonwaxy potato. Storage temperatures of approximately 45° F promote the waxy character of a potato and temperatures between 65–70° F promote nonwaxy character.

SCALLOPED POTATOES

Total Time: 1 1/4 hours (small); 1 1/2 hours (large)
Baking: 350° F oven for 60–75 minutes

1. Preheat oven.
2. Slice pared potatoes very thin.
3. In a 1-quart saucepan, melt the margarine or butter; remove from heat.
4. Stir in the flour and salt.
5. Gradually stir in the milk.
6. Return to heat. Heat to boiling while stirring constantly.
7. Place 1/3 of the potatoes in a casserole; pour 1/3 of the sauce over them. Repeat the layers, ending with a layer of the white sauce.
8. Bake with a cover in a 350° F oven for one hour.
9. Uncover and continue baking until surface is browned (about 15 minutes).

(Serves two)
2	waxy potatoes
1 tbsp	margarine or butter
1 tbsp	flour
1/4 tsp	salt
1 c	milk
	covered casserole dish, 2 cup capacity

(Serves four)
4	waxy potatoes
2 tbsp	margarine or butter
2 tbsp	flour
1/2 tsp	salt
2 c	milk
	covered casserole dish, 1 qt capacity

Note —
For variety, chopped green peppers, pimiento, or onion may be added. Flavor can be varied by adding a dash of curry, pepper, or garlic powder.

Scalloped potatoes may be assembled in a casserole, covered and microwaved on high for 9–10 minutes (small recipe) or 18–20 minutes (large recipe), with the potatoes being stirred when half the time has elapsed. A standing time of 5 minutes after the microwaving period is necessary to complete the cooking.

Potatoes Anna, a variation of scalloped potatoes, is framed by broccoli, boiling onions, and cherry tomatoes.

Au Gratin Potatoes

Total Time: 1 1/4 hours (small); 1 1/2 hours (large)
Baking: 350° F oven for 60–75 minutes

1. Preheat oven.
2. Prepare the recipe for scalloped potatoes, but add grated sharp cheese to the white sauce before placing the layers in the dish.
3. Assemble and bake as described above.

(Serves two)	
	Scalloped potatoes
	(from previous recipe)
2/3 c	grated sharp cheddar cheese

(Serves four)
      Scalloped potatoes
      (from previous recipe)
1 1/3 c   grated sharp cheddar cheese

Hashed Brown Potatoes

Total Time: 30 minutes

1. Wash, pare, and grate potatoes.
2. Place them in a skillet containing 1/6" of hot salad oil.
3. Heat on medium high heat until the bottom side is crisp and golden brown.
4. Turn the entire mass in pancake-fashion to brown the second side.
5. Cook until the second side is also golden brown and crisp.
6. Entire cooking time is approximately 25 minutes. Salt and serve.

> *nonwaxy potatoes*
> *salad oil*

Stuffed Baked Potatoes

Total Time: 1 hour 10 minutes
Baking: 425° F oven for 1 hour

1. Preheat oven.
2. Mash and grease potatoes before baking (about 1 hour at 425° F).
3. When potatoes are easily pierced with a fork, use a paring knife to cut a slice off most of the length of the upper surface of each potato.
4. Scoop the potato pulp into a bowl.
5. Prepare the pulp as for mashed potatoes.
6. Spoon the mashed potato back into the potato shells lightly.
7. If desired, place stuffed potatoes briefly under broiler to brown slightly.

> *nonwaxy potatoes*
> *milk*
> *margarine or butter*

Note: Variations may be created by adding crumbled, fried bacon, grated cheese, or chopped chives to the mashed filling. A pastry tube can be used to add a more decorative appearance when the potatoes are being stuffed.

LEGUMES

KEY CONCEPTS — LEGUMES

1) Legumes of many types are available to provide inexpensive, healthful sources of protein.

2) For efficient use in the body, the proteins from legumes need to be combined with some animal protein or some cereal, such as rice.

3) Dried beans require an extended soaking period and slow cooking to produce the desired tenderness.

BASIC LEGUME COOKERY

LEGUME	CUPS OF WATER/ CUPS OF DRY LEGUMES	SOAKING TIME	COOKING TIME (HOURS)
Split peas	4	1/2 hour	1
Pinto beans	4	None	2
Lentils	6	None	1
Navy beans	3	Boil 2 minutes, soak 1 hour	2
Pink beans	3	Boil 2 minutes, soak 1 hour	1
Great northern beans	3	Boil 2 minutes, soak 1 hour	3
Blackeye peas	4	Overnight or boil 2 min., soak 1 hour	1 1/2
Red kidney beans	4	Overnight	2
Garbanzos	4	Overnight	1/2
Lima beans	3	Boil 2 min., soak 1 hour	1 1/2

Legumes: (front row, left to right) lentils, split peas, pinto beans; (back row) pink beans and kidney beans.

Legumes: (front row, left to right) lima beans, garbanzos, blackeye peas; (back row) navy beans and great northern beans.

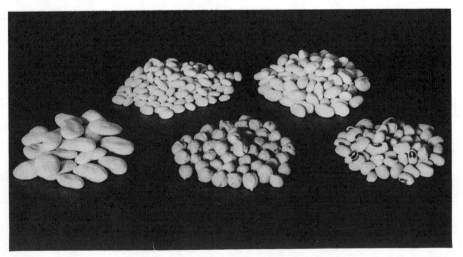

RECIPES

EL RANCHO PINTO BEANS

Total Time: 2 hours

1. Wash beans.
2. Add water and heat to boiling.
3. Reduce heat to simmering and simmer the beans for one hour.
4. Lightly fry the bacon and drain it.
5. Cut it up into small pieces and mix with the other ingredients.
6. Stir into the beans and continue simmering for another hour. Add water as needed. Use a cover throughout the cooking period.

(Serves two)
1/2 c	*pinto beans, dry*
2 c	*water*
3	*strips bacon*
1	*small onion, chopped*
1/4 c	*tomato sauce*
1/4 tsp	*salt*

(Serves four)
1 c	pinto beans, dry
4 c	water
6	strips bacon
1	medium onion, chopped
1	small can tomato sauce
1/2 tsp	salt

SWEET AND SOUR BAKED BEANS (BY PETE PETERSON)

Total Time: 1 1/2 hours
Baking: 350° F for 1 hour

1. Preheat oven.
2. Microwave or fry bacon until crisp.
3. Remove bacon and crumble it.
4. Sauté rings of onion in drippings until tender.
5. Stir in sugar, mustard, garlic powder, salt and vinegar; simmer 20 minutes.
6. Combine in a casserole with the drained butter, lima, and kidney beans and the baked beans with their sauce.
7. Bake at 350° F for 1 hour.

(Small recipe)
4	*slices bacon*
2	*onions, sliced into rings*
1/4 c	*brown sugar*
1/2 tsp	*dry mustard*
1/4 tsp	*garlic powder*
1/2 tsp	*salt*
1/4 c	*cider vinegar*
1	*15 oz can butter beans*
1	*8 oz can lima beans*
1	*8 oz can red kidney beans*
1	*8 oz can baked beans*

(Large recipe)
8	slices bacon
4	onions, sliced into rings
1/2 c	brown sugar
1 tsp	dry mustard
1/2 tsp	garlic powder
1 tsp	salt
1/2 c	cider vinegar
2	15 oz can butter beans
1	1 lb can lima beans
1	1 lb can red kidney beans
1	1 lb can baked beans

PORK CHOPS IN NORTHERN BEANS

Total Time: 3 hours
Baking: 350° F for 1 hour

1. Preheat oven.
2. Wash beans.
3. Cover with the water, heat to boiling, boil 2 minutes, and then let the beans stand in the covered pan for 1 hour.
4. Continue cooking the beans at a simmer until they are tender.
5. Drain well.
6. Combine all of the remaining ingredients except the pork chops and pour over the beans, which have been placed in a casserole.
7. In a skillet, brown the pork chops and arrange on top of the beans.
8. Bake for 1 hour at 350° F.

(Serves two)

3/4 c	*great northern beans, dry*
1 1/2 c	*water*
1	*small can tomato sauce*
1	*small onion, chopped*
2 tbsp	*catsup*
1/8 tsp	*dry mustard*
1 tbsp	*brown sugar*
1 tbsp	*molasses*
2	*pork chops*

(Serves four)

1 1/2 c	great northern beans, dry
3 c	water
1	medium can tomato sauce
1	medium onion, chopped
1/4 c	catsup
1/4 tsp	dry mustard
2 tbsp	brown sugar
2 tbsp	molasses
4	pork chops

CHILI BLACKEYE PEAS

Total Time: 3 hours and 45 minutes
Baking: 350° F for 45 minutes

1. Preheat oven.
2. Wash peas.
3. Put peas and water in a covered saucepan.
4. Heat to boiling and cook for 2 minutes.
5. Let the peas stand for 1 hour, and then continue cooking until tender (approximately 1 1/2 hours).
6. Mix all the remaining ingredients except the cheese, and pour over the peas in a casserole.
7. Bake at 350° F for 45 minutes.
8. Sprinkle grated cheese generously over the top of the dish and return to the oven just long enough to melt the cheese.

(Serves two)

1/2 c	*blackeye peas, dry*
2 c	*water*
1	*small onion, chopped*
1/2	*green pepper, chopped*
1/2	*No. 2 can stewed tomatoes*
1/8 tsp	*garlic powder*
1 1/2 tsp	*Worcestershire sauce*
1/2 tsp	*chili powder*
1/2	*bay leaf*
1/4 tsp	*salt*
1/2 c	*cheddar cheese, grated*

(Serves four)

1 c	blackeye peas, dry
4 c	water
1	medium onion, chopped
1	green pepper, chopped
1	No. 2 can stewed tomatoes
1/4 tsp	garlic powder
1 tbsp	Worcestershire sauce
1 tsp	chili powder
1	bay leaf
1/2 tsp	salt
1 c	cheddar cheese, grated

PORK HOCKS AND LIMA BEAN STEW

Total Time: 3 hours

1. Put hocks and water in large kettle.
2. Add salt, pepper, garlic, bay leaf, onion and cloves.
3. Cover and bring to a boil.
4. Reduce heat and simmer 1 1/2 hours.
5. Meanwhile, rinse beans.
6. Heat beans and water to boiling in a large saucepan; boil 2 minutes.
7. Remove from heat, cover and let soak 1 hour.
8. Drain.
9. Add beans to hocks and continue to simmer 1 hour.
10. Add carrots and simmer 30 minutes more, or until meat and vegetables are tender.
11. Discard bay leaf.
12. Skin hocks with a sharp knife. Arrange with beans and carrots on hot platter.

(Serves two)

2	*fresh pork hocks*
3 c	*water*
3/4 tsp	*salt*
	dash pepper
1	*garlic clove, crushed*
1	*small bay leaf*
1/2	*medium size onion, pared and quartered*
3	*whole cloves*
1/3 lb	*dry lima beans*
1 3/4 c	*water*
2	*carrots, pared and cut into chunks*

(Serves four)

4	fresh pork hocks
1 1/2 qt	water
1 1/2 tsp	salt
1/4 tsp	pepper
2	garlic clove, crushed
1	bay leaf
1	medium size onion, pared and quartered
6	whole cloves
2/3 lb	dry lima beans
3 1/2 c	water
4	carrots, pared and cut into chunks

Pork hocks and lima bean stew (see above recipe) is a hearty recipe particularly well suited to winter weather.

KIDNEY BEAN SALAD

Total Time: Overnight soaking plus 3 hours

1. Wash beans and soak them overnight.
2. Simmer until tender (about 2 hours).
3. Drain and chill.
4. Mix the beans with the remaining ingredients.
5. Cover tightly and refrigerate for at least an hour to blend the flavors.

(Serves two)

1/2 c	*kidney beans*
1 1/2 c	*water*
1/4 c	*celery, chopped*
1/2	*green pepper, chopped*
1/2	*small onion, chopped*
1	*egg, hard cooked*
1/4 c	*pickle relish*
2 tbsp	*mayonnaise*

(Serves four)

1 c	kidney beans
3 c	water
1/2 c	celery, chopped
1	green pepper, chopped
1	small onion, chopped
2	eggs, hard cooked
1/2 c	pickle relish
1/4 c	mayonnaise

SPLIT PEA SOUP

Total Time: 1 1/2 hours

1. Soak peas in the water in a saucepan for 30 minutes.
2. Add remaining ingredients.
3. Cover and simmer for one hour or until the peas are soft enough to be pressed through a sieve easily.
4. Strain.
5. Salt to taste.
6. Serve piping hot. Reheat, if necessary after straining.

(Serves two)

1/2 c	*split peas, dry*
2 c	*water*
1/4 c	*celery, chopped*
1/2	*carrot, chopped*
1 tbsp	*onion, chopped*
1/8 tsp	*thyme*
	piece bay leaf
	ham bone

(Serves four)

1 c	split peas, dry
4 c	water
1/2 c	celery, chopped
1	carrot, chopped
1/2	medium onion, chopped
1/4 tsp	thyme
1	bay leaf
	ham bone

LENTIL SOUP

Total Time: 1 hour and 20 minutes

1. Wash lentils.
2. Cover with the water and simmer for 1 hour or until tender enough to be pureed easily.
3. Add the remaining ingredients to the pureed lentils.
4. Simmer, covered, for 20 minutes.
5. Serve piping hot.

(Serves two)

1/2 c	*lentiles, dry*
3 c	*water*
1/4 c	*ham tidbits*
2 tbsp	*carrot slices*
1 tsp	*dehydrated onion*
	dash salt

(Serves four)

1 c	*lentiles, dry*
6 c	*water*
1/2 c	*ham tidbits*
1/4 c	*carrot slices*
2 tsp	*dehydrated onion*
1/8 tsp	*salt*

BAKED BEANS

Total Time: 4 hours
Baking: 350 ° F oven for 3 hours

1. Preheat oven.
2. Wash beans.
3. Cover with water and heat to boiling.
4. Reduce heat and simmer until tender (about 1 hour).
5. Drain, but save the cooking liquid.
6. Mix the remaining ingredients with the beans and place in a casserole. Add enough of the cooking liquid to cover the beans completely.
7. Cover and bake in a 350° F oven for 3 hours. Add more cooking liquid if needed.

(Serves two)

1/2 c	navy beans, dry
1 1/2 c	water
1/2 c	tomato sauce
1/4 c	catsup
2 tbsp	molasses
1/2 tsp	dry mustard
1/4 c	brown sugar
1	small onion, chopped
	piece bay leaf
1/4 tsp	salt
3	strips bacon, cut up

(Serves four)

1 c	navy beans, dry
3 c	water
1 c	tomato sauce
1/2 c	catsup
1/4 c	molasses
1 tsp	dry mustard
1/2 c	brown sugar
1	medium onion, chopped
1	bay leaf
1/2 tsp	salt
6	strips bacon, cut up

VOCABULARY

Chlorophyll

Carotenoid

Flavonoid

Anthoxanthin

Anthocyanin

Legumes

Waxy potato

Nonwaxy potato

EVALUATION OF LABORATORY PRODUCTS — VEGETABLES

RECIPE	NOTES ON COLOR, TEXTURE, FLAVOR, OR OTHER QUALITIES	COMMENTS OR SUGGESTIONS FOR MAKING OR USING THIS PRODUCT IN THE FUTURE

Chapter 3
Fruits

OSMOTIC PRESSURE

Fruits often are eaten raw to take advantage of their beautiful colors and delightful flavors. They also find their way into a variety of recipes, especially for desserts where their sweetness enhances the pleasure of eating. Whether cooked or raw, fruits always enliven a meal or snack.

Preparation of all fruits needs to begin with careful washing to assure that microorganisms which may have found their way onto the fresh produce have been removed. Clean appearance is no guarantee that micro-

---

KEY CONCEPTS — FRUITS

1. Osmotic pressure can be created in systems consisting of fruit and a sugar solution.

   a) When the sugar solution is more concentrated than is the sugar level inside the cells of the fruit, water is drawn through the cell walls into the sugar solution, promoting a flabby texture in the fruit.

   b) When fruit is cooked in water, water will be drawn into the cells in an attempt to reduce the sugar concentration in the cells; the fruit will become plump and may fall apart.

   c) Fruit cooked in a dilute sugar solution will be pleasingly plump because a very small amount of water will be drawn into the cells.

2. When more than one variety of a fruit is available (apples and pears, for example), select the variety that is best suited to your intended preparation.

   a) Applesauce and coddled apples made with Rome Beauty apples will be bright and translucent, whereas sauce and coddled apples made with Pippens will be rather dark and opaque; the flavor differences are a matter of personal preference.

   b) The color of the skin and the flesh of baked Rome Beauty apples will be more appealing than a baked Pippin, but the tartness of the Pippin may be preferred by some people.

organisms are not present. Assume that fruit may have been harvested under somewhat unsanitary conditions, and you will be careful to even wash bananas in their skins before serving them.

As a general rule, prepare fruit close to the time that it will be served. Cut surfaces of fruit release juices, which causes fruit to become a bit shriveled if it stands too long, especially if sugar has been added to it. Two other cautions are 1) avoid having fresh pineapple in contact with meat or gelatin for more than a few minutes, and 2) be careful about combining various colors of fruit juice lest you discover a new way to make a muddy-looking beverage.

Applesauce and coddled apples are preparations which are useful as illustrations of the control of osmotic pressure in preparing fruits. In applesauce, the fruit is simmered in water. This situation causes water to flow into the cells and tends to rupture the cell walls, resulting in the desired mushy texture. Sugar is then stirred in simply for flavor. Coddled apples are simmered in a sugar syrup. The concentration of sugar used draws only a little water into the cell (just enough to give a plump appearance). If the syrup becomes too concentrated due to evaporation, the fruit will shrivel due to loss of water from the cells.

Frequently it is necessary to make a decision between two or more varieties of a fruit. Each variety has certain characteristics that suit it better for one type of preparation than for another. This is illustrated clearly by preparing applesauce, coddled apples, baked apples, and apple dumplings from three or more varieties of apples. Delicious, Rome Beauty, and Pippin are three varieties that are recommended for comparison because of their distinctly different cooking characteristics.

RECIPES

APPLESAUCE

Total Time: 15 minutes

1. Wash, pare, and quarter apples. Remove all trace of the core.
2. Place in a 1-quart saucepan and add just enough water to cover the bottom of the pan.
3. Simmer in a covered pan until the apples are tender (approximately 10 minutes).
4. Press the apples through a strainer or whirl in a blender to make a puree. Stir in sugar, and garnish with cinnamon, if desired.

(Serves two)
2	apples
2 tbsp	sugar
	cinnamon (optional)

(Serves four)
4	apples
1/4 c	sugar
	cinnamon (optional)

Note —
Apples may be placed in a covered casserole containing 1/4 cup water and microwaved on high, allowing 1 1/2 minutes per apple or until very tender.

CODDLED APPLES

Total Time: 15 minutes

1. Wash and core apples.
2. Cut doughnut-like slices 1/4" thick across the apple.
3. Cover slices with water to prevent discoloration before they are cooked.
4. In a 1-quart saucepan, stir together the sugar and water, and note the liquid level. Use a skillet for the large recipe.
5. Heat to a high simmer.
6. Add several apple slices, and continue simmering until slices are tender (about 10 minutes).
7. Add water as necessary to maintain the original liquid level.
8. When slices are tender, remove them from the syrup with a slotted spoon.
9. Serve as a dessert or as a meat accompaniment.

(Serves two)
2	apples
2 c	sugar
1 c	water

(Serves four)
(If desired, the large recipe may be prepared in a skillet.)
4	apples
2 c	sugar
1 c	water

BAKED APPLES

Total Time: 1 hour
Baking: 375° F for 45–60 minutes

1. Preheat oven.
2. Wash and core apples, being careful to remove all of woody cellulose around the seeds.
3. Peel a strip of skin 1/4" wide around the equator of the apples and place in a casserole dish.
4. Combine the remaining ingredients, and stuff into the center of each apple.
5. Pour 1 cup water into the bottom of the casserole dish. Cover, and bake at 375° F until tender (45 minutes to an hour).
6. Baste every 15 minutes.

(Serves two)
2	apples
2 tbsp	brown sugar
1/4 tsp	cinnamon
1/2 tsp	butter
1 tbsp	raisins

(Serves four)
4	apples
1/4 c	brown sugar
1/2 tsp	cinnamon
1 tsp	butter
2 tbsp	raisins

Note —
Apples may be placed in a covered casserole containing 2 tablespoons water per apple and microwaved on high, allowing 2 minutes per apple.

EVALUATION OF APPLE VARIETIES

TYPE OF APPLE	APPEARANCE AND FLAVOR		
	SAUCE	CODDLED	BAKED
Delicious			
Rome Beauty			
Pippin			

APPLE DUMPLINGS

Total Time: 1 hour
Baking: 400° F for 40 minutes

1. Preheat oven.
2. Combine sugar, water, cinnamon, food coloring, and margarine or butter in a 1-quart saucepan and boil 2 minutes.
3. Wash, pare, and core apples.
4. Mix the flour and salt.
5. With a pastry blender, cut in the shortening to the size of rice grains.
6. While tossing the flour mixture with a fork, slowly add the water.
7. Press together with a fork until dough is in a ball.
8. Roll out on pastry cloth to make a 1/8" thick rectangle 6 1/2 x 13" (13x13" when serving four). Cut squares 6 1/2" inches on a side.
9. Place one apple in the middle of each square.
10. Stuff center of each apple with raisins.
11. Sprinkle each apple generously with sugar and cinnamon.
12. Lightly moisten the edges of a square of dough.
13. Bring up the four corners and pinch them together on top of the apple.
14. Pinch the sides of the dough together.
15. Repeat for each apple.
16. Place in a rectangular cake pan, being sure that apples are at least an inch apart.
17. Pour the syrup over each of the dumplings. Bake at 400° F for 40 minutes, or until dumplings are browned and apples are done.

(Serves two)
1/2 c	sugar
3/4 c	water
1/8 tsp	cinnamon
2	drops red food coloring
1 tbsp	margarine or butter
2	apples, medium size

Dough (Bisquick may be substituted for dough):
1 c	flour
1/2 tsp	salt
1/3 c	shortening
2 2/3 tbsp water	
1 tbsp raisins	
	sugar
	cinnamon

(Serves four)
1 c	sugar
1 1/2 c	water
1/4 tsp	cinnamon
4	drops red food coloring
2 tbsp	margarine or butter
4	apples, medium size

Dough(Bisquick may be substituted for dough):
2 c	flour
1 tsp	salt
2/3 c	shortening
1/3 c	water
2 tbsp raisins	
	sugar
	cinnamon

STRAWBERRY CONSOMME

Total Time: 20 minutes

1. Wash, remove cap, and slice strawberries.
2. Simmer strawberries, rhubarb, cinnamon, sugar, and water for 5 minutes.
3. Strain juice.
4. Add burgundy and soda water to strained juice.
5. Serve either hot or cold with a dollop of sour cream on each serving.

(Serves two)
1 c	strawberries
1 c	fresh rhubarb (or 8 oz frozen rhubarb)
1 1/2"	stick of cinnamon
1/2 c	sugar
1 c	water
1/4 c	burgundy
1/4 c	soda water
2 tbsp	sour cream

(Serves four)
2 c	strawberries
2 c	fresh rhubarb (or 8 oz frozen rhubarb)
3"	stick of cinnamon
1 c	sugar
2 c	water
1/2 c	burgundy
1/2 c	soda water
1/4 c	sour cream

FRUIT COBBLER

Total Time: 45 minutes
Baking: 400° F for 30 minutes

1. Preheat oven.
2. Stir the sugar and cornstarch together and gradually add the canned fruit and juice to make a smooth mixture.
3. Pour into casserole dish and place in 400° F oven to heat while making the dough.
4. Mix the dry ingredients together.
5. Cut in the shortening to the size of rice grains.
6. Add the milk all at once, and stir with a fork until all the ingredients are moistened.
7. Drop from a spoon onto the hot fruit.
8. Sprinkle lightly with sugar and cinnamon, if desired.
9. Bake 30 minutes at 400° F until surface is golden brown.

(Serves two)
6 tbsp	*sugar*
1 1/2 tsp	*cornstarch*
1 1/4 c	*canned fruit and juice*
Dough:	
1/2 c	*flour*
3/4 tsp	*baking powder*
1 1/2 tsp	*sugar*
1/4 tsp	*salt*
4 tsp	*shortening*
3 tbsp	*milk*
	sugar
	cinnamon, if desired

(Serves four)
3/4 c	sugar
1 tbsp	cornstarch
2 1/2 c	canned fruit and juice
Dough:	
1 c	flour
1 1/2 tsp	baking powder
1 tbsp	sugar
1/2 tsp	salt
3 tbsp	shortening
6 tbsp	milk
	sugar
	cinnamon, if desired

BROILED GRAPEFRUIT

Total Time: 10 minutes

1. Cut grapefruit in half. Carefully cut around the circumference of the pulp and separate each section from the membranes.
2. Sprinkle brown sugar over each half.
3. Place on broiler pan, and broil with the upper surface about 3" from the heat. Watch continuously.
4. Remove from the broiler when the sugar is bubbly and brown.
5. Serve hot.

(Serves two)
1	*grapefruit*
1 tbsp	*brown sugar*

(Serves four)
2	grapefruit
2 tbsp	brown sugar

BLUEBERRY COFFEE CAKE

Total Time: 50 minutes (small); 60 minutes (large)
Baking: 350° F oven for 35–40 minutes

1. Preheat oven.
2. Cream the shortening and sugar until light and fluffy.
3. Beat in the well-beaten egg.
4. Sift the dry ingredients together.
5. Add 1/3 of the dry ingredients to the creamed mixture, and stir.
6. Add 1/2 of the milk, and stir.
7. Repeat with the remaining thirds of dry ingredients alternately with the other half of the milk.
8. Pour into a well-greased pan (8x8" for the small recipe, 8x12" for the large).
9. Put blueberries over the surface of the batter.
10. Combine brown sugar, flour, cinnamon, and melted butter in a small bowl.
11. Sprinkle over the blueberries.
12. Bake at 350° F 35–40 minutes until a toothpick inserted in the center comes out clean.

(Serves two)

1/4 c	sugar
1/4 c	shortening
1/2	egg
1 c	flour
1 tsp	baking powder
1/8 tsp	salt
1/4 c	milk
1 c	blueberries, well drained

Topping:

1/4 c	**brown sugar**
1/4 c	**flour**
1/4 tsp	**cinnamon**
1 tbsp	margarine or butter, melted

(Serves four)

1/2 c	sugar
1/2 c	shortening
1	egg
2 c	flour
2 tsp	baking powder
1/4 tsp	salt
1/2 c	milk
2 c	blueberries, well drained

Topping:

1/2 c	**brown sugar**
1/2 c	**flour**
1/2 tsp	**cinnamon**
2 tbsp	margarine or butter, melted

SWEDISH FRUIT SOUP

Total Time: 50 minutes

1. Put apricots, prunes, and water in a saucepan and soak 1/2 hour.
2. In a small bowl, stir the cornstarch and sugar together.
3. Add this mixture, the cinnamon, and lemon to the fruit.
4. Stir while heating to simmering.
5. Simmer, covered, 8–10 minutes, stirring occasionally.
6. Add the raisins and currants, and simmer, covered, an additional 5 minutes.

Traditionally, fruit soup is served chilled as a dessert. It is also a treat when served warm.

(Serves two)

1/4 c	dried appricots
1/4 c	dried prunes
2 c	water
1"	cinnamon stick
1	slice lemon
1 tbsp	cornstarch
1/3 c	sugar
1 tbsp	raisins
1 tbsp	golden raisins
2 tsp	dried currants

(Serves four)

1/2 c	dried appricots
1/2 c	dried prunes
4 c	water
2"	cinnamon stick
2	slices lemon
2 tbsp	cornstarch
2/3 c	sugar
2 tbsp	raisins
2 tbsp	golden raisins
1 tbsp	dried currants

BANANA NUT BREAD

Total Time: 1 hour
Baking: 350° F oven for 40–45 minutes

1. Preheat oven.
2. Cream margarine or butter with sugar until light.
3. Beat in the egg.
4. Sift the dry ingredients together.
5. Combine milk with banana pulp.
6. Add a third of the dry ingredients to the fat-egg mixture and blend.
7. Stir in half of the banana-milk blend.
8. Add a third of the dry ingredients; blend.
9. Stir in the remaining liquid.
10. Add the final third of the dry ingredients and the chopped nuts; blend.
11. Grease loaf pan(s), 8 1/2x4 1/2". Pour in the batter.
12. Bake in preheated oven at 350° F 40–45 minutes until toothpick inserted in center comes out clean.
13. Cut the loaf loose from the edges of the pan, remove from the pan, and cool on a cooling rack.

(Serves two)

6 tbsp	margarine or butter
3/4 c	sugar
1	egg, beaten
1 1/2 c	sifted all purpose flour
1 tsp	baking powder
1/4 tsp	salt
1/4 tsp	soda
2 tbsp	milk
6 tbsp	mashed ripe banana
1/2 c	chopped walnuts

(Serves four)

3/4 c	margarine or butter
1 1/2 c	sugar
2	eggs, beaten
3 c	sifted all purpose flour
2 tsp	baking powder
1/2 tsp	salt
1/2 tsp	soda
1/4 c	milk
3/4 c	mashed ripe banana
1 c	chopped walnuts

RIS A'L'MONDE

Total Time: 1 hour

1. Combine rice, milk, and sugar in saucepan and heat to boiling while stirring.
2. Immediately reduce heat to simmering and simmer until milk is absorbed (25 minutes) stirring frequently to avoid scorching.
3. Remove from heat and stir in cream sherry. Chill in a shallow dish while beating cream.
4. Beat cream until stiff, being careful not to beat until it turns to butter.
5. Fold the whipped cream and chopped almonds into the rice. Spoon into sherbet dishes and chill in refrigerator.
6. Prepare raspberry sauce by draining the syrup from the thawed raspberries and stirring this syrup gradually into the cornstarch.
7. Heat the raspberry-cornstarch mixture to a boil while stirring constantly. Boil 3 minutes.
8. Stir in the raspberries and chill.
9. Spoon some of the chilled sauce over each dish of pudding.

(Serves two)

1/4 c	uncooked rice
3/4 c	milk
1/4 c	sugar
1 tbsp	cream sherry
1/2 c	whipping cream
1/4 c	chopped, toasted almonds
1	10 oz package frozen raspberries, thawed
1 1/2 tsp	cornstarch

(Serves four)

1/2 c	uncooked rice
1 1/2 c	milk
1/2 c	sugar
2 tbsp	cream sherry
1 c	whipping cream
1/2 c	chopped, toasted almonds
2	10 oz package frozen raspberries, thawed
1 tbsp	cornstarch

QUICK LEMON PIE

Total Time: 50 minutes
Baking: 350° F oven 10 minutes for crust and
15 minutes for meringue

1. Preheat oven.
2. Melt margarine or butter and stir in crumbs and sugar.
3. Pack firmly across the bottom and sides of tart pans.
4. Bake at 350° F for 10 minutes. Cool.
5. Beat yolks and stir in the milk, juice, and rind until dispersed uniformly. Pour into graham cracker crusts.
6. Beat egg whites until foamy; add cream of tartar and gradually add the sugar. Continue beating on the electric mixer until peaks just bend over.
7. Spread meringue on tarts, being sure to seal to edges of the crust.
8. Bake at 350° F for 12–15 minutes until pleasing golden brown.
9. Cool at room temperature for 15 minutes before refrigerating.

(Serves two)
3/4 c	*graham cracker crumbs (9 crackers)*
1 tbsp	*sugar*
3 tbsp	*margarine or butter*
2	*eggs, separated*
1/2	*can sweetened condensed milk*
1/4 c	*lemon juice*
	grated rind of 1 lemon
1/4 tsp	*cream of tartar*
1/4 c	*sugar*

(Serves four)
1 1/2 c	graham cracker crumbs (9 crackers)
2 tbsp	sugar
1/3 c	margarine or butter
3	eggs, separated
1	can sweetened condensed milk
1/2 c	lemon juice
	grated rind of 2 lemons
1/2 tsp	cream of tartar
6 tbsp	sugar

CHERRIES JUBILEE

Total Time: 10 minutes

1. In a chafing dish, melt red currant jelly.
2. Blend the cornstarch with the cherry juice until perfectly smooth.
3. Combine the starch slurry with the jelly, stirring rather vigirously while heating to boiling.
4. Add the spices and cherries and continue heating until cherries are warmed through.
5. Warm kirsch in a very small pan before pouring it onto the hot cherry sauce. Immediately ignite with a long match without stirring the kirsch.
6. Spoon flaming cherries jubilee over a scoop of vanilla ice cream.

(Serves two)
1/3 c	*red currant jelly*
1 c	*canned dark sweet (Bing) cherries and their juice, drained*
1 tsp	*cornstarch*
	dash cinnamon
	dash ground cloves
	dash allspice
1/4 tsp	*grated lemon rind*
1 tsp	*grated orange rind*
2 tbsp	*kirsch (cherry brandy)*
1/3 qt	*vanilla ice cream*

(Serves four)
2/3 c	red currant jelly
2 c	canned dark sweet (Bing) cherries and their juice, drained
2 tsp	cornstarch
1/4 tsp	cinnamon
1/4 tsp	ground cloves
1/4 tsp	allspice
1/2 tsp	grated lemon rind
2 tsp	grated orange rind
1/4 c	kirsch (cherry brandy)
2/3 qt	vanilla ice cream

PRUNE BANANA CAKE

Total Time: 75 minutes
Baking: 350° F oven 30 minutes

1. Preheat oven.
2. Simmer prunes 10 minutes.
3. Prepare 8" round cake pan(s) by lining bottom with layer of wax paper which just fits circle.
4. Sift dry ingredients together in mixing bowl.
5. Add shortening, milk, vanilla, and mashed banana and beat at medium speed on electric mixer for 2 minutes.
6. Add egg and beat 2 more minutes.
7. Add pitted, chopped prunes and nuts.
8. Bake at 350° F until toothpick inserted in center comes out clean (30 minutes).
9. Cool on cooling rack.
10. Prepare icing by beating butter, cream, lemon juice, rind and powdered sugar together until light and fluffy.

(One layer)

1/2 c	*cooked prunes*
1 c	*sifted all purpose flour*
3/4 tsp	*baking powder*
1/2 tsp	*soda*
1/2 tsp	*salt*
2/3 c	*sugar*
1/4 c	*shortening*
2 tbsp	*milk*
1/2 tsp	*vanilla*
1 1/2	*bananas (1/2 cup mashed)*
1	*egg*
1/4 c	*chopped walnuts*

Icing:

2 tbsp	**margarine or butter**
1 tbsp	**cream or milk**
1 1/2 tsp	**lemon juice**
1 tsp	**grated lemon rind**
1 1/2 c	**powdered sugar**

(Two layers)

1 c	cooked prunes
2 c	sifted all purpose flour
1 1/2 tsp	baking powder
1 tsp	soda
1 tsp	salt
1 1/3 c	sugar
1/2 c	shortening
1/4 c	milk
1 tsp	vanilla
3	bananas (1/2 cup mashed)
2	eggs
1/2 c	chopped walnuts

Icing:

1/4 c	**margarine or butter**
2 tbsp	**cream or milk**
3 tsp	**lemon juice**
2 tsp	**grated lemon rind**
3 c	**powdered sugar**

FRIED PEACHES

Total Time: 15 minutes

1. Peel and cut peaches in half.
2. Melt the margarine or butter and add the peach halves stuffed with brown sugar.
3. Sauté gently until tender.

Note: These are delicious as an accompaniment to ham and other meats or as a dessert topped with stirred custard or ice cream.

(Serves two)

2	*fresh peaches or 4 canned peach halves, drained*
1 tbsp	*margarine or butter*
4 tsp	*brown sugar*

(Serves four)

4	fresh peaches or 8 canned peach halves, drained
2 tbsp	margarine or butter
3 tbsp	brown sugar

STEWED DRIED FRUIT

Total Time: 15–40 minutes

1. Wash dried fruit well.
2. Cover the fruit with water and simmer in a covered saucepan until fruit is tender.

> *dried fruit*
> *water to cover*

Note: The length of time required to tenderize the fruit varies with the size of the piece and the amount of cut surface. When done, they are plump and lustrous and easily cut. Suggested cooking times for dried fruits are: prunes, 35 minutes; apricots, 30 minutes; peaches, 35 minutes; figs, 35 minutes; and raisins, 10 minutes.

POACHED PEARS

Total Time: 15 minutes

1. Place the first four ingredients in a saucepan and bring to a boil.
2. Peel, halve, and core the pears.
3. Place them in the syrup.
4. Simmer gently until tender (approximately 15 minutes).
5. Chill and serve in sherbet glasses with a dollop of sour cream and a sprinkle of cinnamon.

(Serves two)

3 c	*water*
1 c	*sugar*
1"	*stick cinnamon*
1 tsp	*vanilla extract*
2	*pears*
1 tbsp	*sour cream*
	cinnamon

(Serves four)

4 c	water
1 1/3 c	sugar
2"	stick cinnamon
1 1/2 tsp	vanilla extract
4	pears
2 tbsp	sour cream
	cinnamon

CHERRY CRUNCH PIE

Total Time: 50 minutes
Baking: 275° F oven for 35 minutes

1. Preheat oven.
2. Roll graham crackers into crumbs, blend in the sugar and margarine or butter.
3. Press all but 1/4 of the mixture into a 9" pie plate (use individual pie plates for small recipe).
4. Chill in refrigerator while preparing filling.
5. Mix sugar and cornstarch together in a 1-quart saucepan.
6. Stir in the cherries and heat to boiling, stirring constantly.
7. Remove from the heat; add almond extract, and enough red coloring to turn the filling a bright red.
8. Pour into the chilled crust.
9. In the small bowl, beat the whites to the foamy stage, using an electric mixer.
10. Add the cream of tartar, and gradually add the sugar while beating on high.
11. Beat until the peaks just bend over.
12. Spread the meringue on the pie, and sprinkle the remaining crumbs over the surface of the meringue.
13. Bake in a 275° F oven for 35 minutes.

(Serves two)

7	*graham crackers*
3 tbsp	*sugar*
2 tbsp	*margarine or butter, melted*
1 c	*pie cherries, canned (drained)*
6 tbsp	*sugar*
1 1/3 tbsp	*cornstarch*
1/8 tsp	*almond extract*
	red food coloring (optional)
1	*egg white*
2 tbsp	*sugar*
	pinch cream of tartar

(Serves four)

15	graham crackers
6 tbsp	sugar
1/4 c	margarine or butter, melted
1	No. 2 pie cherries, canned (drained)
3/4 c	sugar
2 2/3 tbsp	cornstarch
1/4 tsp	almond extract
	red food coloring (optional)
3	egg white
6 tbsp	sugar
1/4 tsp	cream of tartar

MINTED TANGERINE FILLING FOR MERINGUES

Total Time: 30 minutes

1. In a small saucepan, combine sugar, cornstarch, and salt.
2. With a wooden spoon, stir in the tangerine juice.
3. Cook over medium heat, stirring constantly, until thickened and clear.
4. Remove from heat. Stir in peel and extract.
5. Cool in refrigerator or at room temperature.
6. Meanwhile, place tangerine pieces in meringue shells.
7. Spoon glaze over fruit.
8. Chill until serving time.

(Serves two)
1/4 c	*sugar*
2 tsp	*cornstarch*
	few grains salt
1/2 c	*fresh squeezed tangerine juice*
1 1/2 tsp	*fresh grated tangerine peel*
1	*drop mint extract*
1	*tangerine, peeled, seeded, cut in bite-size pieces*
or	
1/2 c	*canned mandarin oranges, drained*
2	*baked meringue shells*
	mint sprigs or orange cartwheels

(Serves four)
1/2 c	sugar
1/4 c	cornstarch
	dash salt
1 c	fresh squeezed tangerine juice
3 tsp	fresh grated tangerine peel
2	drops mint extract
2	tangerines, peeled, seeded, cut in bit-size pieces
or	
1 c	canned mandarin oranges, drained
4	baked meringue shells
	mint sprigs or orange cartwheels

VERSATILE LEMON-ORANGE CURD

Total Time: 25 minutes

1. Place all ingredients in the top of a double boiler over hot (not boiling) water.
2. Stir constantly while cooking until thickened (about 15 minutes).
3. Chill thoroughly.
4. Pour over chilled fruit in parfait or sherbet glasses.

Note: Versatile Lemon-Orange Curd is a nourishing and unusual accompaniment which is particularly well-suited to serving with fresh fruits.

(Serves two)
2	*eggs, well beaten*
1 c	*sugar*
2 tbsp	*lemon juice*
2 tbsp	*orange juice*
1 1/2 tsp	*grated lemon peel*
1 1/2 tsp	*grated orange peel*
1/4 c	*margarine or butter*

(Serves four)
4	eggs, well beaten
2 c	sugar
1/4 c	lemon juice
1/4 c	orange juice
1 tbsp	grated lemon peel
1 tbsp	grated orange peel
1/2 c	margarine or butter

STRAWBERRIES ALA MASCARPONE

Total Time: 10 minutes

1. Add honey to mascarpone and stir just until blended. Chill until 10 minutes before serving.
2. Wash strawberries, leaving tops and stems (if present). Drain on paper towel before arranging for service with the mascarpone.
3. Serve mascarpone as a dollop if berries are served individual bowls or in a bowl for dipping.

(Small recipe)
1/3 c	mascarpone
1 tbsp	honey
	fresh strawberries

(Large recipe)
1 c	mascarpone
1/4 c	honey
	fresh strawberries

ORANGE-GRAPE PUNCH

Total Time: 35 minutes
Baking: 325° F for 30 minutes

1. Preheat oven.
2. Stud whole oranges with 10 cloves each; place on baking sheet.
3. Bake for 30 minutes until juices begin to run.
4. Cut oranges in half and place in a heat-proof bowl.
5. Sprinkle with brown sugar.
6. Meanwhile, heat grape juice and water to simmering.
7. Stir into punch bowl along with orange juice.
8. Serve piping hot.

(Makes 3 cups)
1	medium orange
10	whole cloves
2 tbsp	firmly packed brown sugar
2 c	grape juice
2/3 c	boiling water
2/3 c	orange juice

(Makes 1 1/2 quarts)
3	medium oranges
30	whole cloves
1/3 c	firmly packed brown sugar
4 c	grape juice
1 1/3 c	boiling water
1 1/3 c	orange juice

PEARS DELICIOUS

Total Time: 35 minutes
Baking: 325° F for 25 minutes

1. Preheat oven.
2. Place pears cut side up in buttered shallow baking dish.
3. Sprinkle walnuts in hollow of each pear.
4. Pour water, corn syrup and lemon juice over pears.
5. Combine margarine or butter, brown sugar, flour and ground ginger with fork until crumbly and sprinkle over pears.
6. Bake at 325° F until pears are tender (about 25 minutes).
7. Spoon sauce over hot pears to serve.

(Serves two)
2	pears, pared and cored
2 1/2 tbsp	chopped walnuts
2 1/2 tbsp	water
1 1/2 tbsp	light corn syrup
3/4 tsp	lemon juice
1 1/2 tbsp	margarine or butter
2 1/2 tbsp	brown sugar
1 tsp	flour
1/8 tsp	ground ginger

(Serves four)
4	pears, pared and cored
1/3 c	chopped walnuts
1/3 c	water
1/3 c	light corn syrup
1 1/2 tbsp	lemon juice
3 tbsp	margarine or butter
1/3 c	brown sugar
2 tsp	flour
1/4 tsp	ground ginger

GRAPES SUZETTE

Total Time: 35 minutes

1. Wash grapes and stem them.
2. In a heat-proof baking dish, stir the grapes and sour cream to coat the grapes.
3. Sprinkle brown sugar over the mixture.
4. Broil until brown sugar bubbles.
5. Serve immediately.

(Serves two)
1/4 lb	*seedless grapes*
2 tbsp	*sour cream*
1 tbsp	*brown sugar*

(Serves four)
1/2 lb	seedless grapes
1/4 c	sour cream
2 tbsp	brown sugar

VOCABULARY

Berries

Citrus fruits

Drupes

Grapes

Melons

Pomes

Tropical and subtropical fruits

Browning

Osmosis

EVALUATION OF LABORATORY PRODUCTS — FRUITS

RECIPE	NOTES ON COLOR, TEXTURE, FLAVOR, OR OTHER QUALITIES	COMMENTS OR SUGGESTIONS FOR MAKING OR USING THIS PRODUCT IN THE FUTURE

Chapter 4
Salads and Salad Dressings

CARE OF GREENS

STORAGE

Various external conditions influence the flow of water into and out of cells. A succulent will be crisp when conditions draw water into the cell, but will be limp when water is withdrawn. To illustrate the effect of storage conditions on succulents, store lettuce under each of the conditions indicated in the chart, and note the result.

EFFECTS OF VARYING STORAGE CONDITIONS

STORAGE CONDITION	DESCRIPTION OF LETTUCE LEAF	EXPLANATION
Uncovered on counter, room temperature, 24 hours		
Ice water, refrigerated, 24 hours		
Salt water (1 tsp/c of water), refrigerated, 24 hours		
Tightly covered container, refrigerated, 24 hours		

KEY CONCEPTS — SALADS AND SALAD DRESSINGS

1. Salad greens need water in their cells to provide a crisp texture.

    a) Equilibrium between the moisture level in and outside the cells will be established quickly when the greens are stored in a closed container or hydrator drawer in a refrigerator; this assures maximum water in the cells and a crisp texture.

    b) Salad dressing begins to draw water from the cells due to unfavorable osmotic pressure when greens are coated with dressing, which makes it important to add salad dressing to greens just prior to serving.

2. Ingredients for salads need to be washed thoroughly to assure cleanliness and food safety. Careful draining and/or drying will avoid diluting salad dressings and their pleasing flavor accents.

LETTUCE CUPS

To remove attractive lettuce leaf cups from a head of lettuce, first cut out the core of the lettuce head with a sharp knife. Hold the lettuce under cold running water so that the hole resulting from removal of the core is filled with cold water. Let the water stand briefly in the head of lettuce. As the head begins to relax a bit, gently force the leaves apart. Place leaves on paper toweling or on a tea towel. Refrigerate in the hydrator drawer until ready to serve the salad.

RADISH ROSES

Radish roses are a quick, colorful garnish. Wash radishes thoroughly; cut off the root and the stem (unless the leaves are attractive). Cut deeply from the root end in a X or other desired shape, being sure that the segments thus created are fairly thin. Place in a bowl of water to cover. Chill in refrigerator at least 30 minutes.

RECIPES
SPRING SALAD

Total Time: 10 minutes

1. Wash basil leaves, drain, and arrange a bed of leaves on each salad plate.
2. Slice onion into slices 1/8" thick and place one whole slice on each bed of greens.
3. Slice tomato into slices 1/3" thick and arrange one on each onion slice.
4. Top each salad with one slice of cheese and garnish with a fresh basil leaf.
5. Combine lemon juice, vinegar, and olive oil before drizzling over each salad.

(Serves two)
1/2	bunch fresh basil or other greens
1/2	Maui or other white onion
1/2	large tomato
2	slices Mozarella cheese
1 tsp	lemon juice
1 tbsp	rice wine vinegar
1 tbsp	olive oil

(Serves four)
1	bunch fresh basil or other greens
1	Maui or other white onion
1	large tomato
4	slices Mozarella cheese
2 tsp	lemon juice
2 tbsp	rice wine vinegar
2 tbsp	olive oil

CAULIFLOWER CAPER

Total Time: 30 minutes

1. Break cauliflower into flowerets and boil in salted water until just tender (about 5 minutes). Drain and chill.
2. Combine mayonnaise, sour cream, mustard, and lemon juice.
3. Toss cauliflower with dressing to coat completely. Chill.
4. Arrange on lettuce cups and garnish with red pepper strips and chopped parsley.

(Serves two)
1/4	head cauliflower
3 tbsp	mayonnaise
1 tbsp	sour cream
2 tsp	Dijon mustard
1/2 tsp	lemon juice
	pinch of salt
2	lettuce cups
1/8	red bell pepper
2	sprigs parsley

(Serves four)
1/2	head cauliflower
6 tbsp	mayonnaise
2 tbsp	sour cream
4 tsp	Dijon mustard
1 tsp	lemon juice
1/8 tsp	salt
4	lettuce cups
1/4	red bell pepper
4	sprigs parsley

VEGETABLE AND CANADIAN BACON SALAD

Total Time: 20 minutes

1. Caramelize walnuts in melted butter and sugar.
2. Blanch asparagus and snap peas in boiling water 1 minute. Drain.
3. Wash and dice the bell pepper.
4. Clean mushrooms and slice.
5. Wash cherry tomatoes and cut in half.
6. Wash radicchio and Belgian endive before separating leaves.
7. Sauté Canadian bacon briefly to heat.
8. Toss asparagus, peas, tomatoes, mushrooms, bell pepper, oil, vinegar, avocado, salt, and pepper thoroughly.
9. Arrange radichhio cup and endive on individual salad plates before filling cup with salad mixture.
10. Garnish with Canadian bacon and glazed walnuts.

(Serves two)

1 1/2 oz	*walnuts*
2 tsp	*butter or margarine*
2 tbsp	*sugar*
6	*asparagus spears in 1" pieces*
2 oz	*sugar snap peas*
1/4	*yellow bell pepper*
3	*small mushrooms*
4	*cherry tomatoes*
2	*leaves radicchio*
4	*leaves Belgian endive*
2 oz	*Canadian bacon*
2 tbsp	*walnut oil*
1 tbsp	*rice wine vinegar*
1/2	*avocado, diced*
	salt and pepper

(Serves four)

3 oz	walnuts
4 tsp	butter or margarine
4 tbsp	sugar
12	asparagus spears in 1" pieces
1/4 lb	sugar snap peas
1/2	yellow bell pepper
6	small mushrooms
8	cherry tomatoes
4	leaves radicchio
8	leaves Belgian endive
1/4 lb	Canadian bacon
1/4 c	walnut oil
2 tbsp	rice wine vinegar
1	avocado, diced
	salt and pepper

CURRIED CRANBERRY CHICKEN SALAD

Total Time: 15 minutes

1. Cut chicken into bite-sized cubes.
2. Cut apple into 1/4" chunks.
3. Slice celery and onions thinly.
4. Combine mayonnaise, lime juice, and curry powder completely.
5. Add all ingredients and stir to coat all portions of salad.
6. Serve on greens, if desired.

(Serves two)

1 c	*cooked chicken breast*
1/2	*Delicious apple*
1/2	*celery stalk*
1	*green onion*
1/3 c	*mayonnaise*
1 tsp	*lime juice*
3/8 tsp	*curry powder*
1/3 c	*dried cranberries*
2 tbsp	*chopped pecans*
	salad greens (optional)

(Serves four)

2 c	cooked chicken breast
1	Delicious apple
1	celery stalk
2	green onions
2/3 c	mayonnaise
2 tsp	lime juice
3/4 tsp	curry powder
2/3 c	dried cranberries
1/4 c	chopped pecans
	salad greens (optional)

HARVEST SALAD

Total Time: 15 minutes

1. Clean and thinly slice mushrooms, radishes, and celery.
2. Cut tomatoes and chicken into bite-sized chunks.
3. Tear lettuce into bite-sized pieces.
4. Combine all ingredients and toss.

Note: To roast bell peppers, heat under broiler or over gas flame until skin pops and blackens a bit, being sure to turn frequently so that all portions are singed by the broiler heat. Remove from the broiler and immediately cover with damp paper towel. When cool enough to handle easily, pull off the singed skin; carefully wash off any trace of the skin. Remove stem and seeds before dicing or slicing.

(Serves two)
2	*mushrooms*
2	*radishes*
1	*stalk celery*
2	*Roma tomatoes*
3 oz	*cooked chicken breast*
3	*leaves bibb lettuce*
1/4	*roasted yellow bell pepper, diced*
1/4	*roasted green bell pepper, diced*
1 1/2 oz	*pepper cheese, diced*
3 tbsp	*champagne dressing*
	salt and pepper

(Serves four)
4	mushrooms
4	radishes
2	stalk celery
4	Roma tomatoes
6 oz	cooked chicken breast
6	leaves bibb lettuce
1/2	roasted yellow bell pepper, diced
1/2	roasted green bell pepper, diced
3 oz	pepper cheese, diced
6 tbsp	champagne dressing
	salt and pepper

CHICKEN SALAD ALA GRECO

Total Time: 15 minutes

1. Wash romaine leaves and cut into shreds 1/2" thick.
2. Wash and cut tomatoes in pieces.
3. Put romaine, tomato, onion, olives, chicken, and cheese in bowl.
4. Combine lemon juice, olive oil, oregano, and parsley.
5. Toss salad ingredients with dressing, salt, and pepper.

(Serves two)
3	*leaves romaine*
1	*Roma tomato*
1/2	*red onion, coarsely chopped*
1/4 c	*pitted kalamata olives*
1 c	*cooked chicken breast, cubed*
2 oz	*crumbled feta cheese (with basil and sun-dried tomatoes*
1 tbsp	*lemon juice*
1/4 c	*olive oil*
1 1/4 tsp	*chopped fresh oregano*
1 1/4 tsp	*chopped fresh parsley*
	salt and pepper

(Serves four)
6	leaves romaine
2	Roma tomatoes
1	red onion, coarsely chopped
1/2 c	pitted kalamata olives
2 c	cooked chicken breast, cubed
4 oz	crumbled feta cheese (with basil and sun-dried tomatoes
2 tbsp	lemon juice
1/2 c	olive oil
1 tbsp	chopped fresh oregano
1 tbsp	chopped fresh parsley
	salt and pepper

SALAD ROLL UPS

Total Time: 30 minutes

1. On mixer, beat cream cheese to spreadable consistency.
2. Chop garlic very finely.
3. Finely chop red onion, olives, basil, tomatoes, lettuce, and parsley. Stir and blot dry with paper towels.
4. Spread tortilla thickly with cream cheese and a light layer of mustard.
5. Cover tortilla with slices of meat.
6. Add generous layer of mixed vegetables.
7. Roll tortilla into a tight log, beginning from far side and being sure to retain the vegetables within the roll. Wrap the roll carefully in aluminum foil and chill thoroughly.
8. Remove from foil. Slice into pinwheels 1" thick. Secure each with a colored toothpick or place against each other on a serving platter.

Note: These roll ups are a colorful flavorful appetizer that can be prepared a day ahead, if desired.

(Small recipe)

8 oz	cream cheese
1	garlic clove
1/2	red onion
2 tbsp	chopped black olives
1/4	head lettuce or romaine
3	Roma tomatoes, seeded
1/2	bunch parsley (stems removed)
4 oz	thinly sliced turkey
4 oz	thinly sliced salami
3	extra large flour tortillas

(Large recipe)

1 lb	cream cheese
2	garlic cloves
1	red onion
1/4 c	chopped black olives
1/2	head lettuce or romaine
6	Roma tomatoes, seeded
1	bunch parsley (stems removed)
8 oz	thinly sliced turkey
8 oz	thinly sliced salami
6	extra large flour tortillas

MIXED GREENS WITH BEEF AND GORGONZOLA SALAD

Total Time: 20 minutes

1. Wash and blot dry greens.
2. Thinly slice onion and mushrooms.
3. Toast pecans at 350° F.
4. Sauté beef until heated through. Cut into slices 3/8" thick.
5. Combine all ingredients and toss with dressing. Serve immediately.

(Serves 2)

1 1/4 c	mixed greens
1/4	small red onion
2	mushrooms
2 tbsp	pecans
1/2	beef tenderloin (1" thick)
1 tbsp	crumbled Gorgonzola cheese
	salt and pepper
1 tbsp	balsamic vinegar
2 tbsp	olive oil

(Serves 4)

2 1/2 c	mixed greens
1/2	small red onion
4	mushrooms
1/4 c	pecans
1	beef tenderloin (1" thick)
2 tbsp	crumbled Gorgonzola cheese
	salt and pepper
2 tbsp	balsamic vinegar
1/4 c	olive oil

POTATO SALAD WITH TUNA, SNAP PEAS, AND TOMATOES

Total Time: 30 minutes

1. Boil potatoes with skins on until tender. Drain. Cut into cubes.
2. Cut off both ends of each pod before blanching in boiling, salted water for 30 seconds.
3. Thoroughly drain tuna; break into chunks.
4. Stir potatoes, peas, tuna, vinegar, mustard, lemon juice, lemon zest, olive oil, pepper, and chives together to coat vegetables.
5. Serve on bed of arugula garnished with tomatoes.

(Serves 2)

1/2 lb	*small Red Triumph potatoes*
1/8 lb	*sugar snap peas*
3 oz	*canned tuna (white, solid, water pack)*
1 1/2 tsp	*white wine vinegar*
1/2 tsp	*Dijon mustard*
1 tsp	*lemon juice*
1/4 tsp	*lemon zest*
2 1/2 tbsp	*olive oil*
	ground pepper
3 tbsp	*chives, minced*
1 c	*arugula, stemmed*
2	*ripe plum tomatoes (in wedges)*

(Serves 4)

1 lb	small Red Triumph potatoes
1/4 lb	sugar snap peas
6 1/2 oz	can tuna (white, solid, water pack)
1 tbsp	white wine vinegar
1 tsp	Dijon mustard
2 tsp	lemon juice
1/4 tsp	lemon zest
1/4 c	olive oil
	ground pepper
1/3 c	chives, minced
2 c	arugula, stemmed
4	ripe plum tomatoes (in wedges)

PASTA SALAD PRIMA VERDE

Total Time: 1 hour

1. Boil broccoli florets, peas, and pea pods 3 minutes. Drain.
2. Mix together mustard, olive oil, vinegar, scallions, garlic, tomato, and cooked vegetables.
3. Marinate 45 minutes.
4. Meanwhile cook pasta according to package directions to al dente. Drain thoroughly.
5. Toss pasta lightly with vegetables.

(Serves 2)

1/4 c	*broccoli florets*
1/4 c	*peas*
1/2 c	*sugar snap peas*
2 tbsp	*Dijon mustard*
1/4 c	*olive oil*
2 tbsp	*red wine vinegar*
1	*scallion, thinly sliced*
1/2	*garlic clove, minced*
1/2	*tomato, seeded and chopped*
1 c	*uncooked penne or other pasta of choice*

(Serves 4)

1/2 c	broccoli florets
1/2 c	peas
1 c	sugar snap peas
1/4 c	Dijon mustard
1/2 c	olive oil
1/4 c	red wine vinegar
2	scallion, thinly sliced
1	garlic clove, minced
1	tomato, seeded and chopped
2 c	uncooked penne or other pasta of choice

Kashi Vegetable Salad

Total Time: 50 minutes

1. Boil kashi, covered, until water is absorbed. Spread in shallow baking pan and chill briefly in freezer.
2. Meanwhile, combine all vegetables in large serving bowl.
3. Combine oil, soy sauce, vinegar, and mustard in small bowl.
4. Add kashi to vegetables, and toss entire mixture with the dressing. Chill until served.

(Serves 2)

1/2 c	*kashi (uncooked) or bulgur*
1 c	*water*
1/4 c	*sliced mushrooms*
2 tbsp	*diced green pepper*
2 tbsp	*diced red pepper*
2 tbsp	*diced water chestnuts*
2 tbsp	*chopped parsley*
2 tbsp	*diced green onions*
2 tbsp	*diced, seeded tomato*
1/4 c	*olive oil*
1/4 c	*soy sauce*
1 1/2 tbsp	*red wine vinegar*
1 tsp	*Dijon mustard*

(Serves 4)

1 c	kashi (uncooked) or bulgur
2 c	water
1/2 c	sliced mushrooms
1/4 c	diced green pepper
1/4 c	diced red pepper
1/4 c	diced water chestnuts
1/4 c	chopped parsley
1/4 c	diced green onions
1/4 c	diced, seeded tomato
1/2 c	olive oil
1/2 c	soy sauce
3 tbsp	red wine vinegar
2 tsp	Dijon mustard

Raw Spinach Salad

Total Time: 20 minutes

1. Fry the bacon until it is crisp.
2. Drain on paper towel, and crumble into small pieces. Save the drippings for the dressing.
3. Thoroughly wash the spinach, and drain it well.
4. Tear into bite-size pieces, discarding the stems.
5. Warm the drippings and stir in the vbinegar.
6. Stir and pour sparingly over the spinach. Toss the spinach.
7. Top with chopped egg and crumbled bacon.
8. Serve at once.

(Serves 2)

2	*strips bacon*
1/2	*bunch fresh spinach*
1	*egg, hard cooked*
1 tbsp	*vinegar*

(Serves 4)

4	strips bacon
1	bunch fresh spinach
2	eggs, hard cooked
2 tbsp	vinegar

FROZEN FRUIT SALAD

Total Time: At least 2 hours

1. On an electric mixer, whip the cream until stiff.
2. Drain the fruit cocktail or cut fruit into small cubes.
3. Add the other ingredients.
4. Stir well and pour into individual salad molds or larger mold.
5. Cover tightly with aluminum foil.
6. Freeze.

Note: When whipping cream, foam formation will be aided by using cream which has been chilled well. Also be sure to whip the cream until it piles well, but be careful not to whip it enough to break the emulsion and form butter.

(Serves 2)	
1/2 c	*whipping cream, well chilled*
2 tbsp	*mayonnaise*
1	*banana, sliced*
1/2 c	*fruit cocktail, drained (or fresh fruit)*
1/4 c	*salad marshmallows*
1 tbsp	*sugar*

(Serves 4)	
1 c	whipping cream, well chilled
1/4 c	mayonnaise
2	bananas, sliced
1 c	fruit cocktail, drained (or fresh fruit)
1/2 c	salad marshmallows
2 tbsp	sugar

TOSSED SALAD

Total Time: 10 minutes

1. Wash and drain lettuce well; tear into bite-size pieces.
2. In a bowl, combine lettuce, tomatoes, croutons, bacon bits, chopped celery, artichoke hearts, chopped egg, and olives.
3. Add dressing. Toss lightly.
4. Garnish with carrot curls.

Note: Carrot curls are made by first paring large carrots with a vegetable peeler, and then using the peeler to peel off thin slices running the length of the carrot. These slices are wrapped in a curl around the index finger of the left hand and secured with a toothpick. Place in the refrigerator in a bowl of ice water. Chill until just prior to serving. Remove toothpicks, and use curls as a garnish.

(Serves 2)	
1/4	*head lettuce or other lettuce*
1	*stalk celery*
1/4 c	*artichoke hearts*
1	*hard cooked egg*
6	*cherry tomatoes*
1 tbsp	*bacon bits*
	black olives, pitted
	croutons
	carrot curls
	Italian dressing

(Serves 4)	
1/2	head lettuce or other lettuce
2	stalks celery
1/2 c	artichoke hearts
2	hard cooked egg
12	cherry tomatoes
2 tbsp	bacon bits
	black olives, pitted
	croutons
	carrot curls
	Italian dressing

MOLDED STRAWBERRY SALAD

Total Time: At least 2 hours

1. Pour boiling water over gelatin, and stir until gelatin is dissolved completely.
2. Add unthawed strawberries.
3. Stir occasionally, and break up the block of berries as it thaws.
4. When berries are thawed completely, add the sliced banana and chopped pecans.
5. Pour into individual salad molds and refrigerate.
6. Garnish with the sour cream when the salad is served.

(Serves 2)	
1	3-oz package strawberry gelatin
1 c	boiling water
10 oz	frozen strawberries
1	banana
2 tbsp	pecans, chopped
1/2 c	sour cream

(Serves 4)	
1	6-oz package strawberry gelatin
2 c	boiling water
20 oz	frozen strawberries
2	banana
1/4 c	pecans, chopped
1 c	sour cream

MIXED BEAN SALAD

Total Time: 12 hours

1. Drain the beans well.
2. Put them in a large mixing bowl.
3. Add the other ingredients, and mix everything well.
4. Cover tightly, and refrigerate overnight, stirring 1 or 2 times.
5. Just before serving, stir again thoroughly, and then remove the marinade.

(Serves 4)	
8 3/4 oz	Blue Lake green beans, canned
8 3/4 oz	garbanzo beans, canned
8 3/4 oz	wax beans, canned
8 3/4 oz	kidney beans, canned
5 tbsp	diced green pepper
1	small onion, thinly sliced
1/2 c	red wine vinegar
1/4 c	salad oil
2 tbsp	sugar
1/2 tsp	salt
1/2 tsp	black pepper, coarsely ground

(Serves 8)	
1 lb	Blue Lake green beans, canned
1 lb	garbanzo beans, canned
1 lb	wax beans, canned
1 lb	kidney beans, canned
10 tbsp	diced green pepper
1	medium onion, thinly sliced
1 c	red wine vinegar
1/2 c	salad oil
1/4 c	sugar
1 tsp	salt
1 tsp	black pepper, coarsely ground

HOT POTATO SALAD

Total Time: 25 minutes

1. Boil unpeeled, but washed potatoes in salted water (1 tsp salt/qt water) until tender.
2. Fry the bacon crisp, drain on paper towel, and crumble it.
3. Leave 1 tsp bacon drippings in the frying pan.
4. Stir in flour, and gradually stir in the vinegar and water.
5. Heat to boiling, while stirring constantly.
6. Add chopped onion and dry mustard to this dressing.
7. Peel and dice the hot potatoes.
8. Coat with dressing, and serve.   Reheat, if necessary.

(Serves 2)

2	*medium Red Triumph (waxy) potatoes*
3	*slices bacon*
1 tsp	*flour*
3 tbsp	*vinegar*
3 tbsp	*water*
1/4	*medium onion*
1/8 tsp	*dry mustard*

(Serves 4)

4	medium Red Triumph (waxy) potatoes
6	slices bacon
2 tsp	flour
6 tbsp	vinegar
6 tbsp	water
1/2	medium onion
1/4 tsp	dry mustard

POTATO SALAD

Total Time: At least 2 1/2 hours

1. Boil unpeeled, but washed potatoes in salted water (1 tsp salt/qt water) until tender.
2. Peel and cube the potatoes.
3. Stir in the remaining ingredients. If necessary, add more salt.
4. Chill for at least 2 hours (preferably overnight) before serving.

(Serves 2)

2	*medium Red Triumph (waxy) potatoes*
2	*hard cooked eggs, chopped*
1/2	*medium onion, minced*
1/2 tsp	*celery seed*
1/4 c	*mayonnaise*
1 tsp	*prepared mustard*
2 tbsp	*pickle relish*

(Serves 4)

4	medium Red Triumph (waxy) potatoes
4	hard cooked eggs, chopped
1	medium onion, minced
1 tsp	celery seed
1/2 c	mayonnaise
2 tsp	prepared mustard
1/4 c	pickle relish

SEAFOOD MEDLEY

Total Time: 30 minutes

1. Blend all ingredients thoroughly (except lettuce and lemon).
2. Chill, and serve on lettuce leaves, using lemon cartwheels or quarters for garnish.

(Serves 2)

1/2 c	*lobster*
1/2 c	*crab*
1/3 c	*celery, chopped*
1 tbsp	*lemon juice*
1/8 tsp	*curry powder*
1	*hard cooked egg, chopped*
3 tbsp	*mayonnaise*
2	*leaves Bibb lettuce*
1/2	*lemon*

(Serves 4)

1 c	lobster
1 c	crab
2/3 c	celery, chopped
2 tbsp	lemon juice
1/4 tsp	curry powder
2	hard cooked eggs, chopped
6 tbsp	mayonnaise
4	leaves Bibb lettuce
1	lemon

CAESAR SALAD

Total Time: 10 minutes

1. Thoroughly wash romaine and blot dry with paper towels. Break into bite-size pieces and drop in a wooden salad bowl which has been rubbed with a cut clove of garlic.
2. Lightly coddle egg by placing it in boiling water, removing the pan from the heat, and allowing the egg to sit in the water for 2 minutes.
3. Meanwhile, in a separate bowl, mash the anchovy in a spoonful of oil before adding the rest of the oil and the coddled egg. Blend together well and pour over greens in bowl.
4. Toss romaine until all leaves are coated with the dressing.
5. Squeeze lemon over the salad.
6. Garnish with Parmesan cheese, coarse grind black pepper, and salad croutons. Serve immediately.

(Serves 2)

1	*clove of garlic*
1/2	*head of romaine*
1	*egg*
1	*anchovy fillet*
1/4 c	*salad oil (olive oil suggested)*
1/2	*lemon wrapped in square of cheesecloth*
1/4 tsp	*season salt*
	coarse grind black pepper
	Parmesan cheese, grated
1/2 c	*garlic-flavored croutons*

(Serves 4)

1	*clove of garlic*
1	*head of romaine*
2	*eggs*
2	*anchovy fillets*
1/2 c	*salad oil (olive oil suggested)*
1	*lemon wrapped in square of cheesecloth*
1/2 tsp	*season salt*
	coarse grind black pepper
	Parmesan cheese, grated
1 c	*garlic-flavored croutons*

HOT TURKEY SALAD

Total Time: 40 minutes
Baking: 325° F oven for 25 minutes

1. Blend all of the ingredients except the potato chips together in a casserole dish.
2. Sprinkle potato chips on top.
3. Bake uncovered in 325° F oven until salad is heated throughout and the cheese is melted (about 25 minutes).
4. Serve immediately.

(Serves 2)

1 c	roasted turkey, diced
1 c	celery, diced
2 tbsp	blanched, slivered almonds
2 1/2 tbsp	diced green pepper
2 tsp	diced pimiento
1/4	medium onion, minced
1/4 tsp	salt
2 1/2 tsp	lemon juice
1/4 c	salad dressing or mayonnaise
1/4 c	grated Swiss cheese
1/4 c	crushed potato chips

(Serves 4)

2 c	roasted turkey, diced
2 1/4 c	celery, diced
1/4 c	blanched, slivered almonds
1/3 c	diced green pepper
1 1/2 tbsp	diced pimiento
1/2	medium onion, minced
1/2 tsp	salt
1 1/2 tbsp	lemon juice
1/2 c	salad dressing or mayonnaise
1/2 c	grated Swiss cheese
1/2 c	crushed potato chips

GRAPEFRUIT AND AVOCADO SALAD

Total Time: 10 minutes

1. With a sharp knife, peel the rind and membrane surrounding the flesh of the grapefruit, leaving the meat of the fruit completely exposed.
2. Run the knife blade along one side of a membrane and back out along the other side of the grapefruit section. This releases the section from the membranes.
3. Repeat until all sections have been removed.
4. Pare the avocado and slice into thin slices lengthwise.
5. On a leaf of lettuce, alternate grapefruit segments and avocado slices.
6. Garnish with pomegranate seeds.

(Serves 2)

1	grapefruit
1/2	avocado
	pomegranate seeds, if desired
2	lettuce cups

(Serves 4)

2	grapefruit
1	avocado
	pomegranate seeds, if desired
4	lettuce cups

CONFETTI SALAD

Total Time: 2 hours

1. Thoroughly mix the gelatin with the boiling water; stir until no particles of gelatin can be seen.
2. Add the ice and stir slowly until the mixture begins to thicken perceptibly.
3. Remove any remaining ice and then stir in the vegetables.
4. Chill until congealed in mold.
5. To serve, unmold by dipping mold quickly in warm water, shaking to loosen, and then inverting onto the serving plate.
6. Garnish with greens.

(Serves 2)

1	small package of lime gelatin
1 c	boiling water
1/2	tray of ice cubes
1 c	finely grated cabbage
1/2 c	minced celery
1 c	grated carrots
	greens for serving

(Serves 4)

1	large package of lime gelatin
2 c	boiling water
1	tray of ice cubes
2 c	finely grated cabbage
1 c	minced celery
2 c	grated carrots
	greens for serving

COLE SLAW

Total Time: 10 minutes

1. Combine all of the ingredients and mix gently until all pieces are coated with the dressing.

(Serves 2)	
1 c	shredded cabbage
1/2 c	grated carrots
1/4 c	canned pineapple tidbits (optional)
1/2 tsp	celery seed
1/4 c	salad dressing or mayonnaise
1 tbsp	juice from the canned pineapple (optional)

(Serves 4)	
2 c	shredded cabbage
1 c	grated carrots
1/2 c	canned pineapple tidbits (optional)
1 tsp	celery seed
1/2 c	salad dressing or mayonnaise
2 tbsp	juice from the canned pineapple (optional)

MACARONI SALAD

Total Time: 45 minutes

1. Boil the macaroni in salted water just until easily cut. Drain thoroughly and chill in a shallow dish in the refrigerator.
2. Combine all ingredients except the paprika, being sure to coat all the pieces with the dressing.
3. If time permits, chill a couple of hours to help flavors blend.
4. Serve on greens. Garnish with paprika.

(Serves 2)	
1/2 c	uncooked macaroni
2	strips bacon, fried and crumbled
1 tbsp	minced onion
1 tsp	lemon juice
2 tbsp	chopped green pepper
2 tbsp	chopped stuffed olives
1/4 c	chopped celery
1	hard cooked egg, chopped
1/4 c	mayonnaise or salad dressing paprika

(Serves 4)	
1 c	uncooked macaroni
4	strips bacon, fried and crumbled
2 tbsp	minced onion
2 tsp	lemon juice
1/4 c	chopped green pepper
1/4 c	chopped stuffed olives
1/2 c	chopped celery
2	hard cooked eggs, chopped
1/2 c	mayonnaise or salad dressing paprika

CASHEW CHICKEN SALAD

Total Time: 30 minutes plus chilling

1. Stir fry the chicken in the oil about 4 minutes, turning frequently.
2. Add pineapple and salt; continue to fry 5 minutes.
3. Transfer to a refrigerator bowl and chill until 10 minutes before serving.
4. Add the remaining ingredients, stir, and serve garnished with some of the black olives and green onion tops.

(Serves 2)

1 1/2 tsp	*cooking oil*
1	*whole chicken breast, boned, skinned, and cut into bite-sized pieces*
1/4 c	*diced pineapple, drained*
1/2 c	*chopped celery*
1/2 c	*bean sprouts, drained*
1/4 c	*diced water chestnuts or jicama*
1/8 tsp	*curry powder*
2 1/2 tbsp	*sour cream*
2 1/2 tbsp	*mayonnaise*
1/4 c	*cashews*
1/4 c	*green onions, thinly sliced (including tops)*
1/4 c	*black olives, sliced*

(Serves 4)

1 tbsp	cooking oil
2	whole chicken breasts, boned, skinned, and cut into bite-sized pieces
1/2 c	diced pineapple, drained
1 c	chopped celery
1 c	bean sprouts, drained
1/2 c	diced water chestnuts or jicama
1/4 tsp	curry powder
1/3 c	sour cream
1/3 c	mayonnaise
1/2 c	cashews
1/2 c	green onions, thinly sliced (including tops)
1/2 c	black olives, sliced

MOLDED BLACK CHERRY SALAD

Total Time: 2 hours

1. Thoroughly mix the gelatin with the boiling liquid[1]; stir until no particles of gelatin can be seen.
2. Add the ice and stir slowly until the mixture begins to thicken perceptibly.
3. Remove any remaining ice and then stir in the other ingredients.
4. Chill until congealed in individual or ring molds.
5. To serve, unmold by dipping mold quickly in warm water, shaking to loosen, and then inverting onto the serving plate.
6. Garnish with greens.

[1]Note: If there is too little juice to provide the necessary liquid, water should be added to the correct measure.

(Serves 4)

1	*small package black cherry gelatin*
1 c	*boiling juice drained from the cherries[1]*
1/2	*tray of ice cubes*
1/2	*can pitted black cherries, drained*
1/2 c	*chopped celery*
1/2 c	*chopped pecans or walnuts greens to garnish*

(Serves 8)

1	large package black cherry gelatin
2 c	boiling juice from the cherries[1]
1	tray of ice cubes
1	can pitted black cherries, drained
1 c	chopped celery
1 c	chopped pecans or walnuts greens to garnish

SUNSHINE MOLDED SALAD

Total Time: 2 hours

1. Thoroughly mix the gelatin with the boiling juice; stir until no particles of gelatin can be seen.
2. Add the ice and stir slowly until the mixture begins to thicken perceptibly.
3. Remove any remaining ice and then stir in the other ingredients.
4. Chill until congealed in individual molds or ring mold.
5. To serve, unmold by dipping mold quickly in warm water, shaking to loosen, and then inverting onto the serving plate.
6. Garnish with greens.

(Serves 4)	
1	small package lemon gelatin
1 c	boiling juice drained from fruit
1/2	tray of ice cubes
1	small can mandarin oranges, drained
3/4 c	canned pineapple chunks, drained
1	banana, sliced
	greens to garnish

SALAD DRESSING

TRUE FRENCH DRESSING (TEMPORARY EMULSION)

Total Time: 5 minutes

1. Put all ingredients in a container with a tight-fitting lid.
2. Refrigerate.
3. Just before serving, shake vigorously to mix all ingredients thoroughly and form an emulsion.

(Small recipe)	
1/4 c	olive oil
1 tbsp	red wine vinegar
1 tsp	lemon juice
1/4 tsp	paprika
1/4 tsp	dry mustard
1/4 tsp	salt
1/4 tsp	sugar
	dash black pepper

(Large recipe)	
1/2 c	olive oil
2 tbsp	red wine vinegar
2 tsp	lemon juice
1/2 tsp	paprika
1/2 tsp	dry mustard
1/2 tsp	salt
1/2 tsp	sugar
1/4 tsp	black pepper

TOMATO FRENCH DRESSING (SEMI-PERMANENT EMULSION)

Total Time: 10 minutes

1. Mince the onion and chop the green pepper.
2. Put all the ingredients in a mixing bowl.
3. Beat slowly with a rotary beater until all ingredients are thoroughly dispersed.
4. Store in the refrigerator.

(Small recipe)	
1/2 c	vinegar
1/2 c	olive oil
1/2 c	sugar
1/2 tsp	dry mustard
1/2 tsp	salt
1/2	can condensed tomato soup, undiluted
1/2	medium onion
1/2	green pepper

(Large recipe)	
1 c	vinegar
1 c	olive oil
1 c	sugar
1 tsp	dry mustard
1 tsp	salt
1	can condensed tomato soup, undiluted
1	medium onion
1	green pepper

MAYONNAISE (PERMANENT EMULSION)

Total Time: 10 minutes

1. Mix the dry ingredients with the egg yolk and vinegar.
2. Beat well with rotary beater.
3. Very gradually add the oil (1 tsp at a time), beating after each addition until all the oil is emulsified, and no streaks of oil remain.
4. After approximately 1/4 c of oil has been added, the oil can be added in somewhat larger amounts. Continue adding the oil and beating until all the oil has been added. If the emulsion breaks, place an egg yolk in a clean bowl and *very slowly* begin adding the broken emulsion to it, being careful to beat in one addition before adding the next portion.
5. Store in refrigerator in tightly covered container.

Note: If desired, dressing can be thinned with the addition of vinegar or lemon juice.

(Small recipe)	
1/8 tsp	salt
1/4 tsp	sugar
1/2 tsp	dry mustard
	dash cayenne
1	egg yolk
1 tbsp	vinegar
1/2 c	salad oil

(Large recipe)	
1/4 tsp	salt
1/2 tsp	sugar
1 tsp	dry mustard
	dash cayenne
2	egg yolks
2 tbsp	vinegar
1 c	salad oil

COOKED SALAD DRESSING

Total Time: 15 minutes

1. Mix the dry ingredients together in a 1-qt saucepan, and gradually stir in the water.
2. Bring to a boil, while stirring constantly.
3. Remove from the heat.
4. Add a spoonful of the hot mixture to the beaten egg and quickly stir well.
5. Repeat twice.
6. Stir the egg mixture back into the dressing.
7. Cook over very low heat for 5 minutes while stirring slowly. (Be careful to avoid boiling the mixture.)
8. Remove from heat.
9. Stir in the vinegar and margarine or butter.
10. Cool, and store in the refrigerator.

(Small recipe)	
2 tbsp	flour
1/2 tsp	salt
1/2 tsp	dry mustard
2 tbsp	sugar
3/4 c	water
1/4 c	vinegar
1	egg, beaten
2 tbsp	margarine or butter

(Large recipe)	
1/4 c	flour
1 tsp	salt
1 tsp	dry mustard
1/4 c	sugar
1 1/2 c	water
1/2 c	vinegar
2	eggs, beaten
1/4 c	margarine or butter

VOCABULARY

Osmosis

Emulsion

Temporary emulsion

Semi-permanent emulsion

Permanent emulsion

Continuous phase

Interface

Disperse phase

Succulents

EVALUATION OF LABORATORY PRODUCTS — SALADS

RECIPE	NOTES ON COLOR, TEXTURE, FLAVOR, OR OTHER QUALITIES	COMMENTS OR SUGGESTIONS FOR MAKING OR USING THIS PRODUCT IN THE FUTURE

Chapter 5
Starch and Cereal Cookery

STARCHES AS THICKENING AGENTS

Mastering starch cookery is not difficult, but it does require some careful attention throughout preparation, from mixing through heating. You can save yourself from the difficulty of lumpy gravy, sauces, and other starch-thickened products if you make the effort to eliminate every single lump before you begin to heat the mixture. The other essential technique is to stir uniformly throughout the mixture while gelatinizing the starch at a rate that prevents lumping without developing a sticky character in the starch product. You will find many recipes that involve gelatinizing starch; the techniques you learn in this chapter will be used throughout your career working with food. You will also find that your knowledge of gelatinization is important in preparing pastas and other cereal products that are high in starch.

KEY CONCEPTS — STARCH AND CEREAL COOKERY

1) Starches from various sources are useful as thickening agents because they undergo gelatinization when heated sufficiently in the presence of water.

   a) Thickening ability and translucency of starch pastes made with various household starches (tapioca, arrowroot, rice, corn, wheat, flour, and dextrinized or browned flour) differ according to the type of starch used.

   b) The viscosity, appearance, and strength of starch pastes/gels are altered if acid and/or sugar are present during gelatinization.

2) Maximum thickening and optimal palatability can only be achieved if starch is uniformly and smoothly distributed throughout the paste or gel.

   a) The three methods commonly used in cookery to disperse starch uniformly prior to gelatinization are:
      1) mixing thoroughly with fluid fat,
      2) mixing with cold liquid,
      3) mixing with large quantity of dry ingredients.

   b) Thorough stirring throughout a gelatinizing starch paste is required for avoiding the formation of lumps.

THICKENING POWER OF VARIOUS STARCHES

1. In a 1-quart saucepan, make a starch slurry by very gradually adding the cold water to the starch while stirring with a wooden spoon.
2. As the slurry gets thinner, the water can be added rapidly with stirring.
3. Heat the starch mixture to boiling while stirring carefully all across the bottom and around the sides of the pan. Use a medium heat.
4. As soon as the mixture comes to a boil in the center of the pan, pour the hot starch paste into a beaker. Observe each of the types of starch paste for viscosity and translucency; fill in the accompanying chart.

2 tbsp	starch (e.g., tapioca, arrowroot, rice) or flour assigned
1 c	cold water

EFFECT OF SUGAR AND ACID ON STARCH PASTES AND GELS

Acid-containing Paste:

1. Stir the starch and sugar together thoroughly.
2. Add the water gradually and cook as above.
3. Pour into beaker and compare with other sauces.

2 tbsp	cornstarch
2 tbsp	lemon juice or vinegar
14 tbsp	water

Sugar-containing Paste:

1. Combine ingredients.
2. Cook as described above.
3. Pour into beaker and compare with other sauces.

2 tbsp	cornstarch
1/4 c	sugar
1 c	water

VISCOSITY AND APPEARANCE OF SELECTED STARCH PASTES AND GELS

STARCH	VISCOSITY		APPEARANCE
	HOT	COLD	
Tapioca			
Arrowroot			
Rice			
Corn			
Corn plus sugar			
Corn plus acid			
Flour (wheat)			
Browned flour[1]			

[1]Before adding water, heat flour to medium brown in dry skillet while stirring with wooden spoon.

RECIPES FOR STARCH COOKERY

White sauces of varying viscosities are used widely in food preparation. Although the final sauces have somewhat different characteristics, they are all made in the same manner. Thin sauce is used for cream soups, medium sauce is for use in casseroles and creaming vegetables, thick is for making soufflés, and very thick sauce is used as a binding agent to hold ingredients together in croquettes.

Various types of fats may be used to make a white sauce. Margarine and butter add both color and flavor to the sauce. A solid vegetable shortening is a suitable fat to use, and it will not alter the color or flavor. Salad oils are easy to use in white sauces because they are already in liquid form, thus eliminating the need to melt the fat. With the exception of olive oil, salad oils do not greatly influence the color or flavor of the finished sauce.

PREPARING A BASIC WHITE SAUCE

Preparation of a smooth white sauce begins with thorough distribution of the flour in melted fat or oil.

A smooth slurry is maintained as cold milk (or other liquid) is added slowly (careful stirring being used to avoid lumps).

After the mixture is entirely smooth, it is heated at a moderate rate until it comes to a boil throughout the sauce. Stirring must be done continually and at a rate sufficiently fast to maintain uniform heat throughout. Stirring needs to cover the entire bottom of the pan and around the sides, for these are the areas that receive the heat first. A wooden spoon that is flat across the end is ideal for this purpose because each stroke covers a considerable surface area when the mixture is stirred.

The finished sauce should be the desired viscosity (a thick sauce is pictured), and the texture should be completely smooth. Sometimes the fat will begin to separate from the thick and very thick sauces before cooking is completed. This happens when too much water evaporates from the sauce. To remedy this problem, stir a very small amount of water or milk into the sauce. If the fat is still separated, add a little more liquid. Add just enough liquid to unify the sauce.

WHITE SAUCE

Total Time: 5 minutes

1. Melt the margarine or butter.
2. Carefully stir in the flour so that no uncoated flour remains.
3. Add the salt and gradually add the milk while stirring. The milk should be added slowly enough so that the mixture never is lumpy.
4. When all of the milk has been added, begin to heat the sauce over a medium heat. Stir constantly throughout the cooking period. Be careful to stir all parts of the bottom of the pan and all around the sides. Stir rapidly enough so that no lumps form in the thickening sauce.
5. Heat the sauce to boiling.
6. Use immediately. If sauce must be held, cover tightly.

THIN WHITE SAUCE

1 tbsp	margarine (or other fat)
1 tbsp	flour
1/4 tsp	salt
1 c	milk

MEDIUM WHITE SAUCE

2 tbsp	margarine (or other fat)
2 tbsp	flour
1/4 tsp	salt
1 c	milk

THICK WHITE SAUCE

3 tbsp	margarine (or other fat)
3 tbsp	flour
1/4 tsp	salt
1 c	milk

VERY THICK WHITE SAUCE

1/4 c	margarine (or other fat)
1/4 c	flour
1/4 tsp	salt
1 c	milk

WHITE SAUCES

TYPE OF SAUCE	CONSISTENCY	USES
Thin		
Medium		
Thick		
Very Thick		

PUDDINGS

Vanilla Cornstarch Pudding

Total Time: 10 minutes

1. Thoroughly mix the cornstarch, sugar, and salt.
2. Slowly add the cold milk while stirring to make a smooth slurry.
3. Gradually add the scalded milk.
4. Heat to boiling while stirring constantly across the bottom and around the sides of the pan.
5. Continue to heat the pudding until a path remains when a spoon is pulled through it (see illustration).
6. If pudding has any raw starch flavor, cover and place over boiling water for five minutes.
7. Add vanilla and margarine or butter.
8. Pour into custard cups, cover tightly, and chill.

(Serves two)
1 1/2 tbsp	*cornstarch*
2 2/3 tbsp	*sugar*
	few grains salt
1/4 c	*milk*
3/4 c	*scalded milk*
1/2 tsp	*vanilla*
1/2 tsp	*margarine or butter*

(Serves four)
3 tbsp	cornstarch
1/3 c	sugar
	dash salt
1/2 c	milk
1 1/2 c	scalded milk
1 tsp	vanilla
1 tsp	margarine or butter

Chocolate Cornstarch Pudding

Total Time: 10 minutes

1. Melt the chocolate in the milk as it is being scalded.
2. While the milk is being heated, stir the dry ingredients together.
3. Gradually stir in the cold milk to make a smooth slurry.
4. Add the scalded milk and chocolate.
5. Heat over direct heat, stirring constantly, until mixture boils and a spoon leaves a path in the pudding. If pudding tastes starchy, place over hot water for five minutes.
6. Stir in the vanilla and margarine or butter.
7. Pour into custard cups, cover tightly, and chill before serving.

(Serves two)
1 1/3 tbsp	*cornstarch*
1/4 c	*sugar*
	few grains salt
1/4 c	*milk*
1 oz	*(1 square) unsweetened chocolate*
3/4 c	*scalded milk*
1/2 tsp	*vanilla*
1/2 tsp	*margarine or butter*

(Serves four)
2 2/3 tbsp	cornstarch
1/2 c	sugar
	dash salt
1/2 c	milk
2 oz	(1 square) unsweetened chocolate
1 1/2 c	scalded milk
1 tsp	vanilla
1 tsp	margarine or butter

When a cornstarch pudding has thickened sufficiently, a spoon drawn through the pudding leaves a path.

CARAMEL PUDDING

Total Time: 15 minutes

1. Melt the sugar and caramelize it to a medium brown in a small frying pan, stirring it constantly with a wooden spoon.
2. Using a hot pad, carry the frying pan to the sink (being careful not to touch countertops).
3. Immediately add the water.
4. In a 1-quart saucepan, thoroughly mix the cornstarch, sugar, and salt.
5. Gradually stir in the cold milk.
6. Slowly add the scalded milk and caramelized sugar syrup.
7. Heat over medium heat while constantly stirring across the bottom and around the sides of the pan. bring to a boil and continue cooking until the spoon leaves a path through the pudding. If starchy taste remains, heat over hot water for 5 minutes.
8. Stir in the vanilla and margarine or butter.
9. Pour into custard cups, cover tightly, and chill.

(Serves two)	
2 tbsp	sugar (to caramelize)
3 tbsp	boiling water
1 1/2 tbsp	cornstarch
2 tbsp	sugar
	few grains salt
1/4 c	milk
3/4 c	scalded milk
1/2 tsp	margarine or butter
1/2 tsp	vanilla

(Serves four)	
1/4 c	sugar (to caramelize)
1/3 c	boiling water
3 tbsp	cornstarch
1/4 c	sugar
	dash salt
1/2 c	milk
1 1/2 c	scalded milk
1 tsp	margarine or butter
1 tsp	vanilla

ORANGE TAPIOCA PUDDING

Total Time: 25 minutes

1. In a 1-quart saucepan mix the sugar and tapioca together.
2. Add the salt and orange juice.
3. Let stand 5 minutes to rehydrate the tapioca.
4. Heat to a boil, stirring slowly throughout the mixture.
5. Cover and let the pudding cool 20 minutes.
6. Stir and pour into sherbet glasses to serve.

(Serves two)	
1/4 c	sugar
2 tbsp	quick-cooking tapioca
1 1/4 c	orange juice
	few grains salt

(Serves four)	
1/2 c	sugar
1/4 c	quick-cooking tapioca
2 1/2 c	orange juice
	dash salt

RICE PUDDING

Total Time: 1 hour 10 minutes

1. Scald the milk in the top part of a double boiler.
2. When the milk is scalding hot, add the uncooked rice (parboiled is recommended type), sugar, salt, cinnamon, and nutmeg.
3. Place over boiling water and cook until a grain of rice rubbed between the fingers is tender (about 1 hour).
4. Stir occasionally. Keep pan covered when not stirring.
5. During the last 10 minutes of cooking, stir in the raisins and lemon rind.

Note: Serve warm. A stirred custard adds nutritive value and taste appeal to this simple dessert.

(Serves two)	
1/4 c	uncooked rice
2 1/2 tbsp	sugar
1/8 tsp	salt
1/8 tsp	cinnamon
1/8 tsp	nutmeg
1 1/4 c	nonfat milk
1/4 c	seedless raisins
1/2 tsp	grated lemon rind

(Serves four)	
1/2 c	uncooked rice
1/3 c	sugar
1/4 tsp	salt
1/4 tsp	cinnamon
1/4 tsp	nutmeg
2 1/2 c	nonfat milk
1/2 c	seedless raisins
1 tsp	grated lemon rind

PUDDINGS

TYPE OF PUDDING	APPEARANCE	FLAVOR	MOUTH FEEL	CONSISTENCY
Vanilla cornstarch				
Chocolate cornstarch				
Caramel cornstarch				
Orange tapioca				
Rice				

CEREALS AND PASTAS

Cereals are cooked to accomplish two purposes: gelatinize the starch and soften the cellulose. Both of these are achieved by boiling the cereal in water. The amount of water and the cooking time required vary with the type of cereal and the previous treatment of the grain.

To prepare the cooked cereals and pastas, bring the suggested amount of salted water (1 teaspoon salt/quart of water) to a *boil*. Sprinkle the cereal or pasta directly into the boiling water. Granular cereals (cornmeal, farina, cream of wheat) need to be mixed with some cold water before being added to the boiling water if lumps are to be avoided. Specific directions are given in the chart. Stir the product occasionally to keep it from sticking to the bottom of the pan. Cereals are done when thickened and free of a starchy flavor. Pastas are done when just cooked to the point when they can be cut easily, and they no longer have a starchy flavor.

CHART OF CEREAL COOKERY[1]

TYPE OF CEREAL	CUPS OF WATER/ CUP OF CEREAL	BOILING TIME (MINUTES)	METHOD OF PREPARING
Granular			
Cream of wheat	5	15	Slurry with cold water. Stir into boiling water.
Quick cream of wheat	5	5	Same as regular cream of wheat.
Cornmeal	4 1/2	5	Same as regular cream of wheat.
Flaked			
Oatmeal	3	5	Sprinkle on boiling water.
Whole			
Polished rice, long or short	2 3/4	20	Sprinkle on boiling water.
Parboiled rice	2 1/2	20	Sprinkle on boiling water.
Instant and minute rice	1	—	Add to boiling water.
Brown rice	2 1/2	40	Sprinkle on boiling water.
Minute brown rice	1 1/2	15	Sprinkle on boiling water.
Wild rice	3	60	Sprinkle on boiling water.

[1]Add 1 teaspoon salt to each quart of water.

CHART OF PASTA COOKERY[1]

TYPE OF PASTA	QUARTS OF WATER/LB OF PASTA	COOKING TIME (MINUTES)[2]
Egg noodles	4	10–15
Macaroni	4	15–20
Spaghetti	6	15–20
Vermicelli	6	8–10

[1]Add 1 teaspoon salt to each quart of water.
[2]Boil just until *al dente* (yielding to gentle pressure).

CEREALS AND PASTAS RECIPES

PENNE WITH TOMATOES, ZUCCHINI, AND BASIL

Total Time: 20 minutes

1. Boil penne according to package directions. Drain thoroughly.
2. Meanwhile, sauté garlic, zucchini, and tomatoes 2 minutes in the oil.
3. Stir in chopped basil leaves and seasonings.
4. Toss penne with vegetables, and top with grated Romano cheese.

(Serves two)
1 c	*uncooked penne (or other pasta)*
1	*garlic clove, peeled and minced*
1	*yellow zucchini, sliced 1/4" thick*
2	*Roma tomatoes, seeded and chopped coarsely*
1 tbsp	*shredded basil leaves (or pesto)*
1/2 tsp	*lemon zest*
	salt and coarse-grind black pepper to taste
	grated Romano cheese

(Serves four)
2 c	uncooked penne (or other pasta)
2	garlic cloves, peeled and minced
2	yellow zucchini, sliced 1/4" thick
4	Roma tomatoes, seeded and chopped coarsely
2 tbsp	shredded basil leaves (or pesto)
1 tsp	lemon zest
	salt and coarse-grind black pepper to taste
	grated Romano cheese

PESTO

Total Time: 15 minutes

1. Combine piñon nuts, basil leaves, garlic, and cheeses in a blender. Puree until well blended, stopping occasionally to scrape down with rubber spatula.
2. Slowly add olive oil while continuing to puree.
3. Add pepper to taste and puree until smooth.

(Makes about 1 cup)
1/4 c	*piñon nuts*
2 c	*basil leaves*
2	*cloves garlic (peeled)*
1/2 c	*grated Parmesan cheese*
2 tbsp	*grated Romano cheese*
1/2 c	*olive oil*
	black pepper, to taste

Note: Pasta fans may wish to make their own pesto, which can be stored in the refrigerator (covered with a layer of olive oil) for up to a month.

ANGEL HAIR MEDLEY

Total Time: 20 minutes

1. Microwave bacon until crisp, covering with paper towel to block spattering. Blot with paper towel and crumble bacon.
2. Boil angel hair pasta according to package directions. Drain well.
3. Meanwhile, sauté onions and garlic in olive oil until golden brown. Remove and discard garlic.
4. Add dried tomatoes, green pepper, and red chili flakes, and half-and-half. Simmer (with some stirring) until heated and desired consistency is reached.
5. Toss sauce with pasta and serve topped with Romano cheese.

(Serves two)

3	slices bacon
1/4 lb	angel hair pasta
2	green onions, sliced thinly
1	garlic clove, crushed
1 tbsp	olive oil
2 tsp	chopped sun-dried tomato
2 tbsp	chopped green pepper
1/4 tsp	red chili flakes
1/2 c	half-and-half
	grated Romano cheese

(Serves four)

6	slices bacon
1/2 lb	angel hair pasta
4	green onions, sliced thinly
2	garlic clove, crushed
2 tbsp	olive oil
4 tsp	chopped sun-dried tomato
1/4 c	chopped green pepper
1/2 tsp	red chili flakes
1 c	half-and-half
	grated Romano cheese

WILD RICE CASSEROLE

Total Time: 1 1/2 hours
Baking: 375° F for 30 minutes

1. Preheat oven.
2. Gently boil wild rice until tender. Drain.
3. Meanwhile simmer onions, raisins, mushrooms, carrots, and thyme in chicken bouillon 7 minutes.
4. Stir the vegetables into the wild rice and add enough liquid to moisten the wild rice.
5. Place in casserole dish. Bake at 375° F for 30 minutes.

(Serves two)

1/2 c	wild rice
1 c	water
1/2 c	chopped onions
1/4 c	raisins
3	mushrooms, sliced
1/4 c	carrots, thinly sliced
3/4 tsp	dried thyme
1/2	chicken bouillon cube in 1/2 c water

(Serves four)

1 c	wild rice
2 c	water
1 c	chopped onions
1/2 c	raisins
6	mushrooms, sliced
1/2 c	carrots, thinly sliced
1 1/2 tsp	dried thyme
1	chicken bouillon cube in 1/2 c water

NOBLE NOODLES

Total Time: 25 minutes

1. Remove skin and bone from chicken and cut in bite-sized pieces.
2. Wash and slice green onions and mushrooms in thin slices.
3. Microwave peppers and broccoli (in a covered dish containing a tablespoon of water) for 2 minutes.
4. Boil noodles according to package directions just to *al dente* stage. Drain well.
5. In a wok or skillet, stir-fry chicken, green onions and mushrooms in oil olive just until chicken is done. Add the other vegetables and noodles and the seasonings. Stir to blend and continue heating to serving temperature.

(Serves two)

2	*chicken breast halves*
2	*green onions and tops*
3	*mushrooms*
1/2	*green pepper, chopped*
1/2	*red pepper, chopped*
1 c	*small flowerets of broccoli*
1/4 lb	*wide noodles*
2 tbsp	*olive oil*
1/8 tsp	*garlic powder*
1 tsp	*pinch of herbs (basil, rosemary, thyme, oregano, sesame seeds*
1/4 tsp	*salt*
1/8 tsp	*paprika*

(Serves four)

4	chicken breast halves
4	green onions and tops
6	mushrooms
1	green pepper, chopped
1	red pepper, chopped
2 c	small flowerets of broccoli
1/2 lb	wide noodles
3 tbsp	olive oil
1/4 tsp	garlic powder
2 tsp	pinch of herbs (basil, rosemary, thyme, oregano, sesame seeds
1/2 tsp	salt
1/4 tsp	paprika

PASTA SALAD

Total Time: 1 hour

1. Cook pasta according to package directions and drain well.
2. Add other ingredients to pasta and blend thoroughly.
3. Chill at least 45 minutes to blend flavors.

(Serves two)

3/4 c	*uncooked fusilli (or other pasta)*
1 tbsp	*chopped stuffed olives*
1/4 c	*marinated artichoke hearts*
1 tbsp	*green pepper, chopped*
1 tbsp	*green onions and tops, chopped*
1 tbsp	*parsley, chopped*
1/4 tsp	*grated lemon rind*
1/8 tsp	*garlic powder*
1/8 tsp	*paprika*
1 1/2 tbsp	*Italian dressing*

(Serves four)

1 1/2 c	uncooked fusilli (or other pasta)
2 tbsp	chopped stuffed olives
1/2 c	marinated artichoke hearts
2 tbsp	green pepper, chopped
2 tbsp	green onions and tops, chopped
2 tbsp	parsley, chopped
1/2 tsp	grated lemon rind
1/4 tsp	garlic powder
1/4 tsp	paprika
3 tbsp	Italian dressing

STUFFED GRAPE LEAVES

Total Time: 50 minutes
Baking: 325° F for 30 minutes

1. Preheat oven.
2. Brown lamb, onion, and garlic in oil.
3. Stir in tomato sauce, parsley, uncooked rice, salt, and pepper. Simmer 3 minutes.
4. Stir in piñon nuts and currants.
5. Dip grape leaves in hot water to separate before blotting on paper towel and placing shiny side down on cutting board.
6. Put 1 tablespoon of meat mixture near stem end, fold in sides loosely, and roll up loosely to allow rice to expand.
7. Place in oiled, shallow casserole. Weight down rolls with oven-proof plate.
8. Pour boiling water and lemon juice over rolls and cover with foil.
9. Bake at 325° F for 30 minutes. May be served warm or cold.

(Serves two)

2 oz	*ground lamb*
1/2	*medium onion, chopped*
1/2	*clove garlic, minced*
1 1/2 tsp	*olive oil*
3 tbsp	*tomato sauce*
1 tbsp	*parsley, minced*
2 tbsp	*long grain rice*
	salt and pepper to taste
1 tbsp	*piñon nuts*
1 tbsp	*currants*
6	*preserved grape leaves*
1/2 c	*boiling water*
1 1/2 tsp	*lemon juice*

(Serves four)

4 oz	ground lamb
1	medium onion, chopped
1	clove garlic, minced
1 tbsp	olive oil
6 tbsp	tomato sauce
2 tbsp	parsley, minced
1/4 c	long grain rice
	salt and pepper to taste
2 tbsp	piñon nuts
2 tbsp	currants
12	preserved grape leaves
1 c	boiling water
1 tbsp	lemon juice

CRACKED WHEAT STUFFING

Total Time: 20 minutes
Baking: 325° F for 15 minutes

1. Preheat oven.
2. Sauté cracked wheat, onion, and celery in butter.
3. Add salt, pepper, thyme, sage, bouillon cube, raisins, and water.
4. Stir together before baking in 325° F oven for 15 minutes.
5. Stir in nuts.

Note: This can be served as a side dish or used as as stuffing for pork chops or Cornish hens.

(Serves two)

1/2 c	*cracked wheat*
2 tbsp	*chopped onion*
2 tbsp	*chopped celery*
1 1/2 tsp	*butter or margarine*
1/8 tsp	*salt*
	pepper
1/8 tsp	*dried thyme*
1/8 tsp	*sage*
1/2	*chicken bouillon cube*
1/2 c	*hot water*
2 tbsp	*raisins*
2 tbsp	*coarsely chopped walnuts*

(Serves four)

1 c	cracked wheat
1/4 c	chopped onion
1/4 c	chopped celery
1 tbsp	butter or margarine
1/4 tsp	salt
	pepper
1/4 tsp	dried thyme
1/4 tsp	sage
1	chicken bouillon cube
1 c	hot water
1/4 c	raisins
1/4 c	coarsely chopped walnuts

VOCABULARY

Slurry

Gelatinization

Dextrinization

Acid hydrolysis

Syneresis

Starch paste

Retrogradation

Starch granule

Amylose

Amylopectin

Dextrins

Starch

Endosperm

Bran

Germ (embryo)

Polysaccharide

EVALUATION OF LABORATORY PRODUCTS — PASTAS AND CEREALS

RECIPE	NOTES ON COLOR, TEXTURE, FLAVOR, OR OTHER QUALITIES	COMMENTS OR SUGGESTIONS FOR MAKING OR USING THIS PRODUCT IN THE FUTURE

Chapter 6
Milk and Cheese

This chapter moves from a focus on carbohydrates and their behaviors during food preparation to quite a different type of food material — protein. Although milk does contain a carbohydrate (lactose) that influences that tendency of milk to scorch when being heated, the milk proteins have very unique behavior during cooking. The tendency to boil over due to scum formation and curdling are potential problems in milk cookery. Thoughening of cheese and separation of fat when heating cheese products are other results of the high protein content in milk and milk products.

Whenever you are cooking products containing milk and cheese, remember to keep a careful eye on them and avoid any overheating. Your reward will be smooth, highly palatable products. Lack of attention is likely to result in scorching, curdling, and/or tough products, sometimes with fat oozing out. In other words, let the chef beware! The rewards are great — the penalties are dire, including some nasty clean-up problems.

TYPES OF MILK

A wide range of fresh and processed milks is available for consumer selection. Fresh, pasteurized milks include: whole (usually homogenized), reduced fat (2%), lowfat or light (1%), and nonfat or fat free. Special fluid milks and milk products include: sweet acidophilus milk, cultured buttermilk, Lactaid and yogurt. Imitation milks also are available in some areas. Milks often are dried or canned to reduce bulk and promote shelf life. Canned milks commonly available are: evaporated whole milk, evaporated low-fat milk, evaporated nonfat milk, and sweetened condensed milk. Dried milk products (nonfat, low-fat, and whole) are also found in the markets.

To observe and compare the various milks, arrange a display of samples of: 1) packages, 2) the milks as contained in the packages, and 3) the milks ready to serve (reconstitute, as necessary, according to package directions). Record the results in the chart.

KEY CONCEPTS — MILK AND CHEESE

1) Milk and its products contain proteins, which denature and coagulate during heating.

   a. Acids and salts promote coagulation, but must be used to produce the desired result (curd formation in cheesemaking, but a smooth product in such items as cream soups.

   b. Excessive heating causes tightening of the protein coagulum, causing considerable toughening of cheese exposed to very intense heat.

EFFECT OF ADDED INGREDIENTS

Acid:

1. To each of the milks (reconstituted, where appropriate), add the vinegar.
2. Stir and observe changes in texture and viscosity.
3. Explain the change.

2 tbsp	vinegar
1/2 c	milk

Salts:

1. Place the cubes of ham in a custard cup, and add 1/4 c of milk.
2. Pour 1/4 c of milk into a second custard cup.
3. Bake both for one hour at 350° F. Compare the texture of the sauce in each. What caused the difference?

1/4 c	cubed ham
1/4 c	milk

COMPARISON OF MILK PRODUCTS

TYPE OF MILK	PALATABILITY			NUTRITIVE VALUE/CUP		COST/QUART
	FLAVOR	COLOR	VISCOSITY	PROTEIN (GRAMS)	FAT (GRAMS)	CARBOHYDRATE (GRAMS)
Fluid milks Whole (homogenized)						
2%						
1%						
Fat free						
Canned milks Evaporated						
Evaporated nonfat						
Sweetened condensed						
Dried milks Whole						
Low-fat						
Nonfat						

RECIPES

CREAM OF VEGETABLE SOUP

Total Time: 15 minutes

1. In a 1-quart saucepan, combine the oil and flour.
2. Add the salt.
3. Gradually stir in the milk.
4. Heat to boiling, stirring constantly.
5. Add the pureed vegetable.
6. Reheat, if necessary, before serving.

Note: Appropriate pureed fresh or frozen vegetables include spinach, broccoli, onions, celery, and asparagus. For greater variety of texture, vegetables may be chopped, rather than strained.

(Serves two)
1/2 c	pureed, cooked vegetable
1 1/2 tbsp	salad oil
1 1/2 tbsp	flour
1/4 tsp	salt
1 1/2 c	milk

(Serves four)
1 c	pureed, cooked vegetable
3 tbsp	salad oil
3 tbsp	flour
1/2 tsp	salt
3 c	milk

CREAM OF TOMATO SOUP

Total Time: 15 minutes

1. Simmer the tomatoes and seasonings in a 1-quart covered saucepan for 8–10 minutes.
2. Remove bay leaf. Puree tomatoes in blender. Set aside.
3. In a 1-quart saucepan, carefully stir the oil and flour together.
4. Slowly add the milk while stirring.
5. Heat to boiling, stirring constantly.
6. Remove from the heat.
7. Add the strained tomato mixture to the hot white sauce while stirring constantly.
8. If necessary, reheat to serving temperature and serve immediately. Avoid prolonged heating.

(Serves two)

1 1/4 c	*canned tomatoes*
1	*slicd onion*
	piece bay leaf
1/4 tsp	*salt*
	dash white pepper
	few grains garlic powder
1 tbsp	*salad oil*
1 tbsp	*flour*
1 c	*milk*

(Serves four)

2 1/2 c	canned tomatoes
2	sliced onion
	piece bay leaf
1/2 tsp	salt
	dash white pepper
	few grains garlic powder
2 tbsp	salad oil
2 tbsp	flour
2 c	milk

CREAM OF MUSHROOM SOUP

Total Time: 15 minutes

1. In a 1-quart saucepan, saute thinly sliced mushrooms in margarine or butter until mushrooms become slightly translucent. Remove from heat.
2. Stir flour into margarine and mushrooms.
3. Gradually stir in milk and water.
4. Add bouillon and nutmeg.
5. Heat to a boil, stirring constantly.
6. Serve immediately.

(Serves two)

5	*fresh mushrooms*
1 1/2 tbsp	*margarine or butter*
1 1/2 tbsp	*flour*
3/4 c	*milk*
3/4 c	*water*
1	*cube beef bouillon*
	dash nutmeg

(Serves four)

10	fresh mushrooms
3 tbsp	margarine or butter
3 tbsp	flour
1 1/2 c	milk
1 1/2 c	water
2	cubes beef bouillon
1/8 tsp	nutmeg

CREAM OF POTATO SOUP

Total Time: 15 minutes

1. In a 1-quart saucepan, blend the oil and flour.
2. Add the cooked potatoes.
3. Slowly stir in the milk.
4. Add the other ingredients.
5. Heat to boiling while stirring constantly.
6. Serve immediately.

(Serves two)

3/4 c	*boiled potatoes, riced*
1 tbsp	*salad oil*
1/2 tsp	*flour*
1 1/4 c	*milk*
1/4 tsp	*salt*
1 tsp	*chopped pimiento*

(Serves four)

1 1/2 c	boiled potatoes, riced
2 tbsp	salad oil
1 tsp	flour
2 1/2 c	milk
1/2 tsp	salt
2 tsp	chopped pimiento

LEMON CUCUMBER YOGURT SOUP

Total Time: 1 hour

1. Combine chicken broth, onion, salt, dill weed, garlic powder, lemon peel and juice in an electric blender. Blend until smooth.
2. Combine yogurt and sour cream. Add to blender, whirling a few seconds until just blended.
3. Add chopped cucumber; quickly turn blender on and off just to combine. Cucumber will be finely grated but not liquefied.
4. Chill thoroughly (about 50 minutes).
5. Serve in chilled bowls. Garnish with lemon and cucumber slices.

(Serves two)

1/3 c	*chicken broth*
1 1/2 tsp	*finely chopped onion*
1/4 tsp	*salt*
1/4 tsp	*dill weed, crushed*
	few grains garlic powder
1/2 tsp	*grated lemon peel*
1 tbsp	*lemon juice*
1/3 c	*plain yogurt*
1/3 c	*dairy sour cream*
1	*small cucumber, peeled, seeded, and chopped*
	lemon and cucumber slices

(Serves four)

2/3 c	chicken broth
1 tbsp	finely chopped onion
1/2 tsp	salt
1/2 tsp	dill weed, crushed
	few grains garlic powder
1 tsp	grated lemon peel
2 tbsp	lemon juice
2/3 c	plain yogurt
2/3 c	dairy sour cream
2	small cucumber, peeled, seeded, and chopped
	lemon and cucumber slices

BAKED CUSTARD ESPRESSO

Total Time: 55 minutes
Baking: 325° F for 50 minutes

1. Preheat oven.
2. Scald milk and espresso.
3. Add sugar.
4. Combine egg, salt, vanilla, and sugar.
5. Add scalded milk slowly with stirring.
6. Pour into custard cups and arrange in baking pan. Pour boiling water into the large pan halfway up the depth of the custards.
7. Bake at 325° F until a knife can be inserted halfway between the center and the edge of a custard and come out clean.

(Serves two)

1 c	*milk*
1 1/2 tbsp	*instant espresso*
1	*egg, beaten*
2 tbsp	*sugar*
	dash of salt
1/2 tsp	*vanilla*

(Serves four)

2 c	milk
3 tbsp	instant espresso
2	eggs, beaten
1/4 c	sugar
1/8 tsp	salt
1/2 tsp	vanilla

LIME PIE CLASSIC

Total Time: 55 minutes
Baking: 350° F for 10 minutes; 325° F for 30 minutes

1. Preheat oven.
2. Mix graham cracker crumbs, melted butter or margarine, and sugar together, and press into 8" pie plate to form a crust.
3. Bake at 350° F for 10 minutes.
4. Meanwhile, combine egg yolks, milk, lime juice, and enough green food coloring to tint mixture a delicate green.
5. Pour filling into baked pie shell and return to oven that has been reset to 325° F.
6. Bake 20 minutes while preparing the egg white meringue.
7. Make meringue by beating whites on an electric mixer until foamy. Continue to beat while adding cream of tartar and then gradually add the sugar. Beat until tips just bend over when tested with a spatula.
8. Remove pie from oven and spread meringue on pie. Return to oven and bake until meringue is a pleasing golden brown color on its higher surfaces.

(Makes 1 8" pie)	
Crust:	
1 1/4 c	*graham cracker crumbs*
1/4 c	*butter or margarine, melted*
2 tbsp	*sugar*
Filling:	
3	*egg yolks*
1	*14 oz can sweetened condensed milk*
1/2 c	*lime milk juice*
	green food coloring
Meringue:	
3	*egg whites*
1/4 tsp	*cream of tartar*
6 tbsp	*sugar*

NATURAL AND PROCESS CHEESES

Prepare a display of assorted natural and process cheese. Include a range of flavors and firmness. Note the flavor and texture characteristics of each.

Heat 1/2 cup grated cheddar cheese in a double boiler over boiling water for 30 minutes. Do the same with 1/2 cup process cheese. Compare the results.

COMPARISON OF MILK PRODUCTS

TYPE OF CHEESE	TEXTURE	FLAVOR	COMMENTS
Natural cheese			
Process cheeses			
Cheddar heated 30 minutes			
Process heated 30 minutes			

RECIPES
HAM STRATA

Total Time: 20 minutes to prepare;
*   refrigeration 3 hours to overnight;*
*   30–50 minutes for baking*
Baking: 325° F for 30 minutes for small
*   (50 minutes, large)*

1. Preheat oven.
2. Grease a loaf pan for small or 13x9" baking pan for large recipe.
3. Arrange half of bread on bottom of baking dish; distribute ham, cheese, and shallots evenly over the bread. Place remaining bread on top of the ham/cheese layer.
4. Beat eggs in a bowl; then beat in milk and pepper.
5. Pour egg mixture over bread, cover, and refrigerate for at least 3 hours (overnight is satisfactory).
6. Uncover and bake at 325° F until a knife inserted near center comes out clean. The surface should be golden brown and puffy.

(Serves two)

4	slices bread (crusts trimmed)
1/4 c	chopped ham
1/2 c	shredded sharp cheddar cheese
2 tsp	minced shallots
2	eggs
1 c	milk
	ground black pepper

(Serves four)

8	slices bread (crusts trimmed)
1/2 c	chopped ham
1 c	shredded sharp cheddar cheese
4 tsp	minced shallots
4	eggs
2 c	milk
	ground black pepper

CHEESE RAREBIT

Total Time: 15 minutes

1. Fry the bacon until crisp. Drain on paper towels.
2. Melt the margarine or butter and combine with flour in a 1-quart saucepan.
3. Add the salt.
4. Gradually stir in the milk.
5. Heat to boiling, stirring constantly.
6. Remove from heat.
7. Stir in cheese and seasonings until cheese is melted. If necessary, place over low heat to completely melt the cheese.
8. Serve at once over toast.
9. Garnish with crisp bacon strips.

(Serves two)

4	slices bacon (optional)
1 tbsp	margarine or butter
1 tbsp	flour
	dash salt
1/2 c	milk
1/2 c	(2 oz) grated sharp cheddar cheese
1/4 tsp	dry mustard
	dash paprika
2	English muffins, toasted

(Serves four)

8	slices bacon (optional)
2 tbsp	margarine or butter
2 tbsp	flour
1/8 tsp	salt
1 c	milk
1 c	(4 oz) grated sharp cheddar cheese
1/2 tsp	dry mustard
1/8 tsp	paprika
4	English muffins, toasted

CHEESE STICKS

Total Time: 25 minutes
Baking: 400° F oven for 15 minutes

1. Preheat oven.
2. Cut the shortening into the flour and salt until shortening is the size of split peas.
3. Stir in the cheese and seeds.
4. While tossing the mixture with a fork, gradually add the water.
5. Mix until the dough holds together.
6. Roll into a rectangle about 1/4" thick.
7. Cut into strips about 3" long and 1/3" wide.
8. Bake at 400° F about 12 minutes until golden brown.

(Serves two)

1/2 c	flour
1/4 tsp	salt
2 2/3 tbsp	shortening
1 1/3 tbsp	water
1/4 c	sharp cheddar cheese, grated
1 tsp	sesame seeds

(Serves four)

1 c	flour
1/2 tsp	salt
1/3 c	shortening
2 2/3 tbsp	water
1/2 c	sharp cheddar cheese, grated
2 tsp	sesame seeds

QUICHE LORRAINE

Total Time: 55 minutes
Baking: 425° F for 10 minutes;
      375° F for 25 minutes

1. Preheat oven.
2. Mix flour and salt.
3. Cut in shortening to the size of rice grains.
4. Slowly add the water while tossing the flour mixture with a fork.
5. Mix the dough into a ball.
6. Divide small recipe into 2 balls and large recipe into 4.
7. Roll out each ball into a circle large enough to fit a tart pan.
8. Fit in pan and make edging. Prick holes with a fork around the side and bottom.
9. Bake at 425° F until lightly browned. Remove from oven and reduce oven heat to 375° F.
10. While the crusts are baking, fry the bacon crisp, drain well, and crumble it.
11. In a mixing bowl, beat the egg, and add the bacon, onion, sour cream, salt, and grated Swiss cheese.
12. Mix well.
13. Pour the filling into the baked crusts; bake at 375° F 25 minutes, or until a knife inserted halfway between the center and edge of the tart comes out clean.
14. Serve hot.

(Serves two)	
1 c	flour
1/2 tsp	salt
1/3 c	shortening
2 2/3 tbsp	water
2	strips bacon
1/4 c	onion, chopped
1	egg
1/4 c	dairy sour cream
1/8 tsp	salt
4 oz	Swiss cheese

(Serves four)	
2 c	flour
1 tsp	salt
2/3 c	shortening
1/3 c	water
4	strips bacon
1/2 c	onion, chopped
2	eggs
1/2 c	dairy sour cream
1/4 tsp	salt
8 oz	Swiss cheese

MICROWAVE QUICHE

Total Time: 50 minutes
Baking: 425° F for 12–15 minutes;
Microwaving: 9 1/2 minutes on high, 10 minutes
      on low, 5 minutes on browning

1. Preheat oven.
2. Prepare pie crust according to steps 1 through 4 above; roll crust to fit a 9" ceramic or glass quiche pan or pie plate.
3. Fit crust in the pan, make edging, and prick holes with a fork around the side and bottom.
4. Bake at 425° F until golden brown (12–15 minutes).
5. While crust is baking, cook bacon in microwave oven for 6 minutes on high setting. Crumble crisp bacon.
6. Combine salt, nutmeg, cayenne, and flour in a glass mixing bowl.
7. Add milk and beaten eggs while stirring to prevent lumping. Add green chiles.
8. Heat this milk mixture in microwave oven on high for 3 1/2 minutes, being sure to stir carefully after 1 1/2 minutes and after 2 1/2 minutes.
9. Meanwhile, line the bottom of the crust with half the bacon bits and grated cheese.
10. Pour the egg mixture into the baked crust, and garnish with the other half of the bacon and the green onion.
11. Heat on *low* setting in microwave oven for 10 minutes, followed by 5 minutes in the microwave oven with the browning element, turning once.

(Serves four)	
2 c	flour
1 tsp	salt
2/3 c	shortening
1/3 c	water
6	slices bacon
1/4 tsp	salt
1/4 tsp	nutmeg
1/8 tsp	cayenne
1 1/2 tbsp	flour
1	13-oz can evaporated milk (undiluted)
4	eggs, slightly beaten
1 tbsp	canned green chilies, drained, minced
1 1/4 c	grated Swiss cheese
3	small green onions (including the tops), thinly sliced

CHEESE CHOWDER

Total Time: 20 minutes

1. Add the celery to the water when the water boils; cover the pan.
2. After 1 minute, add the carrots and continue boiling until tender. Set aside.
3. In a saucepan, sauté the onion in the margarine. Remove from the heat.
4. Stir in the flour and salt.
5. Gradually add the milk and water.
6. Add the bouillon cube and heat to boiling while stirring constantly.
7. Add the cooked vegetables, their cooking water, and cheddar cheese to the white sauce.
8. Stir until cheese melts. If necessary, reheat over low heat to completely melt the cheese.
9. Serve with croutons.

(Serves two)

1/4 c	grated carrots
1/4 c	minced celery
1/2 c	water
1 tbsp	minced onion
1 tbsp	margarine or butter
1 1/2 tbsp	flour
1/4 tsp	salt
3/4 c	milk
3/4 c	water
1/2	cube chicken bouillon
3/4 c	(3 oz) grated sharp cheddar cheese croutons

(Serves four)

1/2 c	grated carrots
1/2 c	minced celery
1 c	water
2 tbsp	minced onion
2 tbsp	margarine or butter
3 tbsp	flour
1/2 tsp	salt
1 1/2 c	milk
1 1/2 c	water
1	cube chicken bouillon
1 1/2 c	(6 oz) grated sharp cheddar cheese croutons

FONDUE ALA SUISSE

Total Time: 10 minutes

1. Place the cheese and the dry ingredients in a bag and shake them together vigorously so that the cheese is completely coated with the dry ingredients.
2. Heat the sauterne in a chafing dish or in a saucepan over low heat.
3. When it begins to steam, gradually add the coated cheese.
4. As the cheese melts, add more cheese until all the cheese has been added.
5. Stir in the kirsch and keep warm over a candle.
6. Provide bite-sized bread cubes and long-handled fondue forks for dipping the bread cubes in the hot fondue mixture.

(Serves two)

1 1/2 c	(6 oz) grated Swiss cheese
	dash garlic powder
1 tbsp	flour
	dash white pepper
1/4 tsp	salt
10 tbsp	dry sauterne
1 tsp	kirsch
1/4	loaf French bread, cut in bite-sized cubes

(Serves four)

3 c	(12 oz) grated Swiss cheese
	dash garlic powder
2 tbsp	flour
1/8 tsp	white pepper
1/2 tsp	salt
1 1/4 c	dry sauterne
2 tsp	kirsch
1/2	loaf French bread, cut in bite-sized cubes

MACARONI AND CHEESE

Total Time: 1 hour
Baking: 350° F oven for 45 minutes

1. Preheat oven.
2. Bring the water to a boil.
3. Add the macaroni and salt, and continue to boil until the macaroni is white and is just tender when cut against the side of the pan with a fork.
4. Drain in a colander.
5. In a 1-quart saucepan, melt the margarine or butter. Remove from heat; stir in the flour and salt, and gradually add the milk.
6. Heat to a boil, stirring constantly. Remove from the heat.
7. Place a layer of macaroni in the bottom of a casserole dish.
8. Pour one-third of the white sauce over the macaroni and sprinkle with one-third of the cheese.
9. Repeat with a second layer of the macaroni, white sauce, and cheese.
10. Top with the remaining third of each item.
11. Generously sprinkle buttered bread crumbs over the entire surface of the casserole.
12. Bake at 350° F for 45 minutes or until bubbling hot.

(Serves two)

1 c	uncooked elbow macaroni
1 1/2 qt	water
1 1/2 tsp	salt
3 tbsp	margarine or butter
3 tbsp	flour
1/4 tsp	salt
1 1/2 c	milk
4 oz	grated sharp cheddar cheese
1/4 c	buttered bread crumbs

(Serves four)

2 c	uncooked elbow macaroni
3 qt	water
3 tsp	salt
6 tbsp	margarine or butter
6 tbsp	flour
1/2 tsp	salt
3 c	milk
8 oz	grated sharp cheddar cheese
1/2 c	buttered bread crumbs

PIZZA

Total Time: 45 minutes
Baking: 425° F oven for 25 minutes

1. Preheat oven.
2. Brown the sausage carefully and drain off all the fat. Set aside.
3. Meanwhile, mix the flour and yeast.
4. Stir in the lukewarm water to make a stiff dough.
5. Add a little more flour if the dough is sticky to handle.
6. Knead dough on lightly floured board for 5 minutes.
7. Roll dough into circle to fit pizza pans. (Large recipe makes two pizzas.)
8. Mix the sauce and seasonings and spread over the dough.
9. Sprinkle sausage and all of the remaining ingredients over the tomato sauce.
10. Bake at 425° F 25 minutes or until cheese is bubbly and dough is crisp.

(Serves two)

1/4 lb	Italian sausage
1/4 tsp	active dry yeast
1 1/2 c	flour
7 tbsp	lukewarm water
12 oz	tomato sauce or pizza sauce
1/4 tsp	oregano
1/8 tsp	thyme
1/4 tsp	salt
1/8 tsp	pepper
4 tbsp	canned sliced mushrooms
1/4 c	grated Parmesan cheese
1/4 c	sliced black olives
1 c	grated Mozzarella cheese

(Serves four)

1/2 lb	Italian sausage
1/2 tsp	active dry yeast
3 c	flour
14 tbsp	lukewarm water
24 oz	tomato sauce or pizza sauce
1/2 tsp	oregano
1/4 tsp	thyme
1/2 tsp	salt
1/4 tsp	pepper
1/2 c	canned sliced mushrooms
1/2 c	grated Parmesan cheese
1/2 c	sliced black olives
2 c	grated Mozzarella cheese

LASAGNA

Total Time: 1 hour
Baking: 375° F oven for 30 minutes

1. Preheat oven.
2. Brown the sausage and drain off the fat.
3. Add the other ingredients through the tomato paste.
4. Simmer in a covered 1-quart saucepan for 30 minutes, stirring occasionally.
5. Boil noodles in boiling, salted water until just tender.
6. Mix together the ricotta, mozzarella, and Parmesan cheeses, salt, and pepper.
7. In a loaf pan, arrange a layer of noodles topped with a layer of the cheese and the sauce.
8. Repeat the layering until all ingredients are used, ending with the sauce on top.
9. Bake at 375° F for 30 minutes, or until bubbly.
10. Let stand 5–10 minutes, cut in squares, and serve.

(Serves two)

1/4 lb	*Italian sausage*
	dash garlic powder
1/2 tsp	*chopped parsley*
1/8 tsp	*salt*
1/2 c	*stewed tomatoes*
1/4 c	*tomato paste*
2 oz	*lasagna noodles*
3/4 c	*ricotta cheese (or cottage cheese)*
2 tbsp	*grated Parmesan cheese*
1/2 tsp	*salt*
1/8 tsp	*pepper*
1/4 lb	*mozzarella cheese, grated*

(Serves four)

1/2 lb	Italian sausage
1/8 tsp	garlic powder
1 tsp	chopped parsley
1/4 tsp	salt
1 c	stewed tomatoes
1/2 c	tomato paste
4 oz	lasagna noodles
1 1/2 c	ricotta cheese (or cottage cheese)
1/4 c	grated Parmesan cheese
1 tsp	salt
1/4 tsp	pepper
1/2 lb	mozzarella cheese, grated

MICROWAVE CHEESE CAKE

Total Time: 35 minutes
Microwaving: 4 minutes on high, 4 minutes on low.

1. Melt margarine or butter in a 9" pie plate in microwave oven.
2. Add crumbs and mix thoroughly before pressing the crumbs to conform to the plate.
3. Heat 4 minutes in microwave oven on *high*.
4. Meanwhile, mix eggs, cream cheese, sugar, salt, vanilla, and sour cream in a mixing bowl until smooth.
5. Pour into crust and microwave on *low* setting for 3 minutes.
6. Rotate dish a quarter turn and microwave on low for a minute or more until the filling sets.
7. Chill thoroughly (several hours, if possible).

Note: May be served with a topping or plain.

(Serves eight)

1 c	*graham cracker crumbs*
1/4 c	*margarine or butter*
2	*eggs, well beaten*
1	*8 oz package cream cheese (softened in microwave oven)*
1 1/2 c	*dairy sour cream*
1/8 tsp	*salt*
1 tsp	*vanilla*
1/8 tsp	*almond extract*
1/2 c	*sugar*

VOCABULARY

Natural cheese

Process cheese

Ripened cheese

Rennin

Curd

Whey

Curdling

Protein

Lactose

Pasteurization

Evaporated milk

Condensed milk

EVALUATION OF LABORATORY PRODUCTS — MILK AND CHEESE

RECIPE	NOTES ON COLOR, TEXTURE, FLAVOR, OR OTHER QUALITIES	COMMENTS OR SUGGESTIONS FOR MAKING OR USING THIS PRODUCT IN THE FUTURE

Chapter 7
Meats, Poultry, and Fish

Meat usually represents the most expensive item in a meal, so consumers are anxious to have the best possible result. Success in meat cookery requires a knowledge of meat cuts, ability to select them, and an understanding of appropriate methods of cooking the various cuts.

SELECTION

Meat prepration begins with selection. Note first that primal cuts of meat have a circular seal indicating that the meat has been inspected by federal inspectors. Then look for the shield-shaped grading stamp. In

---

KEY CONCEPTS — MEATS, POULTRY, AND FISH

1) Consumers need knowledge of the various types of meats, poultry, and fish so they can select them wisely in the market, handle them safely during storage, and prepare them for optimum palatability.

   a) Identification of meats, their cuts, and their cooking characteristics will result in wise selections and pleasing meat dishes.

   b) Red meats can be divided into tender and less tender cuts, which will determine appropriate cookery methods.

      1. Roasting, broiling, pan broiling, pan frying, and deep fat frying are dry heat methods suited to preparing tender cuts.
      2. Braising and stewing (cooking in liquid) are moist heat methods needed to tenderize less tender cuts.
      3. Moist heat methods may be used on tender cuts to introduce greater menu variety than is generally possible with dry heat methods.

2) Fish and poultry are particularly susceptible to spoilage, but red meats also require careful refrigeration and attention to sanitation to avoid contamination and cross-contamination in the kitchen.

3) Careful attention to final temperatures when cooking meats, poultry, and fish is essential to assuring safe products and to avoiding bacterial, viral, and parasitic infections.

selecting meat cuts, observe the size of the fibers of the meat, look for the amount of fat in the muscle, and check the proportion of meat to bone. Using the following diagrams of the cuts, begin to study cuts at the market and determine their original location on the carcass. From this knowledge of cuts, decide what method of meat cookery will produce the best result.

PREPARATION

Meat preparation may be divided into two basic categories: dry heat methods and moist heat methods. Dry heat methods are well suited to preparing tender cuts of meat, but moist heat methods are preferred for less tender cuts of meat or meats with very mild flavors. Dry heat methods include roasting, broiling, pan broiling, pan frying, and deep fat frying. Braising and stewing are the moist heat methods.

DRY HEAT MEAT COOKERY

ROASTING

Roasting is an excellent dry heat method for large, tender cuts of meat from the rib or loin of beef, pork, and lamb. Ham and leg of lamb also are well suited to roasting.

Select a tender cut of meat that is at least 2" thick for roasting. Wipe the cut surfaces of the meat with a damp paper towel. Place the meat on a rack to hold the cut above the drippings (unless the meat contains its own bone rack) and put the meat and rack in a shallow pan. Insert a meat thermometer into the center of the largest muscle, being careful that it does not rest against bone or in fat. Place the meat (uncovered) in the center of the oven. (If foil or some other covering were used, this would trap moisture from the meat and would change the method into a moist heat cookery method.)

Roast at 325° F for small cuts and 300° F for larger roasts until the thermometer indicates the desired internal temperature. For rare beef, this is 145° F; for medium beef, 160° F, and for well done, 170° F. Fresh pork is always roasted to at least 160° F to insure safety from trichinosis. Lamb is roasted to 160° F for those who prefer medium lamb and to 170° F for those who like lamb well done. Time tables are available for guides to the length of time that may be expected to be required for roasting meats, but the thermometer is the only sure way of knowing that the desired degree of doneness has been reached. When the desired endpoint is reached, the meat is removed from the oven and allowed to stand at room temperature for approximately 15 minutes before carving. Roasts are salted as each slice is carved, because flavoring substances barely penetrate the surface of the meat.

Turkey also is well suited to roasting. A thorough washing of the fowl, both inside and out is done as soon as the neck and the bag containing the giblets are removed from the cavity. Particular attention needs to be given to scrubbing out the cavity and to removing any traces of feathers in the skin. After the turkey has been washed thoroughly under a stream of water in the sink, it should be drained thoroughly. The dressing is an optional item in roasting turkey and may be prepared from a variety of ingredients or from commercially-prepared stuffings. The potential for food spoilage is great if dressing is placed in a turkey several hours in advance of roasting. By far the best practice is to stuff the turkey immediately before beginning to roast the fowl. Stuffing is placed lightly in the body cavity. The turkey now is transferred to a V-shaped rack with the breast down. In this position, it is a simple matter to stuff the neck region of the turkey. This stuffing helps to give the turkey a plump appearance. When lightly stuffed, the flap of skin at the neck is pulled over the dressing and skewered to the back of the bird. The legs are tied together with string.

The thermometer is inserted into the stuffing in the main cavity of the bird if the bird is stuffed. An unstuffed bird is roasted with the thermometer inserted in the thigh. The thermometer is adjusted so that it can be read easily while the turkey is roasting. The turkey and rack are situated in a shallow pan suitable for catching the drippings, and then the assembly is placed in the oven. The oven rack usually needs to be at the bottom rack position because of the large size of turkeys. The turkey itself should be situated an equal distance from the top and bottom of the oven. The oven is set at 300–325° F and the turkey is roasted until the thermometer indicates 165° F in the dressing or 180° F in the thigh. If the turkey is roasted breast down, the juices released during roasting will help to baste the breast. If roasted breast side up on a rack, the breast may be basted occasionally with margarine or butter. However, it is perfectly appropriate to let turkeys roast without any attention until the fowl is done.

BEEF CHART

RETAIL CUTS OF BEEF — WHERE THEY COME FROM AND HOW TO COOK THEM

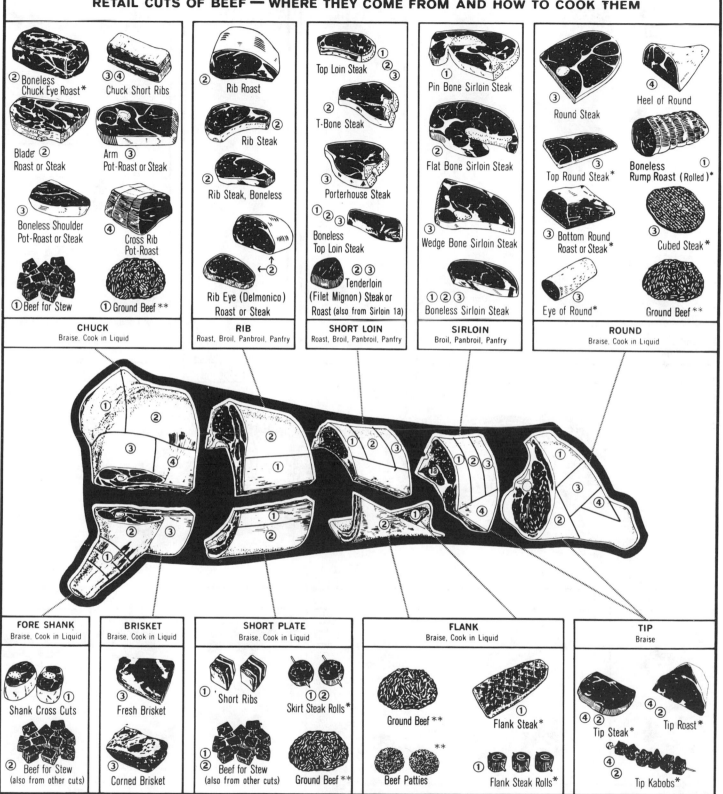

CHUCK
Braise, Cook in Liquid

- ② Boneless Chuck Eye Roast*
- ③④ Chuck Short Ribs
- Blade ② Roast or Steak
- Arm ③ Pot-Roast or Steak
- ③ Boneless Shoulder Pot-Roast or Steak
- ④ Cross Rib Pot-Roast
- ① Beef for Stew
- ① Ground Beef**

RIB
Roast, Broil, Panbroil, Panfry

- ② Rib Roast
- ② Rib Steak
- ② Rib Steak, Boneless
- ② Rib Eye (Delmonico) Roast or Steak

SHORT LOIN
Roast, Broil, Panbroil, Panfry

- ①② Top Loin Steak ③
- ② T-Bone Steak
- ③ Porterhouse Steak
- ①②③ Boneless Top Loin Steak
- ②③ Tenderloin (Filet Mignon) Steak or Roast (also from Sirloin 1a)

SIRLOIN
Broil, Panbroil, Panfry

- ① Pin Bone Sirloin Steak
- ② Flat Bone Sirloin Steak
- Wedge Bone Sirloin Steak
- ①②③ Boneless Sirloin Steak

ROUND
Braise, Cook in Liquid

- ③ Round Steak
- ④ Heel of Round
- ③ Top Round Steak*
- ① Boneless Rump Roast (Rolled)*
- ③ Bottom Round Roast or Steak*
- ③ Cubed Steak*
- ③ Eye of Round*
- ③ Ground Beef**

FORE SHANK
Braise, Cook in Liquid

- ① Shank Cross Cuts
- ② Beef for Stew (also from other cuts)

BRISKET
Braise, Cook in Liquid

- ③ Fresh Brisket
- ③ Corned Brisket

SHORT PLATE
Braise, Cook in Liquid

- ① Short Ribs
- ①② Skirt Steak Rolls*
- ①② Beef for Stew (also from other cuts)
- ①② Ground Beef**

FLANK
Braise, Cook in Liquid

- Ground Beef**
- ① Flank Steak*
- ** Beef Patties
- ① Flank Steak Rolls*

TIP
Braise

- ④② Tip Steak*
- ④② Tip Roast*
- ④② Tip Kabobs*

*May be Roasted, Broiled, Panbroiled or Panfried from high quality beef.
**May be Roasted, (Baked), Broiled, Panbroiled or Panfried.

This chart approved by
National Live Stock and Meat Board

 © National Live Stock and Meat Board

VEAL CHART

RETAIL CUTS OF VEAL — WHERE THEY COME FROM AND HOW TO COOK THEM

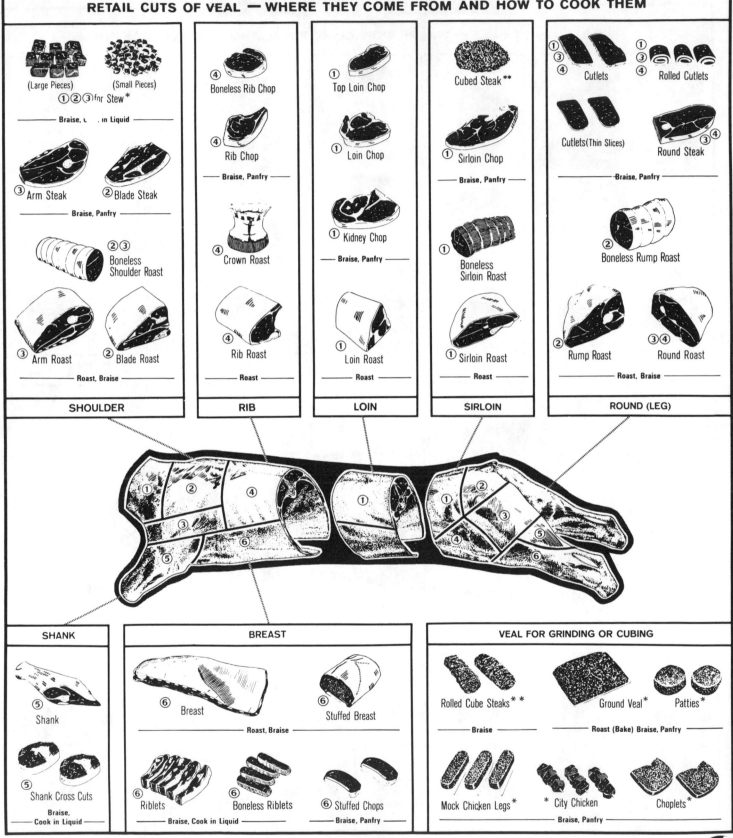

SHOULDER

(Large Pieces)   (Small Pieces)
①②③ for Stew *
— Braise, Cook in Liquid —

③ Arm Steak   ② Blade Steak
— Braise, Panfry —

②③ Boneless Shoulder Roast

③ Arm Roast   ② Blade Roast
— Roast, Braise —

RIB

④ Boneless Rib Chop

④ Rib Chop
— Braise, Panfry —

④ Crown Roast

④ Rib Roast
— Roast —

LOIN

① Top Loin Chop

① Loin Chop

① Kidney Chop
— Braise, Panfry —

① Loin Roast
— Roast —

SIRLOIN

Cubed Steak **

① Sirloin Chop
— Braise, Panfry —

① Boneless Sirloin Roast

① Sirloin Roast
— Roast —

ROUND (LEG)

① ③ ④ Cutlets   ① ③ ④ Rolled Cutlets

Cutlets (Thin Slices)   ③ ④ Round Steak
— Braise, Panfry —

② Boneless Rump Roast

② Rump Roast   ③ ④ Round Roast
— Roast, Braise —

SHANK

⑤ Shank

⑤ Shank Cross Cuts
— Braise, Cook in Liquid —

BREAST

⑥ Breast   ⑥ Stuffed Breast
— Roast, Braise —

⑥ Riblets   ⑥ Boneless Riblets   ⑥ Stuffed Chops
— Braise, Cook in Liquid —   — Braise, Panfry —

VEAL FOR GRINDING OR CUBING

Rolled Cube Steaks **   Ground Veal *   Patties *
— Braise —   — Roast (Bake) Braise, Panfry —

Mock Chicken Legs *   * City Chicken   Choplets *
— Braise, Panfry —

*Veal for stew or grinding may be made from any cut.

**Cube steaks may be made from any thick solid
 piece of boneless veal.

This chart approved by
National Live Stock and Meat Board

PORK CHART

RETAIL CUTS OF PORK — WHERE THEY COME FROM AND HOW TO COOK THEM

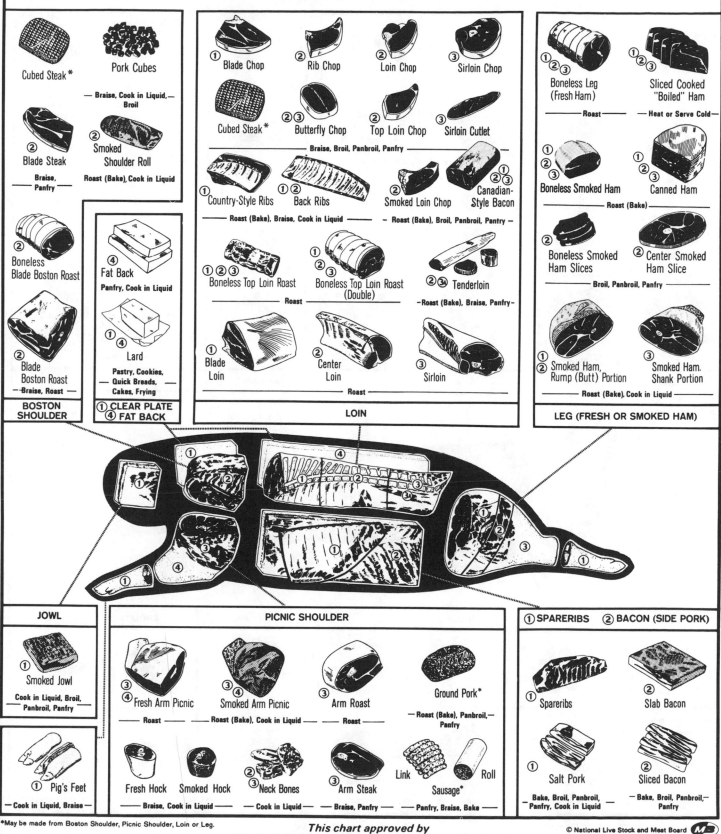

BOSTON SHOULDER

Cubed Steak *

Pork Cubes

— Braise, Cook in Liquid, — Broil

② Blade Steak

Braise, Panfry

② Smoked Shoulder Roll

Roast (Bake), Cook in Liquid

② Boneless Blade Boston Roast

② Blade Boston Roast

— Braise, Roast —

① CLEAR PLATE
④ FAT BACK

④ Fat Back

Panfry, Cook in Liquid

① ④ Lard

Pastry, Cookies, — Quick Breads, Cakes, Frying

LOIN

① Blade Chop

② Rib Chop

③ Loin Chop

③ Sirloin Chop

② ③ Cubed Steak *

② ③ Butterfly Chop

② Top Loin Chop

③ Sirloin Cutlet

— Braise, Broil, Panbroil, Panfry —

① ② ③ Country-Style Ribs

① ② Back Ribs

Smoked Loin Chop

① ② ③ Canadian-Style Bacon

— Roast (Bake), Braise, Cook in Liquid —   — Roast (Bake), Broil, Panbroil, Pantry —

① ② ③ Boneless Top Loin Roast

① ② ③ Boneless Top Loin Roast (Double)

② ③ ④ Tenderloin

— Roast —

—Roast (Bake), Braise, Panfry—

① Blade Loin

② Center Loin

③ Sirloin

— Roast —

LEG (FRESH OR SMOKED HAM)

① ② ③ Boneless Leg (Fresh Ham)

① ② ③ Sliced Cooked "Boiled" Ham

— Roast —   — Heat or Serve Cold —

① ② ③ Boneless Smoked Ham

① ② ③ Canned Ham

— Roast (Bake) —

② Boneless Smoked Ham Slices

② Center Smoked Ham Slice

— Broil, Panbroil, Panfry —

① ② Smoked Ham, Rump (Butt) Portion

③ Smoked Ham. Shank Portion

— Roast (Bake), Cook in Liquid —

JOWL

① Smoked Jowl

Cook in Liquid, Broil, Panbroil, Panfry

① Pig's Feet

— Cook in Liquid, Braise —

PICNIC SHOULDER

③ ④ Fresh Arm Picnic

③ ④ Smoked Arm Picnic

③ Arm Roast

Ground Pork*

— Roast —   — Roast (Bake), Cook in Liquid —   — Roast —   — Roast (Bake), Panbroil,— Panfry

Fresh Hock

Smoked Hock

② ③ Neck Bones

③ Arm Steak

Link   Roll

Sausage*

— Braise, Cook in Liquid —   — Cook in Liquid —   — Braise, Panfry —   — Panfry, Braise, Bake —

① SPARERIBS   ② BACON (SIDE PORK)

① Spareribs

② Slab Bacon

① Salt Pork

Sliced Bacon

Bake, Broil, Panbroil, Panfry, Cook in Liquid

— Bake, Broil, Panbroil,— Panfry

*May be made from Boston Shoulder, Picnic Shoulder, Loin or Leg.

This chart approved by
National Live Stock and Meat Board

© National Live Stock and Meat Board

LAMB CHART

RETAIL CUTS OF LAMB — WHERE THEY COME FROM AND HOW TO COOK THEM

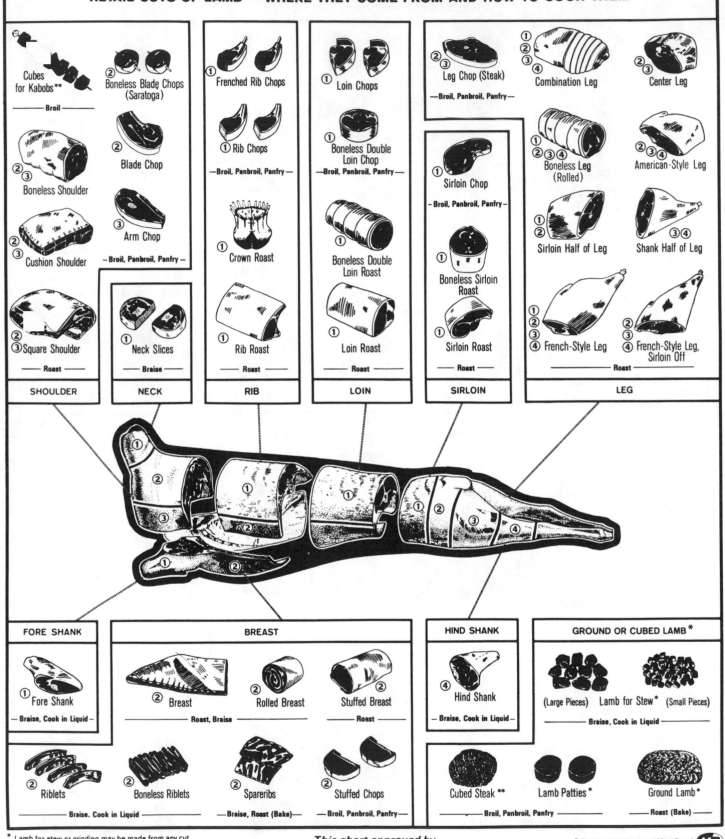

SHOULDER

Cubes for Kabobs ** — Broil —

Boneless Blade Chops (Saratoga) ②

Blade Chop ②

Arm Chop ③

— Broil, Panbroil, Panfry —

Boneless Shoulder ②③

Cushion Shoulder ②③

Square Shoulder ②③ — Roast —

NECK

Neck Slices ① — Braise —

RIB

Frenched Rib Chops ①

Rib Chops ①

— Broil, Panbroil, Panfry —

Crown Roast ①

Rib Roast ① — Roast —

LOIN

Loin Chops ①

Boneless Double Loin Chop ① — Broil, Panbroil, Panfry —

Boneless Double Loin Roast ①

Loin Roast ① — Roast —

SIRLOIN

Leg Chop (Steak) ②③ — Broil, Panbroil, Panfry —

Sirloin Chop ① — Broil, Panbroil, Panfry —

Boneless Sirloin Roast ①

Sirloin Roast ① — Roast —

LEG

Combination Leg ②③④

Center Leg ②③

Boneless Leg (Rolled) ①②③④

American-Style Leg ②③④

Sirloin Half of Leg ①②

Shank Half of Leg ③④

French-Style Leg ①②③④

French-Style Leg, Sirloin Off ②③④ — Roast —

FORE SHANK

Fore Shank ① — Braise, Cook in Liquid —

Riblets ② — Braise, Cook in Liquid —

BREAST

Breast ②

Rolled Breast ②

Stuffed Breast ② — Roast, Braise —   — Roast —

Boneless Riblets ②

Spareribs ②

Stuffed Chops ②

— Braise, Cook in Liquid —   — Braise, Roast (Bake)—   — Broil, Panbroil, Panfry —

HIND SHANK

Hind Shank ④ — Braise, Cook in Liquid —

GROUND OR CUBED LAMB *

(Large Pieces) Lamb for Stew * (Small Pieces) — Braise, Cook in Liquid —

Cubed Steak ** — Broil, Panbroil, Panfry —

Lamb Patties *

Ground Lamb * — Roast (Bake) —

* Lamb for stew or grinding may be made from any cut.

**Kabobs or cube steaks may be made from any thick solid piece of boneless Lamb.

This chart approved by
National Live Stock and Meat Board

© National Live Stock and Meat Board

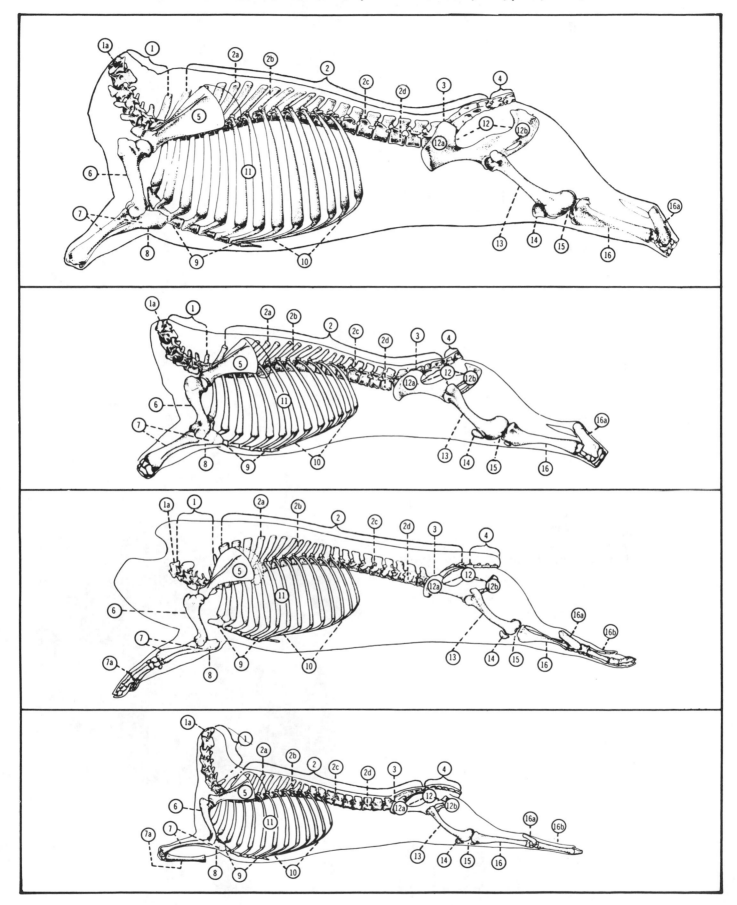

BONE STRUCTURE CHARTS
(on page 125)

1	Neck bone
1 a	Atlas
2	Back bone
2 a	Button
2 b	Feather bone
2 c	Finger bone
3	Slip joint
4	Tail bone
5	Blade bone
6	Arm bone
7	Fore shank bone(s)
7 a	Fore foot bone(s), lower shank
8	Elbow bone
9	Breast bone
10	Rib cartilages
11	Ribs
12	Pelvic bone
12 a	Hip bone
12 b	Rump (aitch) bone
13	Leg (round) bone
14	Knee cap
15	Stifle joint
16	Hind shank bone(s)
16 a	Hock bones
16 b	Hind foot bones, lower shank

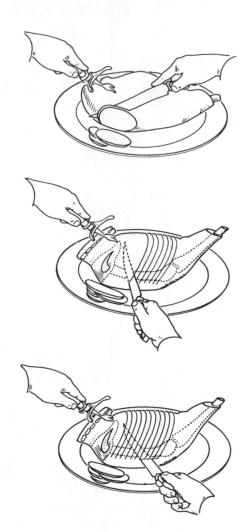

Carving technique for leg of lamb.

The following five tables (pages 127–129) are to be used as guides to help in planning the timing of roasts, as well as meats that are broiled, braised, or cooked in liquid.

CUT	ROASTED (300° F)		BROILED[2]		BRAISED	COOKED IN LIQUID
	(° F)	(MIN/LB)	(° F)	(MIN)	(HOURS)	(HOURS)
Standing rib	140	18–20				
Standing rib	160	22–25				
Standing rib	170	27–30				
Rolled rib	Same as above	Add 10–15				
Steaks:						
1”			140	15–20		
			160	20–30		
1 1/2”			140	25–30		
			160	35–50		
2”			140	30–40		
			160	50–70		
Beef patties:						
1”			140	12–15		
			160	18–20		
Pot roasts:						
Arm or blade					3–4	
Rump					3–4	
Swiss steak					2–3	
Corned beef						3 1/2–5
Fresh beef					3–4	3–4
Stew						2–3

[1]By permission of National Livestock and Meat Board.
[2]Pan broiling or griddle broiling requires approximately one-half the time for broiling.

TIMETABLE FOR COOKING VEAL[1]

CUT	ROASTED (300° F)		BROILED[2]		BRAISED	COOKED IN LIQUID
	(° F)	(MIN/LB)	(° F)	(MIN)	(HOURS)	(HOURS)
Leg	170	25	Veal is seldom			
Loin	170	30–35	broiled			
Rack	170	30–35				
Shoulder:						
Whole	170	25				
Rolled	170	40–45				
Cushion	170	35–35				
Breast:						
Stuffed	170	40–45			1 1/2–2	
Rolled	170	40–45			1 1/2–2	
Loaf	170	25–30				
Birds					3/4–1	
Chops					3/4–1	
Steaks					3/4–1	
Stew						2–2 1/2

[1]By permission of National Livestock and Meat Board.

TIMETABLE FOR COOKING PORK[1]

CUT	ROASTED (300° F)		BROILED[2]		BRAISED	COOKED IN LIQUID
	(° F)	(MIN/LB)	(° F)	(MIN)	(HOURS)	(MIN/LB)
Fresh						
Loin						
Center	170	35–40				
Whole	170	15–20				
Ends	170	45–50				
Shoulder						
Rolled	170	40–45				
Cushion	170	35–40				
Boston Butt	170	45–50				
Leg or ham	170	30–35				
Chops, steaks					3/4–1	
Spareribs		30–34			1 1/2	30
Pork, ham loaf		30–35				
Smoked						
Ham						
Large	160	15–18				
Medium	160	18–22				18–20
Small	160	22–25				
Half	160	30–35				25
Ham slice						
1/2”			160–170	10–12		
1”			160–170	16–20		
Picnic	170	35				
Shoulder butt	170	35				35–45
Bacon				4–5		

[1]By permission of National Livestock and Meat Board.
[2]350° F oven temperature is recommended for fresh pork and 300° F oven temperature for smoked pork.
[3]Rib and loin pork roasts heated at 170° F were shown by Carlin, et al to be safe and more juicy than roasts heated to 185°F. (Carlin, A.F., Blomer, D.M., and Hotchkiss, D.K., Relation of oven temperature and final internal temperature to quality of pork loin roasts, *J. Home Econ.* 57:442-446, 1965.

TIMETABLE FOR COOKING LAMB[1]

CUT	ROASTED (300° F)		BROILED[2]		BRAISED	COOKED IN LIQUID
	(° F)	(MIN/LB)	(° F)	(MIN)	(HOURS)	(HOURS)
Shoulder	160–170	30–35				
Leg						
Whole	160–170	30–35				
Rolled	160–170	40–45				
Cushion	160–170	30–35				
Breast						
Stuffed	160–170	30–35			1 1/2–2	
Rolled	160–170	30–35			1 1/2–2	
Lamb loaf	160–170	30–35				
Chops						
1”			170	12		
1 1/2”			170	18		
2”			170	22		
Lamb patties, 1”				15–18		
Neck slices					1	
Shanks					1 1/2	
Stew						1 1/2–2

[1]By permission of National Livestock and Meat Board.
[2]Pan broiling or griddle broiling requires approximately one-half the time for broiling.

TIMETABLE FOR ROASTING TURKEY[1]

OVEN WEIGHT (LB)	OVEN TEMPERATURE (° F)	COOKING TIME (MIN/LB)
8–10	325	20–25
10–14	325	18–20
14–18	300	15–18
18	300	13–15
20	300	13–15

BROILING

Broiling is a direct heat method particularly well suited to meats that are between 1 and 3" thick and are tender. Thinner cuts become too dry when broiled. Thicker cuts tend to char on the surface before the interior is cooked to the desired endpoint.

To prepare meats for broiling, wipe the surfaces with a damp towel. Use a sharp knife to cut through the fat and connective tissue surrounding the large muscles of steaks. Cuts should be made at 1" intervals to prevent curling of the cut during broiling.

The meat is arranged on a broiler pan with the fat toward the middle of the pan. It is an important safety precaution to use a broiler pan, because the rack is designed to drain the fat away from the meat and protect it from the intense heat of the broiler, thus reducing the risk of a broiler fire.

Position the meat in the broiler so that the top surface of the meat is at least 3" from the heat source. If the cut is very thick, move the meat lower in the broiler so there will be more time for the heat to penetrate the meat before the surface becomes too done. Broil the first side of the meat until it is a pleasing brown and the meat is approximately half done. Salt the cooked side, and then turn the meat.

In the event that broiling meat is browning unusually slowly, raise the broiler pan closer to the heat. If the meat is beginning to burn before the meat has sufficient time to reach the desired interior degree of doneness, the pan should be moved lower in the broiler compartment. Adjustments on rate of broiling are made by moving the meat in relation to the heat rather than adjusting the level of heat, as is done in selecting baking temperatures. Broil the second side until done. Serve. If the meat being broiled is thick enough, insert a ther-

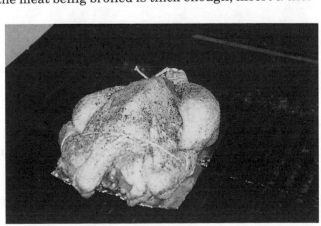

mometer and broil to the desired doneness. Thinner cuts can be tested by cutting a small incision near the bone. It should not be necessary to turn the meat back to its original position. Proper cooking should occur with only the one turning to expose the second side of the cut.

Charcoal broiling is simply an inverted version of broiling. Smoke from the hot coals adds flavor.

A whole roasting chicken is ideal for barbecuing.

PAN BROILING

Pan broiling is another dry heat method and, consequently, is well-suited to many of the same cuts of meat that can be broiled. Pan broiling is particularly good for preparing tender cuts of meat that are less than an inch thick. These thin cuts do not dry out as much when they are pan broiled as when they are broiled.

Preparation of the meat is the same for pan broiling as for broiling. The meat is broiled in a heavy skillet without adding any fat. However, if the skillet is not Teflon-coated, it is possible to warm the skillet slightly and then rub the fat side of the meat cut on the hot metal to provide enough fat to keep the meat from sticking. The meat is cooked until the bottom side is a pleasing brown. Then it is turned over. The cooked surface is salted while the second side is browning. As fat drains from the meat, it is removed from the frying pan so that the meat is pan broiled in an absolute minimum of fat. The meat may be turned as often as needed to cook the meat to the desired doneness without burning the surface.

A thermometer is not used in pan broiling because the cuts used usually are too thin for satisfactory insertion of the thermometer. The important factors in pan broiling are the use of controlled heat, a heavy frying pan, and frequent removal of accumulating fat. Pan broiled meats are popular because of their slightly reduced fat content when served.

Pan broiled meats are attractive to serve if the heat has been controlled properly. To achieve a rare pan broiled steak, a relatively high temperature should be used to brown the outside of the meat quickly before there is sufficient time for the heat to penetrate to the center of the cut. For pork or other cuts that are to be served well done, a somewhat slower rate of heating is to be preferred to allow time for more uniform heat penetration.

PAN FRYING

Thin cuts of meat, such as thin pork chops, thin steaks, and thin lamb chops are well suited to pan frying. Such cuts can be heated adequately in the center before they become too dark on the outside when pan fried.

There are several similarities between pan broiling and pan frying. Meat is prepared for pan frying by wiping the surface with a dampened paper towel and cutting through the connective tissue to make the meat remain flat during the cooking period. A skillet is used for pan frying, just as it is in pan broiling. Here, however, the two methods become distinctly different. A small amount of fat is melted in the skillet before the meat is added for pan frying. Furthermore, the fat is allowed to collect in the pan during pan frying. The heat should be carefully controlled during pan frying to prevent unnecessary splattering and smoking of the fat. After the meat is browned on the first side, it is turned and the first side is salted. Then the second side is browned. It may be necessary to turn the meat more than once to achieve the desired interior temperature without burning the exterior.

DEEP FAT FRYING

A few meats are often prepared by deep fat frying. To be suitable for deep fat frying, the cut must be small enough so that it can be cooked through to the center before the outer portion is overcooked. Chicken can be deep fat fried successfully. Several types of fish and seafood are well suited to deep fat frying.

The key to successful deep fat frying is temperature control. The fat must be maintained at 350° F for larger pieces or 375° F for smaller pieces if the food is to be at its best. Too low a temperature results in a very greasy product. Too high a temperature causes the exterior to burn while the interior is still underdone. Fat for deep fat frying is most effectively maintained at the desired temperature by using a deep fat fryer or a saucepan on a thermostatically-controlled unit.

Foods are prepared for deep fat frying by first cleaning them carefully. Next, it is very important to dry them, because water causes a great deal of splattering when the food is placed in the hot fat. Only a few pieces can be placed in the deep fat fryer at one time. Too much food causes a significant drop in the temperature of the fat and the food will be greasy. When the fat is no longer bubbling right around the edges of the food and the bottom surface is an attractive golden brown, use a slotted spoon to turn the item over very carefully. Avoid any splashing.

To determine when a deep fat fried food is done, time it carefully, look at the color of the exterior, and make a small cut into the center to be sure it is done inside. Drain the food on a paper towel and salt it to taste.

The oil used in the deep fat fryer should be strained each time it is used. By removing extraneous food particles, the useful life of the oil is extended. It is necessary to dispose of the old oil and start with fresh oil when the oil: 1) begins to have a strong odor, 2) becomes rather viscous, or 3) starts to smoke at frying temperatures. A deep fat fried product cannot be any better than the quality of the oil in which it is fried.

MOIST HEAT MEAT COOKERY

There are only two basic methods of moist heat meat cookery, and yet these two methods provide more variety in flavors than can be achieved by the several dry heat meat cookery methods. The two methods of moist heat meat cookery are braising and stewing (also called cooking in liquid).

BRAISING

Meat is prepared for braising by first wiping it clean with a damp paper towel. Frequently it is dipped in flour preparatory to cooking. Sometimes it is dipped in either milk or egg and then in a breading mixture of cracker or bread crumbs. Since less tender cuts of meat are used for braising, many recipes suggest pounding the meat to break the connective tissue before beginning the actual cooking process.

For the first of the two actual steps of braising, either fat is melted in a skillet or a small amount of oil is poured in. The meat is carefully browned on both sides. The second step is the addition of a small amount of liquid and the simmering of the meat in this liquid for a relatively long period of time. During this second phase of braising, the pan is covered with a tight-fitting lid. Occasionally it is necessary to check the level of liquid in the pan to be sure that some liquid still remains. If the level drops, more liquid should be added. Meats are braised until they are fork tender. This means that a fork can be inserted and withdrawn from the meat easily.

Braising is a popular method of preparing meats because it is an effective way of making less expensive, less tender cuts of meat more palatable. It also is an excellent way of introducing a wide variety of flavors to meats.

STEWING (COOKING IN LIQUID)

The chief difference between braising and stewing is the amount of liquid used. Braising uses only a small amount of liquid, while stewing is done by cooking the meat in enough liquid to cover the cut.

Sometimes meats are browned as the first step in stewing. This is usually done when stew meat is being prepared, but is not commonly done when chicken is being stewed. Next, liquid is added to just cover the meat. The meat is simmered with a cover until the meat is fork tender.

This pot roast is being prepared by braising, a basic moist heat cookery method for meat. This slow cooking promotes the conversion of collagen to gelatin, thus tenderizing the meat.

RECIPES
Salmon ala Pesto

Total Time: 20 minutes; Broiling: 10 minutes

1. Preheat oven.
2. Finely chop basil leaves, piñon nuts, and garlic in blender.
3. Slowly pour oil into blender while on puree setting.
4. Stir in cheese, lemon zest, and bread crumbs.
5. Broil salmon steaks on first side 6 minutes before removing from broiler and turning to second side.
6. Spread pesto generously to coat the top surface of the salmon.
7. Continue broiling until salmon flakes when touched with a fork (about 4 minutes).

(Serves two)

1/2 c	basil leaves
1/2 tbsp	piñon nuts
1/2	garlic clove, minced
1 tbsp	olive oil
1/2 tsp	grated Parmesan cheese
1/2 tsp	lemon zest
2 tbsp	bread crumbs
2	salmon steaks

(Serves four)

1 c	basil leaves
1 tbsp	piñon nuts
1	garlic clove, minced
2 tbsp	olive oil
1 tsp	grated Parmesan cheese
1 tsp	lemon zest
1/4 c	bread crumbs
4	salmon steaks

Macadamia Sole Roll-Ups

Total Time: 25 minutes
Baking: 325° F for 12 minutes

1. Preheat oven.
2. Sauté mushrooms, garlic, and macadamia nuts in oil about 3 minutes.
3. Place 1 1/2 tbsp of sauté mixture at end of each filet and roll up.
4. Secure each filet roll with a toothpick; place on aluminum foil on baking sheet.
5. Place filets at least 2" apart on baking sheet.
6. Bake at 325° F until heated through and fish is opaque and flaky (about 12 minutes).
7. Remove toothpick when serving. Garnish with lemon pinwheel.

(Serves two)

1 1/2 tbsp	chopped mushrooms
1/4	clove garlic, minced
1 1/2 tbsp	chopped macadamia nuts
2 tsp	olive oil
2	sole filets
	lemon pinwheels

(Serves four)

3 tbsp	chopped mushrooms
1/2	clove garlic, minced
3 tbsp	chopped macadamia nuts
1 tbsp	olive oil
4	sole filets
	lemon pinwheels

Baked Halibut

Total Time: 35 minutes
Baking: 325° F for 30 minutes

1. Preheat oven.
2. Arrange fish in a shallow baking dish.
3. Spread the undiluted soup over the fish and sprinkle with the seasonings.
4. Place in a 325° F oven for 30 minutes or until the sauce is bubbling and the fish is hot (or microwave oven: 6 minutes on *high*, 2 minutes on *browning*).
5. Serve with a lemon curl garnish.

(Serves two)

3/4 lb	halibut or other white fish filets
1/2	can condensed cream of celery soup
1 tbsp	chopped parsley
	dash poultry seasoning
	dash curry powder
	dash salt
	dill weed
	lemon peel garnish

(Serves four)

1 1/2 lb	halibut or other white fish filets
1	can condensed cream of celery soup
2 tbsp	chopped parsley
1/8 tsp	poultry seasoning
1/8 tsp	curry powder
1/8 tsp	salt
	dill weed
	lemon peel garnish

MEAT LOAF

Total Time: 1 hour (small recipe);
           1 hour 15 minutes (large recipe)
Baking: 350° F oven for 45–60 minutes

1. Preheat oven.
2. In a small amount of water, boil onion and green pepper together 3 minutes.
3. Drain.
4. Beat egg and combine all ingredients.
5. Mix well and shape into loaf in loaf pan.
6. Spread sauce (below) over unbaked loaf. For microwaving, shape a round loaf in a pie plate.
7. Bake small loaf for 45 minutes at 350° F (or cover and microwave on *high* for 6 minutes); bake large loaf 1 hour at 350° F (or cover and microwave on *high* for 12 minutes). Allow 5–10 minutes standing time.

Note: Add onion and green pepper uncooked for stronger flavor.

(Serves two)	
1/4 c	*onion, chopped*
1/4	*green pepper, chopped*
1/2 lb	*ground chuck*
1	*egg*
2	*soda crackers, rolled into crumbs*
1/4 tsp	*salt*
	dash pepper

(Serves four)	
1/2 c	onion, chopped
1/2	green pepper, chopped
1 lb	ground chuck
2	eggs
4	soda crackers, rolled into crumbs
1/2 tsp	salt
1/8 tsp	pepper

MEAT LOAF SAUCE

Total Time: 3 minutes

1. Mix the ingredients.

(Serves two)	
3 tbsp	*brown sugar*
1/4 c	*catsup*
1/2 tsp	*dry mustard*
1/4 tsp	*lemon juice*

(Serves four)	
6 tbsp	*brown sugar*
1/2 c	*catsup*
1 tsp	*dry mustard*
1/2 tsp	*lemon juice*

CHICKEN DIJON

Total Time: 45 minutes
Baking: 400° F for 30 minutes

1. Preheat oven.
2. Sauté garlic, onions, and mushrooms in butter in a small skillet until golden brown.
3. Spread surface of chicken breasts heavily with mustard.
4. Place in shallow baking dish and sprinkle with salt, pepper, and poultry seasoning.
5. Spread sour cream on chicken.
6. Bake at 400° F for 15 minutes.
7. Remove briefly from oven to spread vegetables on top before returning to the oven to finish baking (approximately 15 minutes).

(Serves two)	
1/2	*garlic clove, minced*
1 1/2 tsp	*thinly sliced green onion*
1/8 lb	*mushrooms, thinly sliced*
2 tsp	*butter*
1	*whole chicken breast, boned, skinned, and split*
2 tbsp	*Dijon mustard*
	salt and pepper to taste
1/4 tsp	*poultry seasoning*
1/3 c	*sour cream*

(Serves four)	
1	*garlic clove, minced*
1 tbsp	*thinly sliced green onion*
1/4 lb	*mushrooms, thinly sliced*
1 1/3 tbsp	*butter*
2	*whole chicken breasts, boned, skinned, and split*
1/4 c	*Dijon mustard*
	salt and pepper to taste
1/2 tsp	*poultry seasoning*
2/3 c	*sour cream*

COCONUT-CROWNED CHICKEN

Total Time: 1 1/4 hours
Baking: 350° F oven for 1 hour

1. Preheat oven.
2. Stir salt, pepper, and paprika together before dredging chicken in the mixture.
3. Brown the chicken in olive oil in a skillet.
4. Remove chicken and then sauté onions 2 minutes in the skillet.
5. Add peppers, curry powder, tomatoes, currants, chutney, and wine. Simmer 5 minutes.
6. Add chicken, spooning the vegetables over the chicken before covering and placing in 350° F oven for 40 minutes.
7. Meanwhile, mix melted butter with lime juice, coconut, and almonds.
8. Remove chicken dish from oven to top it with the coconut mixture.
9. Return chicken dish (uncovered) to oven to brown the topping lightly (about 20 minutes.)

(Serves two)

	salt and pepper to taste
2 tsp	*paprika*
1	*whole chicken breast, skinned, boned, and split (or other chicken pieces of choice)*
2 tbsp	*olive oil*
1	*large onion, chopped coarsely*
1	*garlic clove, minced*
1/2	*green bell pepper, strips*
1/2	*red bell pepper, strips*
1/2	*yellow bell pepper, strips*
2 tsp	*curry powder*
1 c	*canned stewed tomatoes*
1/4 c	*dried currants*
1 1/2 tbsp	*Major Grey chutney*
1/4 c	*dry red wine*
2 tbsp	*melted butter*
1 1/2 tbsp	*lime juice*
1/2 c	*shredded coconut*
1/4 c	*sliced almonds*

(Serves four)

	salt and pepper to taste
4 tsp	paprika
2	whole chicken breasts, skinned, boned, and split (or other chicken pieces of choice)
1/4 c	olive oil
2	large onions, chopped coarsely
2	garlic clove, minced
1	green bell pepper, strips
1	red bell pepper, strips
1	yellow bell pepper, strips
4 tsp	curry powder
2 c	canned stewed tomatoes
1/2 c	dried currants
3 tbsp	Major Grey chutney
1/2 c	dry red wine
1/4 c	melted butter or margarine
3 tbsp	lime juice
1 c	shredded coconut
1/2 c	sliced almonds

DEEP FAT FRIED CHICKEN

Total Time: 20–40 minutes

1. Preheat the oil in the deep fat fryer to 350° F while preparing the chicken.
2. Wash the chicken thoroughly.
3. Blot dry with paper towels.
4. Dip each piece of chicken in the batter and then let it drain before putting in the fryer.
5. Fry about 3 pieces of chicken at a time.
6. Put the chicken in the preheated fat and fry about 10 minutes.
7. Make a small incision to be sure the meat is done next to the bone.
8. Drain on paper towels.
9. Place on baking sheet in 150° F oven to keep warm while frying remainder of chicken.

(Serves two)

3	*pieces frying chicken*
1/2 c	*pancake batter*

(Serves four)

6	pieces frying chicken
1 c	pancake batter

BAKED CHICKEN WITH COULIS

Total Time: 50 minutes
Baking: 350° F oven for 20 minutes;
400° F for 25 minutes

1. Preheat oven.
2. Slice tomatoes in 1/4" slices; mash garlic. Spread in shallow baking dish and bake 20 minutes.
3. Meanwhile, stir mayonnaise, mustard, and herbs together. Spread on chicken breasts heavily before rolling in bread crumbs.
4. Place breaded chicken in shallow baking dish.
5. Bake chicken at 400° F for 25 minutes.
6. Now puree tomatoes and garlic, removing any coarse peels. Stir in the vinegar and olives.
7. Reheat the tomato coulis to serving temperature.
8. Serve chicken on a bed of the hot coulis.

(Serves two)

1 lb	*Roma tomatoes*
1	*clove garlic*
1	*chicken breast, boneless, skinless, split*
2 tbsp	*mayonnaise*
2 tbsp	*Dijon mustard*
1/2 tsp	*pinch of herbs*
1/4 tsp	*seasoned salt*
1/4 cup	*fine bread crumbs*
1 1/2 tsp	*balsamic vinegar*
2 tbsp	*sliced black olives*

(Serves four)

2 lb	Roma tomatoes
2	clove garlic
2	chicken breasts, boneless, skinless, split
1/4 c	mayonnaise
1/4 c	Dijon mustard
1 tsp	pinch of herbs
1/2 tsp	seasoned salt
1/2cup	fine bread crumbs
3 tsp	balsamic vinegar
1/4 c	sliced black olives

STEAK WITH MUSHROOM TOPPING

Total Time: 25 minutes

1. Cut edges of steak to prevent curling.
2. Place steak on rack on broiling pan.
3. Position in broiler so top of steak is about 5–6" from heat. For medium doneness, broil steak about 10 minutes on each side.
4. Turn with tongs.
5. Meanwhile, prepare topping by sautéing the mushrooms and onions 2 minutes.
6. In a mixing bowl, combine cheese and sautéed vegetables.
7. Blend in the bread crumbs.
8. During the last 5 minutes of broiling, spread topping on steak. Continue broiling until cheese melts, approximately 3–5 minutes.
9. Serve immediately.

(Serves two)

3/4 lb	*sirloin steak, cut 1 1/2" thick*
1 tbsp	*margarine or butter*
1/2 c	*finely chopped fresh mushrooms*
1/4 c	*finely chopped green onions*
1/3 c	*shredded Cheddar cheese*
2 tbsp	*seasoned bread crumbs*

(Serves four)

1 1/2 lb	sirloin steak, cut 1 1/2" thick
2 tbsp	margarine or butter
1 c	finely chopped fresh mushrooms
1/2 c	finely chopped green onions
2/3 c	shredded Cheddar cheese
1/4 c	seasoned bread crumbs

BABY TURKEY WITH HULA STUFFING

Total Time: 3 1/4 to 3 3/4 hours
Baking: 325° F oven for 3–3 1/2 hours

1. Preheat oven.
2. Wash turkey thoroughly under running water.
3. Sprinkle turkey inside and out with salt and pepper.
4. In a large bowl, mix dressing, lemon juice and rind, pineapple chunks and juice, melted butter, prunes and nuts.
5. Stuff hollows in acorn squash.
6. Spoon remaining stuffing into turkey. Sew or skewer the opening.
7. Roast turkey breast down on a V-shaped rack in a shallow, uncovered pan for 2–2 1/2 hours or until turkey leg can be moved up and down fairly easily.
8. Place stuffed squash halves into oven with turkey and bake for 1 hour or until squash is pierced easily with a fork.

(Serves six)

1	*turkey, thawed or fresh, 8–10 lbs*
	salt and pepper
8 c	*dressing mix*
	grated rind and juice of 1 lemon
1	*can (1 lb 4 oz) pineapple chunks with juice*
1 c	*(1/2 lb) margarine or butter, melted*
1 1/2 c	*chopped California pitted prunes*
1 c	*coarsely broken walnuts, pecans, or macadamia nuts*
3	*small acorn squash, cut into halves, seeds removed*

CURRIED BEEF FRICASSEE

Total Time: 45 minutes

1. Sauté curry powder, meat, onions, and salt in oil to brown the meat (about 5 minutes on medium heat).
2. Add potatoes, carrots, bell peppers, raisins, curry powder, and grated ginger and cook 2 minutes.
3. Add tomatoes, bouillon cube, and water. Cover and simmer slowly for 35 minutes.
4. Prepare rice according to package directions 20 minutes before fricassee is done.

(Serves two)

1 1/2 tsp	*curry powder*
1/2 lb	*sirloin tip, cubed*
1 c	*diced onions*
1/4 tsp	*salt*
1 1/2 c	*cubed Red Triumph potatoes, skin on*
2 tsp	*olive oil*
1/2 c	*carrots in diagonal slices*
1/3 c	*red bell pepper, chopped coarsely*
1/3 c	*raisins*
1 tbsp	*curry powder*
1 1/2 tsp	*grated ginger root*
1 c	*plum tomatoes, diced*
1/2 c	*beef bouillon*
1/2 c	*water*
1 c	*long grain rice*

(Serves four)

1 tbsp	curry powder
1 lb	sirloin tip, cubed
2 c	diced onions
1/2 tsp	salt
3 c	cubed Red Triumph potatoes, skin on
1 tbsp	olive oil
1 c	carrots in diagonal slices
2/3 c	red bell pepper, chopped coarsely
2/3 c	raisins
2 tbsp	curry powder
1 tbsp	grated ginger root
2 c	plum tomatoes, diced
1 c	beef bouillon
1 c	water
2 c	long grain rice

CHICKEN-FRIED STEAK

Total Time: 1 hour 10 minutes

1. On a bread board, pound steak until it is half its original thickness.
2. Trim off any areas of fat and connective tissue.
3. Cut into serving size pieces.
4. Dip each piece briefly in the mixture of beaten egg and milk and then into the crumbs.
5. Shake gently to remove loose crumbs.
6. Brown each piece in oil to a pleasing brown on both sides.
7. Add salt and pepper after browning the first side.
8. Add just enough water to cover the bottom of the skillet.
9. Cover.
10. Reduce the heat to simmering and cook until meat is fork tender. Total braising time is about 1 hour.

(Serves two)

1/2	*round steak, 1/2" thick*
1	*egg*
1 tbsp	*milk*
1/2 c	*fine bread or cracker crumbs*
1 tbsp	*salad oil*
	salt and pepper, to taste

(Serves four)

1	round steak, 1/2" thick
2	eggs
2 tbsp	milk
1 c	fine bread or cracker crumbs
2 tbsp	salad oil
	salt and pepper, to taste

COQ AU VIN

Total Time: 1 hour

1. Coat chicken with flour.
2. Heat oil in a skillet and brown the chicken, shallots, and mushrooms.
3. Remove chicken.
4. Add vegetables and seasonings. Stir while cooking for 2 minutes.
5. Add wine and bouillon. Stir to loosen residue from the pan.
6. Return chicken to pan.
7. Season chicken with salt and pepper before covering pan.
8. Heat on a high simmer for 30 minutes.

(Serves two)

1	*chicken breast, split*
1 tbsp	*flour*
2 tsp	*olive oil*
1 tbsp	*diced shallots*
1/4 lb	*small mushrooms*
1/2 c	*diced Roma tomatoes*
1/2 c	*diced carrots*
1/2 c	*celery in diagonal slices*
1/2 tsp	*dried tarragon*
1/2 tsp	*dried basil*
1/2	*bay leaf*
1/3 c	*dry red wine*
1/2	*chicken bouillon cube in 1/2 c hot water*
	salt and pepper

(Serves four)

2	chicken breasts, split
2 tbsp	flour
1 tbsp	olive oil
2 tbsp	diced shallots
1/2 lb	small mushrooms
1 c	diced Roma tomatoes
1 c	diced carrots
1 c	celery in diagonal slices
1 tsp	dried tarragon
1 tsp	dried basil
1	bay leaf
2/3 c	dry red wine
1	chicken bouillon cube in 1 c hot water
	salt and pepper

LAMB STEW

Total Time: 1 hour 35 minutes

1. Lightly flour 1" cubes of stew meat by putting flour, salt, and pepper in a small bag with the meat and shaking.
2. Brown the meat well in a small amount of oil.
3. Add enough water to just cover the meat.
4. Put on the lid and simmer 1 hour and 15 minutes.
5. Add the other ingredients and cook until the vegetables are tender.
6. Stir in 1 tbsp flour thoroughly blended with 1/4 c water.
7. Stir constantly while heating stew to boiling.
8. Serve.

(Serves two)

1/2 lb	*lamb stew meat, breast*
2 tsp	*salad oil*
8	*boiling onions*
2	*small carrots, diced*
1/4 c	*celery, chopped*
2	*small potatoes, diced*
2	*peppercorns*
	piece bay leaf
1 tbsp	*flour*
1/4 c	*water*

(Serves four)

1 lb	lamb stew meat, breast
1 1/4 tbsp	salad oil
16	boiling onions
4	small carrots, diced
1/2 c	celery, chopped
4	small potatoes, diced
4	peppercorns
2	pieces bay leaf
2 tbsp	flour
1/2 c	water

ISLANDER'S CHICKEN

Total Time: 1 hour

1. Sprinkle chicken with seasoned salt.
2. Sauté in hot oil until well browned on all sides.
3. Drain excess fat.
4. Drain pineapple, and reserve juice for next step.
5. Combine pineapple juice, ginger, orange peel, and honey. Pour over chicken.
6. Cover and simmer 40 minutes or until tender.
7. Remove chicken to a warm serving platter.
8. Mix flour and water together until smooth.
9. Stir into pan drippings, and heat to boiling while stirring.
10. Add pineapple chunks and orange slices. Heat just until fruit is warm.
11. Serve over chicken.

Note: In photograph above, Islander's Chicken is featured with orange slices and accented with Chinese pea pods and water chestnuts.

(Serves two)

2–3	chicken legs and thighs
1/2 tsp	seasoned salt
2 tsp	salad oil
1/2 c	pineapple chunks
1/2 tsp	ginger
1 tsp	grated fresh orange peel
3 tbsp	orange juice
2 tbsp	honey
1 tsp	flour
1 tbsp	water
1/2	orange, peeled, sliced into cartwheels

(Serves four)

4–6	chicken legs and thighs
1 tsp	seasoned salt
1 tbsp	salad oil
1 c	pineapple chunks
1 tsp	ginger
2 tsp	grated fresh orange peel
1/3 c	orange juice
1/4 c	honey
2 tsp	flour
2 tbsp	water
1	orange, peeled, sliced into cartwheels

FRUIT STUFFED PORK CHOPS

Total Time: 1 hour 10 minutes

1. With a sharp knife, cut a slit about 1 1/2" long in the middle of the side of the pork chops.
2. Extend the cut to make a pocket inside the chops parallel with the meat surfaces.
3. Cut thin slices of apple and stuff the pockets with apple and raisins.
4. Lightly flour the chops.
5. Brown well in a small amount of oil.
6. Add enough water to cover the bottom of the skillet.
7. Reduce the heat and simmer the pork chops in the tightly-covered skillet for 1 hour.

Note: Moist heat is used to insure that these thick pork chops will reach a safe interior temperature before they get too dark on the surface.

(Serves two)

2	*loin pork chops, 1" thick*
1/4	*tart apple, cored*
1/4 c	*raisins*
2 tsp	*salad oil*

(Serves four)

4	loin pork chops, 1" thick
1/2	tart apple, cored
1/2 c	raisins
1 tbsp	salad oil

POT ROAST

Total Time: 1 1/2 to 2 hours

1. Lightly flour the meat and brown it well in oil.
2. Salt and pepper are added after the first side is browned.
3. Arrange the onion and lemon on top of the meat.
4. Sprinkle the thyme and marjoram on top.
5. Add just enough water to cover the bottom of the pan.
6. Cover and simmer until fork tender, adding water as needed.
7. Add pared carrots and potatoes the last hour if desired.
8. Total cooking time 1 1/2 to 2 hours.

(Serves two)

1	*small chuck roast*
2 tsp	*salad oil*
1/2	*medium onion, slices*
	dash thyme
	dash marjoram
1/4	*lemon, sliced*

(Serves four)

1	average chuck roast
1 tbsp	salad oil
1	medium onion, slices
1/8 tsp	thyme
1/8 tsp	marjoram
1/2	lemon, sliced

STUFFED FLANK STEAK

Total Time: 3 1/2 hours

1. Lightly score the flank steak.
2. Mix the remaining ingredients and place in the middle of the flank steak.
3. Roll the flank steak with the dressing in the center.
4. Tie securely with string.
5. Lightly coat the exterior of the flank steak with flour.
6. Brown entire flank steak well in a skillet containing 1 tablespoon oil.
7. Add enough water to just cover the bottom of the skillet and put on the lid.
8. Reduce the heat to simmering and cook until the meat is fork tender.
9. Add more water as necessary.
10. Total cooking time is approximately 3 hours.

(Serves two)

1/2	*flank steak*
1 1/2	*slices dry bread, cubed*
1/4	*medium onion, chopped*
1/4 tsp	*salt*
	pinch poultry seasoning
1 tbsp	*margarine or butter, melted*
1/4	*green pepper, chopped*
1/2	*can sliced mushrooms*
1 tbsp	*salad oil*

(Serves four)

1	flank steak
3	slices dry bread, cubed
1/2	medium onion, chopped
1/2 tsp	salt
	pinch poultry seasoning
2 tbsp	margarine or butter, melted
1/2	green pepper, chopped
1	can sliced mushrooms
2 tbsp	salad oil

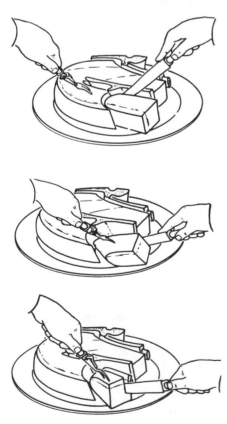

Carving a blade pot roast.

SWISS STEAK

Total Time: 2 hours 15 minutes

1. Cut away extra fat and connective tissue.
2. Pound the meat thoroughly with a meat pounder.
3. After lightly flouring it, brown the meat in oil.
4. Season with salt and pepper.
5. Arrange bay leaf and thin slices of onion over the meat and pour the tomatoes on top.
6. If more liquid is needed, add either tomato juice or water.
7. Cover the pan and reduce heat to simmering.
8. Cook until fork tender, adding additional liquid as needed. Allow 2 hours cooking time.

(Serves two)
1/2	*round steak*
2 tsp	*salad oil*
	piece bay leaf
1/2	*medium onion, sliced*
1/2 c	*stewed tomatoes*

(Serves four)
1	round steak
1 tbsp	salad oil
	piece bay leaf
1	medium onion, sliced
1 c	stewed tomatoes

SAUERBRATEN

Total Time: 2 hours 30 minutes plus 2 days to marinate

1. Put the meat in a bowl just larger than the meat.
2. Make a marinade out of the remaining ingredients and pour over the meat.
3. Cover tightly and place in the refrigerator for two days.
4. Turn the meat occasionally if the marinade does not cover it completely.
5. Take the meat out of the marinade and brown it in oil in a Dutch oven.
6. When the meat has been browned on all sides, add enough of the marinade to cover the bottom of the pan and put on the lid.
7. Simmer until fork tender, adding liquid marinade as needed. Allow 2 hours cooking time.

(Serves two)
	very small rump roast
1 c	*vinegar*
1 c	*water*
1	*medium onion, sliced*
10	*whole cloves*
2	*bay leaves*
10	*peppercorns*
1/4	*green pepper, sliced*
1 tsp	*salt*

(Serves four)
	medium rump roast
2 c	vinegar
2 c	water
2	medium onions, sliced
20	whole cloves
4	bay leaves
20	peppercorns
1/2	green pepper, sliced
1 tbsp	salt

FRICASSEE OF VEAL

Total Time: 1 hour 15 minutes

1. Trim connective tissue and cut meat into serving-sized pieces.
2. Coat the pieces lightly with flour and brown in oil.
3. Mix the seasonings together and sprinkle over the surface of the meat.
4. Add water to cover the bottom of the pan and put on the lid.
5. Simmer 55 minutes.
6. Add the sour cream and continue simmering for about 5 minutes to warm the sour cream. Serve immediately.

(Serves two)
1/2 lb	*thinly cut veal round steak*
2 tsp	*salad oil*
	dash white pepper
	dash salt
1/4 tsp	*paprika*
	dash cayenne
1/2 c	*dairy sour cream*

(Serves four)
1 lb	thinly cut veal round steak
1 1/4 tbsp	salad oil
1/8 tsp	white pepper
1/8 tsp	salt
1/2 tsp	paprika
1/8 tsp	cayenne
1 c	dairy sour cream

LEMON-LAMB SHANKS

Total Time: 2 hours 20 minutes

1. Have a butcher "crack" lamb shanks for easier browning.
2. Combine salt, pepper, paprika, and thyme; rub well over all sides of meat.
3. Lightly coat with flour.
4. Place oil in heavy skillet or Dutch oven.
5. Brown shanks very slowly on all sides.
6. Remove from pan.
7. Sauté onions and garlic in remaining oil until limp and transparent.
8. Make a bouquet garni by placing the peppercorns, bay leaf, and parsley in the center of a cheesecloth square. Tie in bundle fashion with clean string.
9. Return shanks to pan; add lemon peel, juice, water, and bouquet garni.
10. Cover tightly, and simmer slowly for about 2 hours or until tender.
11. Baste and turn occasionally during cooking. Add small amounts of water, if necessary.
12. When fork-tender, place meat on warm serving platter. Remove bouquet garni and discard.
13. While stirring constantly, add 1 tablespoon flour and 2 tablespoons water and heat until mixture boils and thickens.
14. Pour sauce over lamb shanks; garnish with lemon slices.

(Serves two)	
2–3	small lamb shanks
1/4 tsp	salt
1/4 tsp	pepper
1/2 tsp	paprika
1/4 tsp	thyme, crushed
1 tbsp	flour
1 tbsp	salad oil
1/2	medium onion, thinly sliced
1	clove garlic, finely minced
2	whole peppercorns
1	small bay leaf, crushed
1	sprig parsley
1 tbsp	grated lemon peel
1/4 c	lemon juice
1/4 c	water
1/2	lemon, thinly sliced

(Serves four)	
4–6	small lamb shanks
1/2 tsp	salt
1/2 tsp	pepper
1 tsp	paprika
1/2 tsp	thyme, crushed
2 tbsp	flour
2 tbsp	salad oil
1	medium onion, thinly sliced
2	cloves garlic, finely minced
4	whole peppercorns
2	small bay leaf, crushed
2	sprig parsley
2 tbsp	grated lemon peel
1/2 c	lemon juice
1/2 c	water
1	lemon, thinly sliced

VOCABULARY

Elastin

Collagen

Inspection

Grading

Primal cuts

Dry heat meat cookery

Moist heat meat cookery

Deep fat frying

Roasting

Pan frying

Pan broiling

Stewing

Braising

EVALUATION OF LABORATORY PRODUCTS — Meats, Poultry, and Fish

Recipe	Notes on Color, Texture, Flavor, or Other Qualities	Comments or Suggestions for Making or Using This Product in the Future

Chapter 8
Egg Cookery

Egg cookery requires subtlety and attention if you are going to get the best possible results. In particular, you will find that temperature and time need to be controlled so that the proteins in eggs and egg products are heated to just the right end point.

To illustrate the behavior of eggs in food preparation, you will have opportunities in this chapter to prepare eggs in and out of the shell, as well as using them in recipes where they are combined with other ingre-

---

KEY CONCEPTS — EGG COOKERY

1) Eggs contain a variety of proteins in the yolks and whites, and these proteins contribute important functions in food preparation.

   a) Careful timing and temperature control are essential to achieving the correct degree of doneness in soft- and hard-cooked eggs, as well as fried, baked, poached, and scrambled eggs.

   b) Whites can be beaten to a foam that adds considerable volume to a fluffy omelet and to a soufflé.

   c) Egg white foams gain optimum stability when they have some acid and/or sugar added to them and when they are beaten to the correct endpoint, but not over-beaten.

   d) French omelets are less tender than fluffy omelets because the protein is concentrated and is not distributed throughout the volume provided by the egg white foam in fluffy omelets.

   e) Egg yolks bind the fat in the sauce that is a part of a soufflé and help to keep the sauce distributed in the egg white foam during baking.

   f) The thickening provided by egg proteins in custards and other mixtures is effective, but considerably less dramatic than the thickening that occurs when starch is the thickening agent.

   g) Overheating of egg proteins causes tightening of the proteins, which results in loss of volume in over-baked soufflés and syneresis and porosity in custards and egg-thickened sauces.

dients in different ways. Omelets and soufflés demonstrate the dramatic changes that occur as the result of coagulating eggs. Egg white foams play a significant role in soufflés and are the main component of meringues. Custards are used to illustrate the crucial importance of heating egg proteins just to the correct point to achieve optimum thickening.

RECIPES (IN THE SHELL)

SOFT-COOKED EGGS

Total Time: 8 minutes

	eggs

1. In a covered saucepan, heat enough water to boiling to just cover the eggs when they are added. As soon as the water boils, reduce the heat to low and add eggs using a slotted spoon to dip each egg in and out of the water once before depositing in the pan. Simmer the eggs for 3–4 minutes. Remove from the water, hold very briefly under cold water, and serve.

HARD-COOKED EGGS

Total Time: 25 minutes

	eggs

1. Use the same procedure outlined for soft-cooked eggs, but increase the simmering time to 20 minutes. Then remove the eggs and place them under cold, running water for several minutes to cool them rapidly.

RECIPES (OUT OF THE SHELL)

FRIED EGGS — METHOD 1

Total Time: 5 minutes

	eggs
2 tsp	salad oil

(Eggs may be fried by two methods. The first method requires a minimum amount of fat.)

1. Melt just enough margarine or butter in the frying pan to cover the bottom of the skillet.
2. Add the egg gently and cook over low heat.
3. As soon as the white begins to set, add 1 or 2 teaspoons water and quickly cover the pan.
4. Cook just until the whites are coagulated and the yolk is covered with a thin veil of coagulated white.

FRIED EGGS — METHOD 2

Total Time: 5 minutes

	eggs
2 tbsp	salad oil

(The other method for frying eggs uses fat in a large enough quantity to spoon the fat over the eggs.)

1. Melt enough fat in the skillet so that the fat can be basted with a spoon across the surface of the yolk.
2. While the eggs are frying slowly, baste each yolk frequently with the hot fat to coagulate the white covering the surface of the yolk.
3. Cook until the white is coagulated, and the yolk is covered with a thin layer of coagulated white.
4. Season with salt and pepper to serve.

POACHED EGGS

Total Time: 8 minutes

eggs
toast
salt
pepper

1. Fill a saucepan with 2–3" of water and heat to boiling.
2. Remove from the heat, and very carefully slide egg into the pan.
3. Return to heat and maintain water at simmering, but be careful not to boil it.
4. Poach egg until the white is completely coagulated, and the yolk is still fluid.
5. Remove egg from water using a slotted spoon.
6. Serve plain or on buttered toast.
7. Season with salt and pepper.

SCRAMBLED EGGS

Total Time: 7 minutes

(Serves two)	
2	*eggs*
2 tbsp	*milk*
1/8 tsp	*salt*
	pepper to taste

(Serves four)
4	eggs
1/4 c	milk
1/4 tsp	salt
	pepper to taste

1. Melt just enough butter or margarine in frying pan to cover the bottom of the pan.
2. In a small bowl, combine the eggs (which have been broken separately into a small custard cup and transferred to the mixing bowl), milk, and seasonings.
3. Beat slowly with a rotary beater to completely blend the yolk and white. Avoid forming a foam on the mixture.
4. Pour into the frying pan, and heat over a medium low heat to coagulate the egg.
5. Stir occasionally with a narrow spatula or wooden spoon so that the eggs will cook in fairly large pieces without becoming the least bit brown.
6. Cook until all portions are coagulated, but still slightly shiny.

FRENCH OMELET

Total Time: 12 minutes

(Serves two)	
3	*eggs*
3 tbsp	*water*
1/8 tsp	*salt*
	dash of pepper
	margarine or butter

(Serves four)
6	eggs
6 tbsp	water
1/4 tsp	salt
1/8 tsp	pepper
	margarine or butter

1. With a rotary beater gently, but thoroughly blend all of the ingredients so that there are no unblended portions of yolk and white. Avoid developing any foam.
2. Melt enough margarine or butter to just coat the bottom of the skillet and heat until bubbling, but not brown.
3. Add the egg mixture and cook over medium heat.
4. As the egg begins to coagulate, use a narrow spatula to lift up portions of the omelet and let uncoagulated egg run underneath.
5. Continue lifting only as long as there is uncoagulated egg to fill in.
6. When the egg is all coagulated, but still shiny on the surface, check the bottom of the omelet. If it is not a golden brown, turn up the heat briefly to brown it.
7. Fold omelet in half and transfer to serving platter.

Note: For variety, cheese, crumbled bacon, minced green onion, or chopped black olives and mushrooms may be added before folding the omelet. Cheese sauce or tomato sauce may be used as a topping for the omelet.

FLUFFY OMELET

Total Time: 25 minutes
Baking: 325° F oven for 15 minutes

1. Preheat oven.
2. Carefully separate eggs individually over a custard cup, being certain that no yolk is permitted to get into the whites.
3. Beat egg yolks until very thick and lemon-colored, preferably using an electric mixer.
4. Wash the beaters to remove all traces of yolk.
5. Beat the whites to the foamy stage.
6. Add the salt, cream of tartar, and water to the whites, and continue beating until the peaks just fold over.
7. Begin to melt the margarine or butter in a skillet over low heat so that it is bubbling, but not browned when the folding of the yolk and white foams is completed.
8. Pour all of the yolk foam down the side of the bowl containing the egg white foam.
9. Gently, but efficiently use a rubber spatula to fold the yolks into the whites. Folding is done by scraping the spatula down the inside of the bowl farthest away from you. Drag spatula clear across the bottom of the bowl and up the side nearest you. Spread the material on the spatula across the surface of the mixture.
10. Turn the bowl a quarter of a turn and repeat the process.
11. Repeat this process 4 times (the bowl has now made one complete revolution).
12. On the fifth stroke pull the spatula only half-way across the bottom of the bowl and then cut up through the middle and spread the mixture across the top of the omelet.
13. Contintue this 5-stroke cycle until the mixture is entirely homogeneous and no layer remains on the bottom of the bowl.
14. Immediately pour the folded mixture into the bubbling, but not browned margarine.
15. Heat 30 seconds on medium heat.
16. Immediately transfer the omelet (in its pan) to an oven preheated to 325° F.
17. Bake about 15 minutes until a knife inserted in the center of the omelet comes out clean.
18. Fold the omelet in half and transfer to a serving platter.

Note: Serve with a cheese sauce, Spanish sauce, or other sauce suitable for a main dish.

(Serves two)	
2	*eggs*
2 tbsp	*water*
1/8 tsp	*salt*
1/4 tsp	*cream of tartar*
1/2 tbsp	*margarine or butter*

(Serves four)	
4	eggs
4 tbsp	water
1/4 tsp	salt
1/2 tsp	cream of tartar
1 tbsp	margarine or butter

LEMON FLUFFY OMELET

Total Time: 25 minutes
Baking: 325° F oven for 15 minutes

1. Preheat oven.
2. Carefully separate the eggs individually over a custard cup.
3. Beat egg yolks until very thick and lemon-colored, perferably using an electric mixer.
4. Thoroughly wash the beaters.
5. Beat the whites to the foamy stage.
6. Add the salt, lemon juice, and water.
7. Continue beating while gradually adding the sugar.
8. Beat until the peaks just bend over.
9. The folding and baking steps of this omelet are the same as for the Fluffy Omelet (above).

Note: This is a sweet omelet that makes an excellent dessert when served with Lemon Sauce.

(Serves two)	
2	*eggs*
2 tsp	*lemon juice*
1 1/3 tbsp	*water*
2 tbsp	*sugar*
1/8 tsp	*salt*
1/2 tbsp	*margarine or butter*

(Serves four)	
4	eggs
1 1/3 tbsp	lemon juice
2 2/3 tbsp	water
1/4 c	sugar
1/4 tsp	salt
1 tbsp	margarine or butter

LEMON SAUCE

Total Time: 5 minutes

1. Mix the sugar and cornstarch together well with a wooden spoon.
2. Gradually stir in the water.
3. Heat to boiling, while stirring constantly.
4. Remove from heat, and stir in the lemon juice and rind.
5. Serve warm over hot omelet.

(Serves two)

1/4 c	*sugar*
1 1/2 tsp	*cornstarch*
1/2 c	*water*
2 tsp	*lemon juice*
1/2 tsp	*grated lemon rind*

(Serves four)

1/2 c	sugar
1 tbsp	cornstarch
1 c	water
1 1/3 tbsp	lemon juice
1 tsp	grated lemon rind

PRINCIPLES OF PREPARING SOUFFLÉS

Soufflés are egg foam products which combine the principles of starch cookery with the problems of preparing and utilizing a stable foam. The total preparation involves 5 key steps:

1) gelatinization of a starch mixture to yield a smooth thick white sauce;
2) combination of the hot starch paste with beaten egg yolks;
3) formation of a stable egg white foam;
4) incorporation of the sauce into the egg white foam; and
5) baking of the starch-foam mixture.

CHEESE SOUFFLÉ

1/4 c	margarine or butter
1/4 c	flour
1/8 tsp	salt
1 c	milk
1/4 lb	grated sharp cheddar cheese
4	eggs (separated, one at a time over a custard cup)
1/2 tsp	cream of tartar

For the most efficient preparation of a soufflé, assemble all ingredients before beginning to prepare the product. Cheese soufflé is used in this series to demonstrate the principles of preparing soufflés. The ingredients are shown above. The necessary utensils, including the soufflé dish, should then be assembled. If a soufflé dish slightly smaller than the necessary size is used, an aluminum foil or paper collar about 1 1/2" high can be fitted onto the inside lip of the dish.

Before beginning preparation of the white sauce, it is important to begin preheating the oven so that the correct oven temperature will be reached before the soufflé is ready to bake. The oven rack positions should be checked to be certain the top rack is just below the center of the oven and then the oven temperature is set at 325° F. This moderately low oven

temperature allows time for the heat to penetrate the center of the soufflé before the outer region is overbaked, yet it is sufficiently hot to set the structure before the sauce begins to drain toward the bottom of the foam.

One means of helping to disperse starch uniformly in a starch-containing product is to blend the starch with melted fat or with an oil. The preparation of the sauce for a soufflé begins with melting the solid fat in a heavy saucepan that will distribute the heat uniformly. Heavy aluminum is a suitable pan material for starch cookery. The margarine or butter should be heated just enough to melt it. Browning is to be avoided because of its influence on the flavor and appearance of the finished sauce.

The first ingredients added to the melted margarine or butter are flour and salt. These may be added all at once. A wooden spoon is an excellent choice for stirring these ingredients into the margarine or butter. It is very important to be sure that a smooth paste is formed and that all of the flour is stirred into the margarine. Dry clumps of flour at this time point are potential sources of lumps in the finished sauce. The melted margarine or butter is a very effective agent in dispersing the starch granules contained in the flour.

With the pan removed from the heat, cold milk is stirred into the starch-margarine slurry. The milk is added gradually at first with stirring so that the slurry can be thinned smoothly rather than having lumps of thick slurry interspersed with the fluid milk. It is essential that the mixture be perfectly smooth before proceeding to the gelatinization process in the next step. Otherwise, the finished sauce is certain to contain lumps from the dry flour.

As soon as a smooth slurry of the ingredients has been made, the sauce is returned to the heat. As the sauce begins to heat, it is necessary to stir it carefully to insure uniform heating of all of the starch mixture. A wooden spoon is a very useful utensil because it does not scratch the surfaces of coated pans. It also has the advantage of not becoming hot in

the hand during the heating period. Stirring of gelatinizing starch mixtures is an important technique if lump-free sauces are to be made. The starch mixture will be hottest where it comes in contact with the pan. Consequently, continuous stirring is required around the sides of the pan and across the bottom. The heat should be adjusted to a setting that will bring the sauce to a boil in less than 5 minutes, but it should not be so hot that the sauce begins to form lumps or to scorch on the bottom of the pan.

The sauce will be hot all across the bottom as well as around the sides. Good stirring technique will intersperse a careful stirring all around the sides with a thorough stirring across the bottom of the pan. The technique across the bottom of the pan is comparable to the parallel lines or "push-pull" technique sometimes taught in penmanship. It is very important to be certain that the entire bottom surface is stirred throughout the heating period. A stirring technique featuring a "Figure 8" pattern does not accomplish this, but leaves areas where the mixture will gelatinize unevenly. Unless stirring is done at a moderate rate and throughout the entire mixture, uneven gelatinization will occur and an occasional stirring of an area will simply result in scraping loose gelatinized portions which then become lumps in the finished sauce.

Gelatinization of the sauce will be completed when the entire mixture boils. In a soufflé recipe, this will result in a thick sauce of a sufficient viscosity to leave a very discernible path if the wooden spoon is pulled through the sauce. The viscosity of the sauce is critical to the finished product. Too thin a sauce will tend to drain from the egg white foam before the structure is set, and the soufflé will have a heavy layer in the bottom. Too thick a sauce will not fold well into the egg whites. Sometimes a sauce may begin to separate at this point, with

fat being visible around the edges. This is most likely to occur in the preparation of a chocolate soufflé because of its higher fat content. However, it may happen with any soufflé if the rate of heating the sauce has been extremely slow. Very slow cooking results in excessive evaporation and the sauce will separate. Although such sauces look very bad, they are remedied easily by stirring in just enough water or milk to reform the smooth sauce. This step must be taken if the sauce separates. Otherwise, fat will continue to ooze from the sauce during the remainder of the soufflé preparation.

When the sauce has reached the correct viscosity, the pan is removed from the heat and the grated cheese is added all at once and stirred into the sauce.

If the sauce is not warm enough to completely melt the cheese, the sauce is returned to a very low heat and stirred slowly as the cheese melts. The cheese must all be melted before proceeding to the next step. Any unmelted cheese at this point will result in pockets of cheese in the finished soufflé. A low heat is used to melt the cheese without causing undue toughening of the protein in the cheese. If the

sauce should happend to separate during this process, water or milk should be added as described before. Add only enough liquid to reform the sauce. Excess liquid will make the sauce too thin to remain suspended in the egg white foam.

After the cheese is completely melted and the sauce is of the correct consistency, the pan containing the sauce is set aside, away from the heat. The egg yolks are beaten to mix them thoroughly and to incorporate some air in them. this beating can be done easily with a fork or with an egg beater. A spoonful of the warm sauce is stirred rapidly into the beaten egg yolks. The sauce must not be in contact with the yolks without stirring because the hot sauce will begin to coagulate the egg yolk protein that it touches, and lumps of unevenly coagulated yolk will be the result.

As soon as the first spoonful of sauce is stirred into the yolks to form a homogeneous mixture, the process is repeated again with another spoonful of the hot sauce. This process is repeated for a total of approximately 4 cooking spoonfuls of the sauce. Exact measurement of the sauce is not at all important, but efficient stirring as soon as the hot mixture comes in contact with the eggs is essential in this step. This method of combining egg yolk protein with the hot sauce is used as a means of diluting the concentration of the egg yolk protein, thus elevating the coagulation temperature of the protein before the yolks are in contact with a large quantity of the hot sauce.

When approximately 1/4 cup of the hot sauce has been stirred carefully into the yolks to give a smooth and homogenous mixture, the egg yolk-cheese sauce mixture then is ready to be poured back into the main panful of sauce. The yolk-cheese sauce mixture should be poured slowly into the saucepan, and stirring should be done continuously as the yolk mixture is being added. The purpose of this step is to blend the yolks uniformly with the hot mixture and to avoid uneven coagulation of the yolks. When a perfectly homogeneous blending of the yolk-cheese sauce mixture with the white sauce has been completed, the sauce is set aside to wait for the formation of the egg white foam. Note that the entire process of combining the egg yolks with the cheese sauce was done without the addition of any heat. There is no need to coagulate the yolk proteins at this time. The coagulation will be completed during the baking process.

The egg white foam is a vital part of all soufflés. It is important to be certain that there is absolutely no trace of yolk in the whites or on the beaters that will be used, for any trace of fat will impair formation of the egg white foam. The addition of cream of tartar slows foam formation, making an electric mixer a useful tool. Cream of tartar is added all at once at the foamy stage. (If a dessert soufflé were being prepared, sugar would be added gradually beginning at the foamy stage.)

Beating the egg white foam to the correct end point is a critical step in soufflé preparation. The foam should be beaten until the beater can be withdrawn from the mixture to leave peaks that bend over on the end, but that do not fall over. Underbeaten whites will result in a soufflé with smaller volume than optimum and a tougher product. There may also be a tendency toward layering in the bottom. Overbeaten egg whites will not blend readily with the sauce, but will tend to break into chunks. The overfolding that is required to distribute the sauce uniformly will cause a loss of volume in the finished product and consequently a somewhat less tender soufflé. Chunks of egg white are likely to be evident in the baked soufflé if whites are overbeaten.

As soon as the egg whites are beaten to the point where the peaks just bend over, all of the sauce is poured carefully, but efficiently down the side of the bowl containing the egg whites. The sauce will collect in the bottom of the bowl with the whites on top. Avoid pouring the sauce on top of the foam, because this pushes some of the air out of the foam, and it is the air in the foam which is needed to give maximum volume to the soufflé. All efforts from this point onward are directed toward minimizing the loss of air from the foam. Work should proceed quickly, yet gently until the soufflé is in the oven.

Now all of the sauce needs to be folded as efficiently as possible to give a homogenous blending of foam with sauce.

A rubber spatula is a useful utensil for efficient folding. Folding is actually a repeating 5-step process. The first step is done by running the rubber spatula down the far side of the bowl, scraping across the very bottom of the bowl, dragging the spatula with its load of sauce up the near side of the bowl, and then lightly and gently spreading the sauce across the top of the foam. With a little practice, this folding movement, that is, scraping along the side, across the bottom, up the near side, and across the foam can be done very efficiently, yet gently. The pupose of folding is to bring up the sauce from the bottom of the bowl and distribute it across the foam. The goal is to make a light, completely homogeneous mixture, with no traces of the yellow sauce showing.

When the first folding step has been completed and the sauce spread across the foam, the mixing bowl is rotated one-fourth of a turn or 90°. Then the folding process is repeated by once again scraping the spatula down the far side of the bowl, across the bottom, up the near side, and spreading the sauce across the surface of the foam.

Again, the bowl is rotated 90° and the folding is repeated. The bowl then is rotated another 90° and the folding is repeated. At this point, the folding step has been repeated a total of 4 times, and the bowl has been rotated 90° degrees before each fold.

After the fourth folding operation, the bowl is rotated 90° degrees to return to its original position. The folding so far has not been involving the center portion of the foam. To incorporate the sauce into the center of the foam, a special folding stroke is done once each time the cycle of 4 strokes is completed. This special stroke is started in the same way that the other strokes begin, that is, by scraping the spatula carefully down the far side of the bowl. The stroke across the bottom of the bowl proceeds only halfway across. Then the spatula is brought up sideways, bearing its load of sauce through the middle of the foam, and the sauce is spread over the top of the foam.

Following this special stroke, folding again proceeds by scraping down the far side of the bowl and continuing the first folding stroke without rotating the bowl. Then rotation of the bowl continues. Every fifth fold is done by coming up through the middle of the soufflé. Folding needs to be continued just until there is no more sauce remaining on the bottom of the bowl, and the soufflé mixture has a homogeneous appearance. Overfolding is to be avoided since this merely reduces volume by releasing air from the foam unnecessarily.

As soon as folding has been completed, the soufflé mixture should be poured immediately into the dish. The bowl should be held as low as possible, and the mixture should be transferred as gently as possible to minimize loss of air from the foam during the transfer. A spatula can be used to expedite the transfer without undue damage to the foam.

When the soufflé has been placed in the baking dish, run a rubber spatula in a circle around the surface of the soufflé at a distance about 1 to 1 1/2" from the edge of the dish. This gently breaks the surface of the soufflé and aids in creating a picture-perfect soufflé with an attractive surface when the baked product is served. This circle should be traced very quickly to avoid any delay at this critical point.

The soufflé is placed gently on the top oven rack that has been positioned previously just below the center of the preheated oven. The rack is pushed in, the door is closed, and the time is noted. Most soufflés will require approximately 55 minutes to bake in a 325° F oven. A timer may be set as a guide to indicate when testing should be done. If possible, the soufflé should be baked in an oven with a window so that the progress of baking can be watched. There will be very little change in appearance during the initial baking period while the heat is penetrating into the soufflé. The outer region then will begin to rise along the side of the dish, and the surface will begin to brown. As the coagulation temperature of the egg proteins is reached around the edge, the structure will set. However, the inner portion of the soufflé will not yet have reached the coagulation temperature. The air in the soufflé will continue to expand and to stretch the uncoagulated portions. This increase in volume will

continue until the protein structure coagulates. It is very important to avoid opening the oven door during the baking process. If cooler air comes in contact with the soufflé, the heated air in the soufflé will be cooled. The result is reduced pressure within the soufflé, and the soufflé will begin to fall. Soufflés should not be tested for doneness until the correct amount of time has elapsed. Their structure is most delicate just before the protein coagulates.

Prepare for testing the soufflé by having everything set for service of the food. Hot pads and a table knife will be needed for the actual testing. With these items in hand, gently open the oven door and pull the rack out. If the soufflé appears to be shaking considerably, it is not done, and the rack should be returned immediately, and the door closed gently. If the soufflé does not shake much, quickly pull out the rack far enough to test the soufflé with the knife. Insert the knife as far as possible vertically in the middle of the soufflé.

Immediately withdraw the knife and check for clinging particles of soufflé. The knife will appear moist, but will not be coated with the soufflé if the soufflé is done. If the soufflé passes this test, serve it immediately. If not, quickly and gently return the soufflé to the oven position and close the door to continue baking. It is important to bake soufflés to the correct degree of doneness. If they are underbaked, they will fall because the protein structure will not be coagulated sufficiently to hold up the weight of the suspended sauce. If the soufflé is baked too long, there will be a shrinking and toughening of the soufflé due to the changes in the denatured protein.

The baked soufflé as it comes from the oven will have its maximum volume. The structure of even a properly baked soufflé is very delicate and there will be some loss of volume as the cooler air of the room begins to cool the air within the soufflé. The volume then becomes dependent on the strength of the cell walls themselves. A well prepared soufflé will have a good volume and will also have a pleasingly browned surface. The soufflé should show limited shrinkage when served. Evaluation of a soufflé requires not only an examination of the total volume achieved and an assessment of the overall external appearance, but it also requires a careful look at the interior cross section of the soufflé. Interior evaluation needs to extend from the upper surface clear to the bottom of the soufflé. In particular, the lower area should be examined for any suggestion of a layer. This layer could be caused by improper beating of the whites, by inadequate folding, by too thin a sauce, or by delayed baking after folding was completed. The cross section should also be reviewed for areas of cheese, which would be caused by failure to melt all of the cheese before adding the yolks. Lumps also should be noted. These might be caused by faulty blending of ingredients in the sauce, by poor stirring techniques while the starch was being gelatinized, or by uneven coagulation of the yolks while the yolks and cheese sauce were being combined. The other possible error that can be observed by looking at a cross section of a soufflé is lumps of white. These are caused by overbeating the egg whites. Preparation of a soufflé requires understanding of the principles of starch cookery and the formation and use of egg white foams. When attention is paid to the procedures that these require during preparation, a soufflé of high quality can be prepared quickly. A cheese soufflé has been used to demonstrate the principles, but any baked soufflé can be prepared by following these same guidelines.

RECIPES
CHEESE SOUFFLÉ

Total Time: 65 minutes (small); 75 minutes (large)
Baking: 325° F oven for 45 minutes (small) or
55 minutes (large)

1. Preheat oven.
2. Melt margarine in a 1-quart saucepan.
3. Stir in the flour and salt with a wooden spoon.
4. Gradually stir in the milk to make a slurry.
5. When all the milk is added, return pan to the heat.
6. Stir constantly with wooden spoon while heating to boiling; remove from heat. If fat separates, stir in just enough milk to make a smooth sauce.
7. Add cheese to hot sauce. Heat, if necessary, to melt cheese.
8. While the cheese is melting, beat the egg yolks.
9. Stir a spoonful of the hot sauce into the egg yolks. Be sure to stir immediately to avoid lumps of coagulated egg yolk.
10. Repeat three more times.
11. Then add the egg yolk-cheese sauce mixture back into the remaining sauce while stirring. Cover and set aside.
12. Beat the egg whites to the foamy stage. Add the cream of tartar and continue beating until the peaks just bend over. Be careful to beat to just the right stage.
13. Gently pour the cheese sauce down the side of the bowl containing the beaten egg whites.
14. With a rubber spatula, fold the yolk mixture and whites together completely and efficiently. Remember to 1) drag the spatula down the far side of the bowl, 2) across the bottom, 3) up the near side, and 4) end the stroke by spreading the sauce from the bottom of the bowl across the upper surface of the whites.
15. Rotate the bowl a quarter of a turn after each stroke.
16. On the fifth stroke come up through the middle of the mixture.
17. Continue this 5-stroke cycle until absolutely no sauce remains in the bottom of the bowl and the entire mass is homogeneous.
18. Quickly and gently pour the soufflé mixture into a 1-quart casserole (2-quart soufflé dish for large recipes).
19. With a table knife, trace a circle about an inch from the edge in the upper portion of the soufflé.
20. Place the soufflé on the middle rack of the oven and bake at 325° F for 55 minutes for the large soufflé or 45 minutes for the small one.
21. Test by inserting a knife in the center of the soufflé. It is done when the knife comes out clean. Serve immediately.

(Serves two)	
2 tbsp	margarine or butter
2 tbsp	flour
1/8 tsp	salt
1/2 c	milk
1/2 c	(1/8 lb) grated sharp cheddar cheese
2	eggs, separated
1/4 tsp	cream of tartar

(Serves four)	
1/4 c	margarine or butter
1/4 c	flour
1/4 tsp	salt
1 c	milk
1 c	(1/4 lb) grated sharp cheddar cheese
4	eggs, separated
1/2 tsp	cream of tartar

BROCCOLI SOUFFLÉ

Total Time: 65 minutes (small); 75 minutes (large)
Baking: 325° F oven for 45 minutes (small) or
        55 minutes (large)

1. Preheat oven.
2. Put frozen broccoli in boiling salted water, and boil 2 minutes.
3. Drain thoroughly, and chop broccoli very fine. Set aside.
4. Melt margarine or butter in a 1-quart saucepan.
5. Stir in the flour and salt with a wooden spoon.
6. Slowly add the milk, while stirring with a wooden spoon.
7. Return to the heat and bring to boiling while stirring constantly.
8. Remove from the heat.
9. Beat the egg yolks.
10. Add a spoonful of the hot sauce to the egg yolks and stir immediately.
11. Repeat three more times.
12. Pour the egg yolk mixture back into the white sauce, stirring constantly.
13. Add the lemon juice, nutmeg, pimiento, and chopped broccoli to the sauce.
14. Cover and set aside while beating the egg whites.
15. Beat the whites to the foamy stage, add the cream of tartar, and continue beating until the whites just bend over.
16. Fold the white sauce into the egg whites as outlined for the cheese soufflé.
17. Pour into a 3/4-quart soufflé dish (1 1/2-quart for large recipe).
18. Bake in preheated oven at 325° F for 55 minutes (large recipes) or 45 minutes (small recipe) until a knife inserted in the center comes out clean.
19. Serve immediately.

(Serves two)	
1/2	package frozen broccoli
1 1/2 tbsp	margarine or butter
1 1/2 tbsp	flour
1/8 tsp	salt
1/2 c	milk
2	eggs, separated
1/2 tsp	lemon juice
	few grains nutmeg
1 1/2 tsp	minced pimiento
1/8 tsp	cream of tartar

(Serves four)	
1	package frozen broccoli
3 tbsp	margarine or butter
3 tbsp	flour
1/4 tsp	salt
1c	milk
4	eggs, separated
1 tsp	lemon juice
	dash nutmeg
1 tbsp	minced pimiento
1/4 tsp	cream of tartar

SPOONBREAD

Total Time: 35 minutes (small); 45 minutes (large)
Baking: 375° F oven for 20 minutes (small) or
        30 minutes (large)

1. Preheat oven.
2. In a saucepan, slowly stir milk into the cornmeal.
3. Heat, while stirring with wooden spoon, until mixture boils and is thick. Remove from the heat.
4. Add the margarine, salt, and baking powder.
5. Beat the egg yolks.
6. Add a spoonful of the hot cornmeal mixture to the yolks and stir.
7. Repeat 3 more times and then stir the yolk mixture back into the cornmeal.
8. Cover and set aside while beating the whites.
9. Beat the egg whites to the foamy stage. Add cream of tartar and continue beating until the peaks just bend over.
10. Fold the yolk and white mixtures together, as outlined in the cheese soufflé recipe.
11. Pour into a small casserole dish (use 1 1/2-quart casserole for large recipe) and bake in a 375° F oven for 20 minutes (small) to 30 minutes (large), until a knife inserted in the center comes out clean.
12. Serve at once with marargine or butter.

(Serves two)	
1/4 c	cornmeal
1 c	milk
2 tsp	margarine or butter
1/4 tsp	salt
1/4 tsp	baking powder
2	eggs, separated
1/4 tsp	cream of tartar

(Serves four)	
1/2 c	cornmeal
2 c	milk
1 1/3 tbsp	margarine or butter
1/2 tsp	salt
1/2 tsp	baking powder
4	eggs, separated
1/2 tsp	cream of tartar

.Note: This dish, which may be described as a cornmeal soufflé, is served in place of potatoes.

CHOCOLATE SOUFFLÉ

Total Time: 65 minutes (small); 75 minutes (large)
Baking: 325° F oven for 45 minutes (small) or
55 minutes (large)

1. Preheat oven.
2. Melt margarine or butter and chocolate over hot water.
3. Stir in flour and salt, using a wooden spoon.
4. Slowly add the milk, while stirring.
5. Place the sauce over direct heat and bring to a boil.
6. Stir carefully as the mixture thickens.
7. If sauce separates, stir a small amount of water into the sauce. Add just enough water to unite the sauce.
8. Beat the egg yolks.
9. Add a spoonful of the chocolate sauce to the yolks, and stir it in immediately.
10. Repeat three more times.
11. Pour the yolk mixture back into the chocolate sauce, while stirring.
12. Cover and set aside.
13. Beat the egg whites to the foamy stage; add cream of tartar and gradually begin adding the sugar.
14. Beat until the peaks just fold over.
15. Stir the vanilla into the chocolate sauce.
16. Pour the chocolate sauce carefully down the side of the bowl containing the beaten egg whites.
17. Fold as outlined in the procedure for the cheese soufflé.
18. Pour into a small soufflé dish (1 1/2-quart soufflé dish for large recipe) and bake in a 325° F oven for 45 minutes (small) or for 55 minutes (large), until a knife inserted in the center comes out clean.
19. Serve immediately with a large dollop of whipped cream on each portion (optional).

(Serves two)

2 tbsp	margarine or butter
1 oz	unsweetened chocolate
2 tbsp	flour
1/8 tsp	salt
1/2 c	milk
2	eggs, separated
1/4 tsp	cream of tartar
1/4 c	sugar
1/2 tsp	vanilla
	whipped cream

(Serves four)

1/4 c	margarine or butter
2 oz	unsweetened chocolate
1/4 c	flour
1/4 tsp	salt
1 c	milk
4	eggs, separated
1/2 tsp	cream of tartar
1/2 c	sugar
1 tsp	vanilla
	whipped cream

ORANGE SOUFFLÉ

Total Time: 1 hour 30 minutes
Baking: 325° F oven for 1 hour (small) or
70 minutes (large)

1. Preheat oven.
2. Melt the margarine or butter, and stir in the flour and salt, using a wooden spoon. Remove from the heat.
3. Gradually add the milk, and stir constantly while heating to boiling. The sauce will be very thick.
4. Remove from the heat and cover.
5. Stir the orange and lemon juices and rinds into the sauce.
6. Beat the egg yolks.
7. Add a spoonful of the white sauce to the yolks and stir.
8. Repeat three more times and then stir the yolk mixture back into the white sauce.
9. Cover while beating the egg whites.
10. Beat the egg whites to the foamy stage; add cream of tartar and gradually begin adding the sugar while beating the whites until the peaks just bend over.
11. Pour the yolk mixture down the side of the bowl containing the whites and fold as outlined in the procedure for cheese soufflé.
12. Pour into a 1-quart casserole (use 2-quart for large recipe).
13. Bake in a preheated oven at 325° F for 1 hour.
14. Test with a knife inserted in the center of the soufflé to be sure it is done before removing from the oven.
15. Serve with lemon sauce (see Lemon Fluffy Omelet) or with whipped cream as soon as it comes from the oven.

(Serves two)

2 tbsp	margarine or butter
2 tbsp	flour
1/8 tsp	salt
1/3 c	milk
1 1/2 tbsp	orange juice
1/2 tbsp	lemon juice
1/4 tsp	lemon rind, grated
2	eggs, separated
1/4 tsp	cream of tartar
1/4 c	sugar
	lemon sauce or whipped cream

(Serves four)

1/4 c	margarine or butter
1/4 c	flour
1/4 tsp	salt
2/3 c	milk
3 tbsp	orange juice
1 tbsp	lemon juice
1/2 tsp	lemon rind, grated
4	eggs, separated
1/2 tsp	cream of tartar
1/2 c	sugar
	lemon sauce or whipped cream

MOCHA MINI-SOUFFLÉ

Total Time: 30 minutes
Baking: 400° F oven for 10–12 minutes

1. Preheat oven.
2. Melt chocolate chips in microwave oven (about 20 seconds) until soft.
3. Meanwhile beat yolks with coffee briefly.
4. Begin beating egg whites in separate bowl, adding sugar at foamy stage while continuing beating at high speed until soft peaks form.
5. Stir chocolate into yolk mixture and then add all at once to white foam.
6. Lightly fold until no chocolate layer remains and the mixture is homogeneous.
7. Pour into buttered 1/2 cup soufflé dishes (3 for small; 6 for large).
8. Bake at 400° F until top is crisp (about 11 minutes).
9. Dust lightly with sifted powdered sugar to serve.

(Serves three)	
3 oz	semisweet chocolate chips
1	egg, separated
1	egg white
2 tbsp	strong coffee
1 1/2 tbsp	sugar
	powdered sugar

(Serves six)	
6 oz	semisweet chocolate chips
3	eggs, separated
1	egg white
1/4 c	strong coffee
3 tbsp	sugar
	powdered sugar

MERINGUES

SOFT MERINGUE

Total Time: 20 minutes
Baking: 350° F oven for 12–15 minutes

1. Preheat oven.
2. Prepare pie filling or heavy paper (if meringues are being prepared as separate samples).
3. Beat egg white to foamy stage.
4. Add the cream of tartar and gradually begin adding the sugar.
5. Continue beating until all of the sugar is dissolved and the peaks just bend over.
6. Spread gently on pie filling or on baking sheet.
7. Bake in 350° F oven until golden brown.

(Two tart topping)	
1	egg white
1/8 tsp	cream of tartar
2 tbsp	sugar

(1 pie topping)	
3	egg whites
1/4 tsp	cream of tartar
1/4 c	sugar

BAKED ALASKA

Total Time: 15 minutes
Baking: 450° F oven for 8 minutes

1. Preheat oven.
2. On a small wooden board, arrange 3" circles of cake 1/2" thick.
3. Make soft meringue.
4. Place a scoop of ice cream on each cake round.
5. Use a rubber spatula to quickly frost each serving with a thick layer of meringue, being sure to completely cover the ice cream and cake with the meringue.
6. Bake at 450° F until meringue is lightly browned.
7. Serve immediately.

(Serves two)	
1	egg white
1/8 tsp	cream of tartar
2 tbsp	sugar
2	3" circle cakes
1/2 pt	ice cream

(Serves four)	
3	egg whites
1/4 tsp	cream of tartar
6 tbsp	sugar
4	3" circle cakes
1 pt	ice cream

OEUFS A LA NEIGE

Total Time: 45 minutes

1. Heat 2" of water to simmering in a saucepan or deep skillet.
2. Prepare soft meringue and drop by tablespoon into simmering water.
3. At the end of 1 minute, roll the meringue over, and finish poaching the second side.
4. Remove with a slotted spoon, and drain on paper towel.
5. Prepare stirred custard and chill.
6. To serve, put meringues in glass bowl.
7. Add fresh fruit, and pour chilled stirred custard to float the meringues.

(Serves two)
Meringue:
1	*egg white*
1/8 tsp	*cream of tartar*
2 tbsp	*sugar*

Stirred Custard:
1	*egg*
2 tbsp	*sugar*
	dash salt
1 c	*milk, scalded*
1/2 tsp	*vanilla*
1/2 c	*fresh fruit*

(Serves four)
Meringue:
2	egg whites
1/4 tsp	cream of tartar
1/4 c	sugar

Stirred Custard:
2	eggs
1/4 c	sugar
1/8 tsp	salt
2 c	milk, scalded
1 tsp	vanilla
1 c	fresh fruit

HARD MERINGUE

Total Time: 2 hours 15 minutes
Baking: 275° F oven for 1 hour

1. Preheat oven.
2. Using an electric mixer, beat egg whites to foamy stage.
3. Add the cream of tartar and very slowly begin to add the sugar while beating.
4. Continue beating the whites until peaks stand up straight. Finish beating with rotary beater if electric mixer begins to overheat.
5. Line a baking sheet with brown paper and spoon two mounds of meringue for each egg white used.
6. With a rubber spatula, swirl each mound into a shell shaped like a nest.
7. Bake at 275° F for an hour.
8. Turn off oven at end of one hour and leave meringue shells in oven to continue baking as oven cools.

Note: Meringue shells may be served with ice cream and/or fruit in the center. Hard meringues can have other ingredients, such as chopped nuts or glazed fruits, added to them prior to being dropped onto a cookie sheet by the spoonful to make cookies.

(Serves two)
2	*egg whites*
1/2 c	*sugar*
1/8 tsp	*cream of tartar*

(Serves four)
4	egg whites
1 c	sugar
1/4 tsp	cream of tartar

MACAROONS (MERINGUE COOKIES)

Total Time: 35 minutes
Baking: 325° F oven for 20 minutes

1. Preheat oven.
2. On electric mixer, beat egg whites to the foamy stage; add cream of tartar and vanilla.
3. While beating on high speed, very gradually add sugar.
4. Beat until peaks barely bend over.
5. Fold in coconut and pecans.
6. Drop by teaspoons onto Teflon-lined baking sheet.
7. Bake at 325° F for 20 minutes.

(1 dozen cookies)	
1	egg white
1/4 tsp	cream of tartar
1/4 tsp	vanilla
1/4 c	sugar
2/3 c	flaked coconut
3 tbsp	chopped pecans

(2 dozen cookies)	
2	egg whites
1/2 tsp	cream of tartar
1/2 tsp	vanilla
1/2 c	sugar
1 1/3 c	flaked coconut
1/3 c	chopped pecans

EGGS AS THICKENING AGENTS: QUICHE AND CUSTARD

(Custard recipes may be made using milks with varying levels of fat and can be compared with results obtained by others in the laboratory.)

MEXICAN QUICHE

Total Time: 40 minutes (small); 50 minutes (large)
Baking: 350° F oven for 20 minutes (small);
30 minutes (large)

1. Preheat oven.
2. Crumble and brown the sausage until well browned. Drain well.
3. Line shells with chiles and sausage.
4. Combine eggs, milk, cheeses, and seasonings; pour over sausage.
5. Bake at 350° F for 20–30 minutes, until golden brown and custard is set half-way between edge and center.
6. Let stand 5 minutes to finish setting before serving.

(Serves two)	
2	tart shells, baked
2 oz	canned green chiles
1/3 lb	sausage
2	eggs, lightly beaten
2/3 c	milk
3 tbsp	grated Swiss cheese
2 tbsp	grated Parmesan cheese
1/8 tsp	salt
	pinch of pepper

(Serves four)	
4	tart shells, baked
4 oz	canned green chiles
2/3 lb	sausage
4	eggs, lightly beaten
1 1/3 c	milk
1/3 c	grated Swiss cheese
1/4 c	grated Parmesan cheese
1/4 tsp	salt
	dash of pepper

STIRRED CUSTARD

Total Time: 20 minutes

1. While milk is scalding, combine beaten egg, salt, and sugar.
2. Add the scalded milk slowly into the other ingredients.
3. Strain the mixture.
4. Cook over simmering, not boiling, water while stirring constantly until thick enough to lightly coat a silver spoon.
5. Cool quickly by setting pan in a pan of ice water.
6. Stir in vanilla.

Note: Serve chilled over puddings and other desserts. (If custard begins to curdle while cooling, beat with rotary beater to help produce a smooth product.)

(Serves two)	
1	egg, beaten slightly (add an extra egg if thicker product desired)
	dash salt
2 tbsp	sugar
1 c	milk, scalded
1/2 tsp	vanilla

(Serves four)	
2	eggs, beaten slightly (add an extra egg if thicker product desired)
	dash salt
1/4 c	sugar
2 c	milk, scalded

BAKED CUSTARD

Total Time: 45 minutes
Baking: 325° F oven for 40 minutes

1. Preheat oven.
2. Follow the recipe for Stirred Custard through first 3 steps.
3. Stir in vanilla.
4. Pour the strained mixture into custard cups.
5. Sprinkle nutmeg on top of each custard.
6. Put cups in rectangular baking pan, and pour boiling water 1" deep around the cups.
7. Bake at 325° F for 40 minutes.
8. Test by inserting knife half-way between the center and the edge of the custard. When it comes out clean, the custard is done. The center will still be soft, but it will coagulate from the residual heat in the custard.
9. Serve chilled.

Note: Baked custards are baked in a pan of hot water to help protect them from the intense heat of the oven. They can be varied through the use of imaginative toppings.

(Serves two)	
1	*egg, beaten lightly*
2 tbsp	*sugar*
	dash salt
1 c	*milk, scalded*
1/2 tsp	*vanilla*
	nutmeg
	boiling water

(Serves four)	
2	eggs, beaten lightly
1/4 c	sugar
1/8 tsp	salt
2 c	milk, scalded
1 tsp	vanilla
	nutmeg
	boiling water

MICROWAVED CARAMEL FLAN

Total Time: 20–25 minutes

1. Microwave sugar and water in glass measuring cup on *high* 5 1/2 minutes for small (11 minutes for large).
2. Pour into 2 or 4 custard cups and cool after swirling up sides of cups.
3. Microwave milk in glass measuring cup on high 2 1/2 minutes for small (5 minutes for large).
4. Combine eggs, sugar, salt, and vanilla; slowly stir in scalded milk.
5. Pour custard into caramel-lined custard cups, cover, and microwave on low 6 minutes for small (12 minutes for large) until set.
6. Chill and unmold.

(Serves two)	
1/4 c	*water*
1/4 c	*sugar*
	ingredients small Baked Custard (above)

(Serves four)	
1/2 c	*water*
1/2 c	*sugar*
	ingredient large Baked Custard (above)

CREAM PUDDINGS

(Pudding recipes may be made using milks with varying levels of fat and can be compared with results obtained by others in the laboratory.)

VANILLA CREAM PUDDING

Total Time: 15 minutes

1. Combine the ingredients and cook them in the same way as when making a cornstarch pudding.
2. After the pudding is thick enough to leave a path with a spoon, remove from the heat.
3. Beat the egg yolk slightly.
4. Take a spoonful of the hot pudding, and stir it rapidly into the egg yolk.
5. Repeat three more times.
6. Immediately stir the egg yolk-pudding mixture back into the pudding.
7. Cook for 5 minutes over boiling water or else use direct heat controlled so that the pudding does not boil.
8. Stir slowly throughout this period of cooking.
9. Remove from heat, and stir in vanilla and butter.
10. Pour into custard cups or individual serving dishes, cover tightly, and chill.

(Serves two)	
1 1/2 tbsp	*cornstarch*
2 2/3 tbsp	*sugar*
	few grains salt
1/4 c	*milk*
3/4 c	*scalded milk*
1	*egg yolk*
1/2 tsp	*vanilla*
1/2 tsp	*butter or margarine*

(Serves four)	
3 tbsp	cornstarch
1/3 c	sugar
	dash salt
1/2 c	milk
1 1/2 c	scalded milk
2	egg yolks
1 tsp	vanilla
1 tsp	butter or margarine

CHOCOLATE CREAM PUDDING

Total Time: 15 minutes

1. Combine the ingredients (mix cocoa with cornstarch and sugar) in the same way as when making a cornstarch pudding.
2. After the pudding is thick enough to leave a path with a spoon, remove from the heat.
3. Beat the egg yolk slightly.
4. Take a spoonful of the hot pudding, and stir it rapidly into the egg yolk.
5. Repeat three more times.
6. Immediately stir the egg yolk-pudding mixture back into the pudding.
7. Cook for 5 minutes over boiling water or else use direct heat, controlled so that the pudding does not boil.
8. Stir slowly while the yolk is being coagulated.
9. Remove from heat, and stir in vanilla and butter or margarine.
10. Pour into custard cups or individual serving dishes, cover tightly, and chill.

(Serves two)	
1 1/3 tbsp	*cornstarch*
2 2/3 tbsp	*cocoa*
	few grains salt
1/4 c	*sugar*
1/4 c	*milk*
3/4 c	*scalded milk*
1	*egg yolk*
1/2 tsp	*vanilla*
1/2 tsp	*butter or margarine*

(Serves four)	
2 2/3 tbsp	cornstarch
1/3 c	cocoa
	dash salt
1/2 c	sugar
1/2 c	milk
1 1/2 c	scalded milk
2	egg yolks
1 tsp	vanilla
1 tsp	butter or margarine

BUTTERSCOTCH CREAM PUDDING

Total Time: 15 minutes

1. Combine the ingredients, and cook them in the same way as when making a cornstarch pudding (see Ch. 5, p. 95).
2. After the pudding is thick enough to leave a path with a spoon, remove from the heat.
3. Beat the egg yolk slightly.
4. Take a spoonful of the hot pudding, and stir it rapidly into the egg yolk.
5. Repeat three more times.
6. Immediately stir the egg yolk-pudding mixture back into the pudding.
7. Cook for 5 minutes over boiling water or else use direct heat controlled so that the pudding does not boil.
8. Stir slowly throughout this period of cooking.
9. Remove from the heat, and stir in vanilla and butter or margarine.
10. Pour into custard cups or individual serving dishes, cover tightly, and chill.

(Serves two)	
1 1/2 tbsp	*cornstarch*
2 2/3 tbsp	*brown sugar*
	few grains salt
1/4 c	*milk*
3/4 c	*scalded milk*
1	*egg yolk*
1/2 tsp	*vanilla*
1 1/2 tbsp	*butter or margarine*

(Serves four)	
3 tbsp	cornstarch
1/3 c	brown sugar
	dash salt
1/2 c	milk
1 1/2 c	scalded milk
2	egg yolks
1 tsp	vanilla
3 tbsp	butter or margarine

VOCABULARY

Chalazae

Vitelline membrane

Soufflé

Hard meringue

Soft meringue

Cream of tartar

Syneresis

Ferrous sulfide

Coagulation

Denaturation

Ovalbumin

Isoelectric point

Candling

Fluffy omelet

French omelet

EVALUATION OF LABORATORY PRODUCTS — Eggs

Recipe	Notes on Color, Texture, Flavor, or Other Qualities	Comments or Suggestions for Making or Using This Product in the Future

Chapter 9
Breads

GLUTEN

You are likely to find that making breads of various types is one of the most satisfying and relaxing experiences you will have in preparing food. Creativity is very possible when formulating and shaping breads. The rewards are fairly fast in coming if you are making quick breads; a bit of patience is necessary when making yeast breads because of the need for carbon dioxide formation to leaven them.

In this chapter, you will learn about gluten, the protein complex required for the strong structure needed in various breads. Then you will learn about basic types of quick breads and some variations. The unique aspect of making quality yeast breads is managing temperatures in any part of the preparation where yeast is present to ensure viability of the yeast and the consequent production of carbon dioxide.

By manipulating a simple dough of flour and water, you can develop the gluten of the flour to make gluten balls. Washing of the dough then removes the starch, leaving the protein. In the unbaked gluten ball, the cohesive and elastic nature of gluten can be observed easily. After baking, the structural contribution the denatured gluten makes to baked products can be appreciated. The differences in the gluten of cake and all purpose flours also are apparent.

KEY CONCEPTS — BREADS

1) Gluten, a mixture of proteins in wheat, can be developed into a cohesive, rather elastic complex if some liquid is manipulated with wheat flour; the structure of breads depends heavily on optimal gluten development.

2) Quick breads include biscuits, muffins, popovers, pancakes, waffles, cake doughnuts, and variations of these; all are leavened with steam, and most also obtain added volume from baking powder or acids and baking soda.

3) The preparation of yeast breads requires extensive kneading to develop a strong gluten network and care to avoid killing the yeast by exposing to high temperatures.

GLUTEN BALLS — A BASIC DEMONSTRATION

Total Time: 65 minutes
Baking: 450° F oven for 15 minutes, then 300° F oven
for 30 minutes

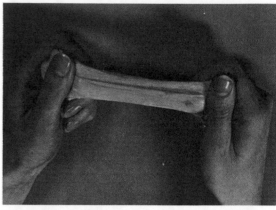

(1 ball)	
1 c	all purpose or cake flour
	water

1. Preheat oven.
2. Use either cake flour or all purpose flour; add just enough water to make a stiff dough.
3. Knead the dough hard for 5 minutes to develop the gluten.
4. Put the ball of dough in a tightly-woven cloth, and work it under cold running water to wash out the starch. Keep manipulating the dough until the water runs clear and has no trace of milkiness.
5. Scrape the cream-colored gluten from the cloth with a knife and work into a ball. If patches of white remain, wash the gluten some more to completely remove the starch.
6. Place on a cooky sheet and bake 15 minutes at 450° F in a preheated oven.
7. Turn the temperature down to 300° F and continue baking an additional 30 minutes. With a sharp knife, cut the gluten balls in half and examine the texture.

Gluten is an elastic, protein complex which is developed when wheat flour and water are manipulated together.

Baked cake flour and all purpose flour gluten balls.

COMPARISON OF GLUTEN FROM ALL PURPOSE AND CAKE FLOURS

	ALL PURPOSE FLOUR GLUTEN BALL	CAKE FLOUR GLUTEN BALL
Approximate height baked		
Exterior appearance		
Interior appearance		

PRINCIPLES OF PREPARING BISCUITS AND MUFFINS

Quick breads are defined as any breads that are not leavened by yeast. They are termed *quick* because they can be baked quickly rather than having to wait for the action of yeast to leaven the bread. Cake doughnuts, fritters, pancakes, waffles, popovers, many coffee cakes, biscuits, and muffins are classified as quick breads. Air and steam are leavening agents in all of these, but many of them also are leavened by the carbon dioxide which is generated from baking powder. Popovers are leavened primarily by steam, but muffins, biscuits, pancakes, doughnuts, and most other quick breads rely on baking powder for their primary source of leavening.

Quick breads range in viscosity from the fluid batters of pancakes and popovers, to the thicker batter of muffins, and finally to doughs such as biscuits and dougnuts which can be handled and cut out before baking or frying. The methods of cooking these batters and doughs vary from one type of quick bread to another. Doughnuts and fritters are fried in deep fat, while pancakes are baked on a griddle, waffles in a waffle iron, and the other quick breads are baked in an oven.

Biscuits and muffins are typical examples of quick breads, that is, breads which are not leavened by yeast. Like all quick breads, the recipes for biscuits and muffins include all purpose flour, salt, and liquid (usually milk). In addition to these basic ingredients, biscuits contain baking powder and solid shortening, while muffins are made with melted shortening, eggs, baking powder, and sugar added.

BISCUITS

Since the preparation time for mixing biscuits is rather short and since proofing or rising time is not required, the oven should be preheating before mixing begins. The oven temperature is set at 425° F. This temperature allows sufficient time for carbon dioxide to be generated from the baking powder to expand the biscuits before the gluten of the flour denatures and loses its extensiblity, thus promoting optimum volume. Although this is a high temperature, there is an adequate amount of time during baking to bake the dough throughout before the biscuit surface becomes too brown. At this temperature, the crust browns readily, but there is much less risk of burning than is the case at a higher temperature.

The fat used in biscuits traditionally is a solid fat which is cut into the sifted dry ingredients with a pastry blender or two knives until the pieces are the size of cooked rice grains. The cutting in of fat should be done with a light, tossing motion to avoid packing the dough. At first it will be necessary to scrape the fat from the pastry blender occasionally. The small pieces of fat which are formed by the cutting in of the shortening will melt during baking to help create layering or flakiness in the finished product.

When the cutting in of the fat has been completed, a fork is used to make a well in the center of the dry ingredients. The milk is poured into this well all at one time. This single addition of liquid is in contrast to the very gradual addition of water which is done in making pastry. By having

all of the milk present at one time, this somewhat sticky ratio of milk and flour can be mixed efficiently without developing the gluten excessively.

Efficient and effective mixing of the milk and dry ingredients is done easily with a table fork. Stirring is done with quick, light motions. Attention should be directed toward scraping the edges and the bottom of the bowl while stirring. This helps to get the entire mixture stirred uniformly. Also, it is necessary to cut through the center of the mass of dough frequently to help moisten all portions of the dough uniformly. Satisfactory mixing should be accomplished in approximately 20 strokes.

Lightly flour a bread board over an area of about 12" x 12", brushing this entire area well with the hand to rub the flour into the surface of the board. When the board has been floured, push any extra flour to the edge of the floured area, leaving only a very light dusting of flour on the surface. Scrape all of the dough from the bowl onto the floured area in preparation for kneading.

Kneading is done to help finish the uniform mixing of ingredients, to develop the gluten in the flour, and to promote the desired flakiness. The kneading action in making biscuits is much lighter than that used for yeast rolls. Biscuits are kneaded with the finger tips, while rolls are kneaded with a vigorous push with the heel of the hand.

The kneading action is begun by lifting the dough at the far edge. The far edge of the dough is folded over to the near edge. This folding of two layers of dough aids in creating the desired layered or flaky texture of kneaded biscuits.

The kneading action is completed by pressing the near edge of the dough toward the folded rear edge. This action is accomplished using a gentle, light motion with the finger tips of both hands. This gentle, kneading action promotes development of gluten, but is not done vigorously enough to tear the gluten strands.

The dough now is turned 90° so that the elongated dough mass is extending away from the person kneading the dough. As the dough is rotated, it may tend to stick to the floured board. If this happens, the dough should be

lifted, and a very small amount of flour should be dusted on the kneading area. A minimum of flour should be used on the board to avoid producing a tough, dry biscuit. When the dough has been rotated, the kneading process is repeated by lifting the far edge, folding to the near edge, and pressing lightly toward the fold with the finger tips. Again the dough is rotated 90° and the lifting, folding, and pressing steps are repeated. A smooth rhythm can be developed so that kneading becomes a quick and effective technique in which the lifting, folding, and pressing of the dough blend into a continuous, fluid motion. During the kneading, the development of the gluten can be felt in the finger tips as the dough becomes somewhat tighter, smoother, and slightly resistant to pressure. An appropriate amount of kneading can be done in 20 strokes or less.

When kneading is completed, use a minimum of flour on the board and roll the dough gently with a lightly floured rolling pin to a uniform thickness of 1/2". If desired, the dough can be rolled thinner to produce crisper biscuits. During the baking period, the biscuits will just about double in height. To obtain a uniform thickness, the pressure on the rolling pin should be lightened near the edge of the dough. Light pressure is used throughout the rolling process to avoid undue stretching and damage to the gluten. This helps to promote the desired flakiness and tenderness.

Use a lightly floured biscuit cutter to cut out the biscuits. The cutting is done by applying a firm, uniform pressure on the cutter handle straight down all the way through the dough. Careful cutting is essential so that the biscuits will be a uniform thickness around the edge. Attention to cutting will help to maintain the shape of biscuits and minimize the tendency to bend over during baking. Biscuits should be cut as close together as possible to obtain the maximum number of biscuits from the first rolling of the dough.

The dough left from the first cutting can be kneaded enough to make a cohesive mass which can again be rolled and cut. Although biscuits from the second rolling will be a little less attractive and slightly less tender than the first rolling, they still are very satisfactory if the dough is kneaded and rolled gently.

The cut biscuits are transferred individually from the bread board to a baking sheet. If soft sides are desired, the biscuits should be placed so that their sides touch each other. This arrangement also helps to direct the biscuits up straight so the sides will remain straight as the biscuits rise during baking. For biscuits with crisper sides, arrange the biscuits on the baking sheet with a space of at least 1/2" between biscuits on all sides. Since biscuits rise upward without spreading, this spacing allows the hot oven air to circulate well between the biscuits.

When all of the biscuits are arranged on the baking sheet, they may be brushed with milk on the upper surface. This small amount of liquid aids in dissolving any dry baking powder that may be on the surface. In addition, the protein and lactose contained in the milk aid in developing a pleasing brown color and a slight sheen during baking. Biscuits can be made without brushing them with milk, but their top surface is likely to have small brown flecks of undissolved baking powder, and they will not brown as readily. The use of milk on the surface is strictly a matter of individual preference.

The sheet of biscuits is baked on a central rack position in a 425° F oven for approximately 12 minutes. Biscuits made from dough rolled 1/2" thick are done when their upper surface is a pleasing, medium brown, and they have baked for at least 12 minutes. Thinner biscuits will be done in a slightly shorter time. For the most pleasing results, biscuits should be served hot when they come from the oven.

The evaluation of biscuits begins with an examination of the exterior. The sides of the biscuit should be straight, and the top and bottom should be flat and perpendicular to the sides. If the bottom edge tends to curve upward toward the sides, the dough contained a bit too much liquid in proportion to flour. If the sides are not perpendicular to the top and bottom, the biscuits were cut with uneven pressure on the cutter or the dough was not rolled to a uniform thickness.

The bottom and top surface should be evaluated for appearance. They should be pleasing, medium golden brown color. Too light a color is an indication of underbaking, due either to too low an oven temperature or too short a time for baking. Too dark a color may be due to too high an oven temperature or too long a time for baking. If the rack position is too high, the upper surface may fail to brown satisfactorily. Conversely, a very low rack position results in excessive browning or even burning of the bottom crust.

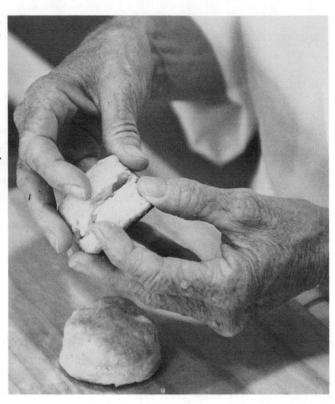

The sides of biscuits provide a clue to the flaky interior. Biscuits which are flaky will exhibit a number of short cracks on the sides. These cracks are caused when the biscuits are rising during baking. Corectly kneaded biscuits will have several of these cracks in the sides. Volume also is of interest because a high biscuit implies quality to most people. Biscuits with the correct amount of baking powder and proper mixing should double in volume during baking.

Biscuits, when broken apart, should reveal a flaky interior. This can be judged by rubbing a finger across the exposed interior surface. This motion will begin to peel off layers of the biscuit. In addition to appearance, biscuits are evaluated on the basis of flavor and tenderness. The flavor should be pleasing, with a minimum aftertaste from baking powder and no trace of burning. An excessive amount of double-acting baking powder contributes a metallic aftertaste, a problem not noted if a tartrate baking powder is used. The crust of biscuits should be somewhat crisp, and the crumb should be tender. Tenderness in biscuits is promoted by using an adequate quantity of milk and by avoiding excessive mixing and kneading, either of which would develop the gluten too much.

RECIPES

BISCUITS

Total Time: 25 minutes
Baking: 425° F oven for 12 minutes

1. Preheat oven.
2. Sift dry ingredients together in a mixing bowl.
3. Cut in the shortening with a pastry blender until the pieces are about the size of split peas.
4. Make a well in the mixture and pour all the milk in at once. Stir with a fork to mix the dough and moisten all the ingredients.
5. Turn dough out onto a lightly floured bread board.
6. Knead lightly with the fingertips by first lifting the far edge of the dough and folding it over toward you to meet the front edge of the dough.
7. Then press lightly with the fingertips.
8. Turn the dough a quarter of a turn, and knead.

(Makes 6 biscuits)

1 c	*all purpose flour, sifted*
1 1/2 tsp	*baking powder*
1/4 tsp	*salt*
3 tbsp	*shortening*
6 tbsp 1/2 tsp	*milk*

(Makes 12 biscuits)

2 c	all purpose flour, sifted
1 tbsp	baking powder
1/2 tsp	salt
1/3 c	shortening
3/4 c	milk

BISCUITS (CONTINUED)

10. Keep repeating this kneading action until the dough has been kneaded at least 10 times.
11. With a lightly floured rolling pin, roll out the dough 1/3–1/2" thick (dough will double in height during baking).
12. With a floured, sharp biscuit cutter, cut out the biscuits as close together as possible.
13. Transfer the biscuits to a cookie sheet. For crisp sides, spread the biscuits apart. For soft sides, place the biscuits so that their sides are touching.
14. After cutting all the biscuits possible from the first rolling, rework the dough a little and roll again for a second cutting.
15. Brush the surface of the biscuits lightly with milk if a slightly shiny top is desired.
16. Bake at 425° F for about 12 minutes until the tops are a golden brown. Serve hot.

BUTTERMILK BISCUITS

Total Time: 30 minutes
Baking: 425° F oven for 15 minutes

1. Preheat oven.
2. Stir dry ingredients (flour, baking powder, and salt) together in mixing bowl.
3. Cut in shortening with a pastry blender until the pieces are about the size of split peas.
4. Make a well in the ingredients and add the buttermilk. Stir with a fork just until ingredients are all moistened.
5. Flour bread board moderately and turn the dough out onto it.
6. Keep hands floured while lightly kneading the dough until it begins to work together enough to be rolled 1/2" thick.
7. With a floured biscuit cutter, cut biscuits and arrange on a baking sheet so that they touch each other.
8. Bake at 450° F about 15 minutes until golden brown. Serve hot.

(Makes 6 biscuits)
1 c	*all purpose flour*
2 tsp	*baking powder*
1/8 tsp	*salt*
3 tbsp	*shortening*
1/2 c	*buttermilk*

(Makes 12 biscuits)
2 c	all purpose flour
4 tsp	baking powder
1/4 tsp	salt
1/3 c	shortening
1 c	buttermilk

MUFFINS

The recipe for muffins is different from biscuits in that it contains sugar and eggs. An additional difference is the use of salad oil or melted shortening rather than solid fat. The ratio of liquid to flour in muffins is 1:2, that is, 1 cup liquid to 2 cups of flour. This is a slightly higher ratio of liquid to flour than is found in biscuits.

Muffins, like biscuits, may be baked at 425° F, although they also may be baked successfully at 400° F. The oven should be preheated while the muffins are being mixed. Before beginning to mix the ingredients, the cups in the muffin pan should be greased lightly to facilitate removal of the baked muffins.

The muffin method of mixing, in summary, is a three-step process: 1) mixing of the dry ingredients, 2) mixing of the liquid ingredients, and 3) combining the liquid and dry ingredients to make the finished batter. The first step in this total process is the preparation of the dry ingredients. These are combined by sifting all of them together into a mixing bowl in preparation for incorporation with the liquid ingredients.

Preparation of the liquid ingredients is started by gently beating the egg until it is blended thoroughly, but not foamy. The milk is added to the egg and beaten very gently. Thorough blending of the egg and milk is important. Underblended egg will cause muffins to have a somewhat waxy quality on the interior and may even result in streaks of egg showing in the baked muffins. The final step in combining liquid ingredients is to stir in the melted shortening.

Make a well in the dry ingredients and pour the liquid mixture into the well. All of the liquid is added at one time to reduce the total amount of mixing. A wooden spoon is a convenient utensil to use for stirring the liquid and dry ingredients together. Stirring needs to be done throughout the mixture as uniformly as possible. Care should be taken to stir in the dry ingredients from the sides and bottom of the mixing bowl. It is also necessary to cut through the batter with the mixing spoon. The objective of the mixing procedure is to

moisten all of the dry ingredients without developing the gluten too much. Since the ratio of 1 part liquid to 2 parts flour is very sticky, gluten develops very readily with stirring.

The appearance of muffin batter changes quickly as mixing progresses. At the beginning, there will be many regions where dry ingredients are visible and also areas where the liquid is draining from the batter. In these dry regions, the gluten is not yet developing, and the baking powder is not moistened enough to permit the chemical reaction needed to release carbon dioxide for leavening. A muffin batter which still has areas of dry ingredients visible and pools of liquid is undermixed.

Stirring of muffin batter should be continued until all of the dry and liquid ingredients are blended to the point where no dry areas remain and the liquid is not evident at the edges of the bowl. At this stage of mixing, the batter will still be lumpy. The gluten will be developed sufficiently to provide the necessary structural framework to allow the muffin to expand without falling during baking and to hold the baked muffin together without being excessively crumbly.

Sometimes people overmix muffins because they do not recognize the appearance of properly mixed muffin batter. Muffin batter should not be mixed to the point where it begins to look smooth because the muffins will have a less attractive appearance and will be less tender.

Muffins will have the best appearance if enough batter for a single muffin is placed in a muffin cup at one time. To do this, the mixing spoon is filled with batter by cutting toward the side of the mixing bowl; then a second spoon or spatula is used to scrape the batter gently into the pan. The cup should be filled a little more than half full.

This process is repeated until the batter is gone. The batter should be scooped from the bowl with a minimum amount of manipulation. The practice of scraping down the sides of the bowl and stirring the batter after each spoonful is removed is detrimental to the quality of the batch of muffins. When all of the batter has been spooned into the pans, any spilled batter should be wiped from the pans before baking the muffins.

Muffins are baked approximately 20 minutes until they are a pleasing, golden brown. The pan should be positioned on a rack in the center of the oven. If more than one pan is to be baked at the same time, the pans should be at least an inch from the sides, front, and back of the oven and a comparable distance should be allowed between pans. This arrangement is important to avoid blocking the flow of hot oven air needed for satisfactory browning.

To avoid developing a soggy crust, muffins should be removed from the cups after the baked muffins have been taken from the oven. Fresh muffins are best when served while still hot from the oven. However, quick breads (including muffins) can be frozen very successfully. If they are to be frozen, muffins should be cooled to room temperature on a rack before packaging them for freezing.

The exterior of baked muffins clearly reflects the amount of mixing. The surface of undermixed muffins will be rough and jagged. Specks of dry flour are likely to be in evidence. Correctly mixed muffins have a cauliflower-like top. The surface has softly rounded bumps, the result of adequate gluten development. Batter that has been overmixed will result in muffins with a very smooth surface, which is similar to the appearance of yeast rolls.

The shape of the upper crust of muffins also is modified by the amount of mixing. Undermixed muffins are only very slightly rounded, and the volume is small due to the failure of some of the dry baking powder to react. There may be evidence of some liquid draining to the edge of the upper surface. Properly mixed muffins will have a rounded top surface and a greater volume than the undermixed muffins. With increasing mixing beyond optimum, the rounded contour will change to a humped or peaked shape.

The interior of muffins also reflects the amount of mixing. Undermixed muffins will not have the gluten developed sufficiently, and they will tend to crumble readily. There also may be evidence of dry flour. Properly mixed muffins will be quite coarse, yet relatively uniform in texture, but will crumble just a little. Overmixed muffins will have some tunnels that extend upward toward the peak. These tunnels are created by pockets of gas expanding upward along strong gluten strands before the protein was denatured during baking. The regions between the tunnels generally will be comprised of comparatively small cells.

In addition to evaluating texture and volume, muffins are rated on the basis of flavor and tenderness. The flavor should be well rounded and pleasing, with no suggestion of any burning. The interior should not have any regions of dry ingredients nor any suggestion of waxiness. Muffins should be tender, but they will be just a little bit crumbly.

The undermixed muffin (left) has poor volume and crumbly texture when compared with the properly mixed muffin (center). The overmixed muffin (right) has tunnels and a peaked top.

RECIPES

MUFFINS

Total Time: 30 minutes
Baking: 425° F oven for 20 minutes

1. Preheat oven.
2. Grease the muffin pan.
3. Sift all the dry ingredients into the mixing bowl.
4. In a separate bowl, beat the egg well.
5. Add salad oil and milk to the egg and beat until well blended.
6. Pour the liquid ingredients into the dry ingredients, and mix with a wooden spoon just enough to moisten all the ingredients. The batter will look lumpy, but no dry flour will show.
7. Scoop a spoonful of batter from the mixing bowl. Using a second spoon, push the batter into a greased muffin pan. Be sure to get enough batter at one time to fill muffin cup slightly more than half full.
8. Repeat this procedure until all the muffin batter is used. Avoid stirring the batter when spooning batter from the bowl.
9. Bake in a 425° F oven 20 minutes or until the tops are golden brown.
10. Remove muffins from pan as soon as they are taken from the oven.
11. Serve while hot.

(Makes 6 muffins)	
1 c	all purpose flour, sifted
2 tbsp	sugar
1 1/2 tsp	baking powder
1/4 tsp	salt
1/2	egg
2 tbsp	salad oil
1/2 c	milk

(Makes 12 muffins)	
2 c	all purpose flour, sifted
1/4 c	sugar
1 tbsp	baking powder
1/2 tsp	salt
1	egg
1/4 c	salad oil
1 c	milk

POPOVERS

Total Time: 55 minutes
Baking: 425° F oven for 45 minutes

1. Preheat oven.
2. Grease popover pan or custard cups and place in a 425° F oven to preheat while making the batter.
3. Combine all the ingredients and beat until smooth.
4. With the aid of the hot pads, put the hot popover pan on a heat-resistant counter.
5. Quickly pour batter into the hot cups, filling them half full.
6. Immediately bake at 425° F.
7. Bake 40 minutes.
8. Puncture with a cooking fork to let out steam, and bake 5 more minutes.
9. Remove from pan and serve.

(Makes 4 popovers)	
1/2 c	all purpose flour, sifted
1/8 tsp	salt
1/2 c	milk
1	egg

(Makes 8 popovers)	
1 c	all purpose flour, sifted
1/4 tsp	salt
1 c	milk
2	eggs

Note: When a popover is broken open (above right) a very large central cavity should be found inside. The walls surrounding the cavity should be rather thin and not doughy. Although the walls will be a bit moist, the general impression is one of crispness and chewiness rather than of sogginess. Failure to achieve the desired cavity may be due to baking at too low a temperature. A low oven temperature allows heat to penetrate to the interior and begin to coagulate the gluten and egg proteins before enough steam pressure has built up inside to stretch the batter and form the large cavity that is the hallmark of a good popover.

PANCAKES

Total Time: 15 minutes

1. Sift the dry ingredients into a mixing bowl.
2. Beat the liquid ingredients together in another bowl, and then pour them into the dry ingredients.
3. Mix with a rotary beater just until the batter is smooth.
4. Bake on a griddle hot enough to make drops of water dance on it.
5. Pour batter from the pitcher to make pancakes the diameter desired. Pour far enough apart so that the sides do not touch.
6. Bake until golden brown on the bottom, and the bubbles that form have popped.
7. Flip over and bake the second side to a golden brown.
8. Serve at once, or hold in a 150° F oven with paper towels separating the pancakes.

(Makes 4 pancakes)
10 tbsp	all purpose flour, sifted
1 tsp	sugar
1/4 tsp	salt
1 1/2 tsp	baking powder
1/2	egg
1/2 c	milk
1 tbsp	salad oil

(Makes 8 pancakes)
1 1/4 c	all purpose flour, sifted
2 tsp	sugar
1/2 tsp	salt
1 tbsp	baking powder
1	egg
1 c	milk
2 tbsp	salad oil

WAFFLES

Total Time: 15 minutes

1. Preheat waffle iron.
2. Sift dry ingredients together in a mixing bowl.
3. Beat egg in another mixing bowl and then beat in the other liquid ingredients.
4. Make a well in the dry ingredients, and add all of the liquid ingredients.
5. Beat with a rotary beater just until batter is smooth.
6. Pour batter carefully onto hot waffle iron, being sure to use enough batter just to reach the edge of the iron.
7. Carefully close over; bake without opening the iron until steam no longer is escaping.
8. Check to be sure waffle is a pleasing brown. Remove from iron and serve immediately.

(Makes 4 waffles)
1 1/4 c	all purpose flour, sifted
2 tsp	baking powder
1 1/2 tsp	sugar
1/4 tsp	salt
1	egg
1 1/8 c	milk
1/3 c	salad oil

(Makes 8 waffles)
2 1/2 c	all purpose flour, sifted
4 tsp	baking powder
1 tbsp	sugar
1/2 tsp	salt
2	eggs
2 1/4 c	milk
2/3 c	salad oil

CAKE DOUGHNUTS

Total Time: 1 hour 30 minutes
Deep fat fryer: 375° F oven for 15 minutes

1. Preheat fat.
2. Mix the dry ingredients together.
3. In a separate bowl, beat the eggs well.
4. Stir in the milk and melted shortening.
5. Combine the dry and liquid ingredients, and mix well.
6. Chill dough 1 hour before rolling on a well-floured board.
7. Begin preheating oil in fryer during last 5 minutes of chilling period.
8. Roll dough a little less than 1/2" thick and cut with a floured doughnut cutter.
9. Use a wide spatula to transfer the doughnuts from the bread board to the deep fat fryer which contains fat preheated to 375° F.
10. Fry on one side until a pleasing golden brown, and then turn over and brown the second side.
11. Drain on paper towels after they are fried.

(Makes 10 doughnuts)

1 3/4 c	all purpose flour, sifted
6 tbsp	sugar
1 1/2 tsp	baking powder
1/4 tsp	salt
1/4 tsp	cinnamon
1/4 tsp	nutmeg
1 1/2	eggs
1/4 c	milk
2 2/3 tbsp	shortening, melted
	salad oil for fryer

(Makes 20 doughnuts)

3 1/2 c	all purpose flour, sifted
3/4 c	sugar
1 tbsp	baking powder
1/2 tsp	salt
1/2 tsp	cinnamon
1/2 tsp	nutmeg
3	eggs
1/2 c	milk
1/3 c	shortening, melted
	salad oil for fryer

The oil for frying the doughnuts should be heated just long enough to bring the oil to 375° F, the temperature best suited to frying doughnuts. Several doughnuts may be fried at one time; there should always be enough surface area in the fryer to permit a doughnut to rise up in a flat position on the surface of the oil. The heat for the deep fat fryer or kettle should be high enough to maintain the oil at 375° F, with only a very slight drop in temperature when new doughnuts are added for frying. Remove the doughnuts with a chopstick or slotted spoon after they have become a pleasing brown on the second side. Drain them of exces oil by placing them on paper towels.

Evaluation of cake doughnuts begins with the external appearance. They should be a uniform, pleasing brown on both the top and bottom. Ideally, homemade cake doughnuts will be perfectly round, with an open, cylindrical center. Poor exterior color may range from pale (a condition caused by using too low a frying temperature) to very dark. Excessive browning may be the result of too high a frying temperature or too long a time for frying. The doughnuts should be double the volume of the original dough thickness. The interior of doughnuts should be evaluated for uniformity of cell size and for doneness. Properly mixed doughnuts will have a relatively small and uniform cell size. Sometimes doughnuts may be doughy in the center. This problem usually is caused by using too high a temperature for frying. With too high a temperature, the exterior will become a deceptively pleasing brown before the interior is done. Excessive moistness in the center also may be caused by rolling the dough so thick that the heat cannot penetrate the doughnut before the exterior browns.

When a doughnut is broken open for evaluation, the amount of oil penetration also should be noted. A doughnut that has been fried well at the proper temperature will have only slight evidence of greasiness below the outer surface. If the oil is at too low a temperature during frying, the dougnut will have a greasy crumb. This excess oil will give a doughnut a greasy mouthfeel when it is eaten. This problem is avoided by being sure the oil is maintained at 375° F throughout the frying period and by not overcrowding the oil by frying too many doughnuts at a time. The final evaluation is done by tasting the doughnut. Doughnuts should have a rich, fried flavor without seeming to be greasy and should be a pleasing flavor blend of the ingredients. They also should be tender. Tough doughnuts are caused by too much handling and manipulation of the dough or by working in too much flour.

COFFEE CAKE

Total Time: 45–50 minutes
Baking: 350° F oven for 25 minutes (small) or
            35 minutes (large)

1. Preheat oven and grease bottom of pan. Use loaf pan for small recipe and 8" square pan for large one.
2. Cream the shortening, vanilla, and sugar, and then beat in the egg yolk.
3. Sift the dry ingredients together and add by thirds, alternately with milk.
4. Beat egg white with rotary beater until peaks just bend over.
5. Fold into batter.
6. Put half the batter in the pan.
7. Mix the remaining 5 ingredients together, and sprinkle half of the mixture on the cake batter in the pan.
8. Put the remaining batter on top, and add the other half of the topping.
9. Bake at 350° F until a toothpick inserted in the center comes out clean.

(Makes 1 small coffee cake)
Batter:

2 tbsp	shortening
1/2 tsp	vanilla
1/2 c	sugar
1	egg, separated
1/8 tsp	salt
3/4 c	all purpose flour, sifted
1 tsp	baking powder
1/4 c	milk

Topping:

6 tbsp	brown sugar
1/2 tsp	cinnamon
1 1/2 tsp	flour
1 1/2 tsp	margarine or butter, melted
1/4 c	walnuts, chopped

(Makes 1 large coffee cake)
Batter:

1/4 c	shortening
1 tsp	vanilla
1 c	sugar
2	eggs, separated
1/4 tsp	salt
1 1/2 c	all purpose flour, sifted
2 tsp	baking powder
1/2 c	milk

Topping:

3/4 c	brown sugar
1 tsp	cinnamon
1 tbsp	flour
1 tbsp	margarine or butter, melted
1/2 c	walnuts, chopped

BLUEBERRY MUFFINS

Total Time: 30 minutes
Baking: 425° F oven for 20 minute

1. Preheat oven and grease muffin pans.
2. Drain the blueberries thoroughly in a strainer.
3. Sift all the dry ingredients into the mixing bowl.
4. In a separate bowl, beat the egg and stir in the salad oil and milk.
5. Pour the liquid ingredients into the dry ingredients; mix with wooden spoon.
6. Add the blueberries, sprinkle with the sugar, and just barely stir them in.
7. Put the batter in muffin pans, and bake at 425° F 20–25 minutes. Serve at once.

(Makes 6 muffins)

1 c	all purpose flour, sifted
2 tbsp	sugar
1 1/2 tsp	baking powder
1/2 tsp	salt
1/2	egg
1/4 c	milk
2 tbsp	salad oil
1/3 c	blueberries
1 tsp	sugar

(Makes 12 muffins)

2 c	all purpose flour, sifted
1/4 c	sugar
1 tbsp	baking powder
1 tsp	salt
1	egg
1/2 c	milk
1/4 c	salad oil
2/3 c	blueberries
1 tbsp	sugar

CALIFORNIA CORN BREAD

Total Time: 30 minutes
Baking: 425° F oven for 20–25 minute

1. Preheat oven.
2. Mix dry ingredients in mixing bowl.
3. In another bowl, blend the liquid ingredients.
4. Pour liquid ingredients all at once into a well in the dry ingredients, and stir with a wooden spoon just until all ingredients are moistened.
5. Pour into greased baking pan.
6. Bake in 400° F for 20–25 minutes until wooden toothpick inserted in center comes out clean.

(Small recipe)

1/2 c	*all purpose flour*
1/2 c	*yellow cornmeal*
2 tbsp	*sugar*
1 1/2 tsp	*baking powder*
1/8 tsp	*salt*
1/2 c	*whipping cream*
2 tbsp	*vegetable oil*
2 tbsp	*honey*
1	*egg, slightly beaten*

(Large recipe)

1 c	all purpose flour
1 c	yellow cornmeal
1/4 c	sugar
1 tbsp	baking powder
1/4 tsp	salt
1 c	whipping cream
1/4 c	vegetable oil
1/4 c	honey
2	eggs, slightly beaten

BRUSCHETTA

Total Time: 35 minutes
Broiling: 3 minutes each side

1. Preheat oven.
2. Mix tomatoes, basil, oregano, garlic, olive oil, salt, and pepper and let stand 20 minutes.
3. Brush each side of bread slices with oil.
4. Place bread on baking sheet and broil each side until golden brown, turning once.
5. Distribute tomato mixture uniformly on the toasted bread.
6. Return to broiler for a minutes just to warm.

(Serves two)

1 1/2	*Roma tomatoes (ripe), diced*
5	*fresh basil leaves, thinly sliced*
1/4 tsp	*oregano*
1/4	*garlic clove, minced*
1 tbsp	*olive oil*
	salt and pepper to taste
2	*thick slices crusty Italian bread*
2 tsp	*olive oil*

(Serves four)

3	Roma tomatoes (ripe), diced
10	fresh basil leaves, thinly sliced
1/2 tsp	oregano
1/2	garlic clove, minced
2 tbsp	olive oil
	salt and pepper to taste
4	thick slices crusty Italian bread
4 tsp	olive oil

CREAM PUFFS

Total Time: 1 hour
Broiling: 450° F 15 minutes, then 325° F 25 minutes

1. Preheat oven.
2. Stir the butter or margarine into the boiling water.
3. As soon as the butter is melted, add the salt and flour all at once.
4. Stir vigorously while continuing to cook the mixture until it forms a ball. Remove from heat.
5. After cooling about 2 minutes, beat in the eggs, adding them one at a time and beating hard to make a smooth mixture.
6. Drop individual puffs on a teflon-lined jelly roll pan, using about 1 tbsp of dough for each. Place them at least 3" apart. (Note: Puffs for appetizers are made using only about 1/2 tsp of dough.)
7. Bake 15 minutes at 450° F. Reduce heat to 325° F and bake an additional 25 min.
8. Cool on a wire rack. Split and fill with ice cream, cream filling, or other desired filling just before serving.

(Makes 6 puffs)

1/2 c	*water, boiling*
1/4 c	*butter or margarine*
1/2 c	*flour*
1/8 tsp	*salt*
2	*eggs*

(Serves four)

1 c	water, boiling
1/2 c	butter or margarine
1 c	flour
1/4 tsp	salt
4	eggs

EVALUATION OF LABORATORY PRODUCTS — QUICK BREADS

RECIPE	NOTES ON COLOR, TEXTURE, FLAVOR, OR OTHER QUALITIES	COMMENTS OR SUGGESTIONS FOR MAKING OR USING THIS PRODUCT IN THE FUTURE

YEAST BREADS

PRINCIPLES OF PREPARING YEAST BREADS

Yeast breads, in contrast to quick breads, require a relatively long production time to provide sufficient opportunity for carbon dioxide formation by the yeast. The types of yeast breads are numerous, ranging from simple formulas of flour, yeast, and water to rich doughs containing eggs, sugar, salt, milk, and butter, in addition to the flour and yeast. Crusty breads with a chewy, rather tough crumb result when eggs and fat are not included. A softer crust and more tender crumb are produced when the formula is richer. Despite these variations in the characteristics of the end products, the procedures followed in preparing the various yeast breads are basically the same.

Active dry yeast works quickly and well in yeast doughs when the yeast is softened before being incorporated in the dough. The other ingredients can be assembled and measured while the yeast is being hydrated. Yeast is hydrated by stirring the granules into lukewarm water, that is, water at approximately body temperature. The yeast used in breads is *Saccharomyces cerevisiae*, a single-celled plant which produces carbon dioxide from sugar in doughs. This plant will be killed if subjected to high temperatures, and carbon dioxide will not be produced for leavening. For this reason, temperatures of liquids and doughs in contact with hydrated dry yeast should be monitored and should not exceed 105° F. If the dry yeast is mixed directly with the other dry ingredients, the liquid can be 125° F because the mixture will cool adequately before the yeast is hydrated in the dough.

If milk is used in a yeast bread, it is scalded in a saucepan before being added to other ingredients. The milk is scalded sufficiently when the hot milk clings to the sides of the pan as the pan is tipped. Boiling is not necessary. Originally, scalding was required to kill microorganisms that might be present in raw milk. Even now pasteurized milk is scalded for yeast breads because the hot milk melts the fat to give excellent distribution of fat throughout the dough. This hot liquid also aids in producing a dough sufficiently warm to promote active gas production by the yeast.

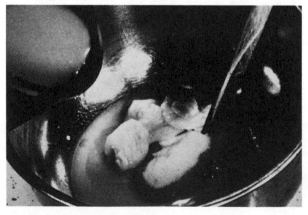

While the milk is being scalded and the yeast is hydrating, the next step in the straight dough method is to measure the sugar, salt, and fat into a mixing bowl. Many yeast bread recipes include at least a small amount of sugar to serve as food for the yeast. Without added sugar in the formula, yeast will have only a little sugar available from the flour in the dough, and gas production will be slow and limited. Increasing the sugar in a bread formula will increase the sweetness of the flavor and also promote tenderness of the bread and browning of the crust. The salt in the formula serves as an inhibitor to yeast growth, thus acting to regulate gas production. Fat in yeast breads promotes tenderness of the crumb and crust. Also, the flavor is enhanced by fat. If butter or margarine is the fat used, the color of the end product will be more yellow than if other fats are used.

The scalded milk is poured directly into the mixing bowl containing the sugar, salt, and fat. This mixture should be stirred occasionally until the fat is melted. Since the egg is quite cool, the temperature of the mixture will drop, and the egg proteins will not coagulate.

Approximately half a cup of flour is stirred into the mixture. This will result in a very lumpy mixture. The purpose of this small amount of flour is to tie up the fat so that the yeast will not be coated by the fat when the softened yeast is added. There is no need to try to eliminate the lumps of flour at this stage. Subsequent steps will develop a smooth mixtures.

The temperature of the mixture needs to be checked at this point to be sure that it is not so hot that the hydrated yeast will be killed when added. The simplest satisfactory way of checking the temperature is to insert a well-washed finger directly into the mixture.

If the mixture feels approximately body temperature or only very slightly warm, the softened yeast can be added immediately. If the mixture feels warm or hot, it should be cooled to approximately body temperature before adding the yeast. A thermometer can also be used to check the temperature. The mixture should not be warmer than 105° F when the yeast is added. Higher temperatures kill the yeast and result in a bread dough that will not rise well.

After the yeast has been stirred into the other ingredients, approximately half the flour is added to give a mixture sufficiently viscous to permit vigorous beating. This dough is beaten vigorously for about 3 minutes. During this period, the mixture will become quite smooth and will begin to develop a cohesive quality as a result of gluten development. This is an important step toward achieving the rather tenacious crumb structure needed in breads.

When the gluten has been developed sufficiently, all purpose flour is added gradually to make a soft dough. As mixing progresses, flour should be mixed throughout the dough by cutting through the dough with a wooden spoon. Unless mixing is done with these cutting strokes, the dough will have many areas in the interior which are very sticky and difficult to manage. Flour should be added just to the point where the entire dough mass can be handled by hand without being sticky. At this point, the dough will be difficult to stir. The

actual amount of flour needed varies from one part of the country to another because of the variable nature of the protein contained in flours on the market. For this reason, there is no need to sift and measure flour for yeast breads. The exact amount needed is determined by the handling characteristics of a specific dough.

The dough then is turned out onto a lightly floured board. Additional flour needs to be available to keep the dough from sticking during the kneading process. When the dough is resting on the board, it should be soft enough to sag, but not to flow.

The kneading of yeast doughs is designed to develop gluten. Breads need to have a structure strong enough to hold together when butter or margarine, jams, and sandwich fillings are spread on them. This characteristic results when gluten develops to the correct point during kneadings. Kneading of yeast doughs is a very vigorous, rhythmic process which is done with the heel of both hands. Each kneading stroke is done by grasping the far edge of the dough, folding it to the front edge, and then pushing away vigorously with the heels of both hands. This stroke makes the dough into an elongated mass.

This mass is rotated 90° so that the length of the dough extends away from the operator. The far edge again is folded to meet the front edge, and the dough is pushed vigorously with the heel of both hands. This rotation, folding, and pressing procedure is repeated rapidly and vigorously for 5 minutes or more, until the dough shows blisters under the surface when it is stretched. Kneading should develop into a rhythmic, rapid, and vigorous process. Sufficient gluten development is essential for uniform cell size and adequate cell wall strength in the finished bread. During kneading, more flour may be needed on the board to keep the dough from sticking. However, excess flour should be avoided because too much flour results in a less tender and rather dry product.

When kneading is complete, the dough should be soft, but not sticky. This dough then is ready for the first rising period. Since this first rising usually requires about an hour, the surface of the dough needs to be protected to prevent drying. Protection can be provided by putting a few drops of salad oil in a large bowl, dragging the dough through the oil, and then placing the oiled side of the dough upward in the bowl.

Aluminum foil or a clean towel can be used to provide additional protection from air currents. The bowl then should be placed in a warm place to facilitate yeast growth and carbon dioxide production. Hot places such as an oven with a high pilot light may be so warm that the yeast will be killed; hence such places should be avoided. However, doughs can be placed in the refrigerator or even in the freezer if baking is to be delayed. Doughs will rise very slowly in the refrigerator and not at all in the freezer.

Dough is allowed to rise without disturbance until it has doubled in volume. Under normal room conditions, this first rising will require approximately 1 hour. If this proofing is being done in the refrigerator, between 9 and 12 hours may be required to double the volume. Frozen, unshaped doughs will need to be thawed and then allowed to rise to double their volume. The cooler the actual temperature of the dough, the slower will be the production of carbon dioxide by the yeast. Yeast activity is accelerated by warmer temperatures until temperatures above 105° F are reached. Temperatures higher than this cause permanent damage to the yeast, whereas cool temperatures retard gas production but do not kill the yeast.

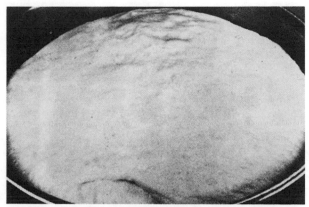

The first rising stretches existing gluten strands and expands pockets of carbon dioxide and air. After the dough has doubled, the fist is used to force the extra gas from these pockets and reduce the strain on these stretched strands of gluten. This procedure helps to promote cells of uniform size and to avoid large, coarse cell areas in the bread. It also helps to keep gluten strands from being stretched so far that they break.

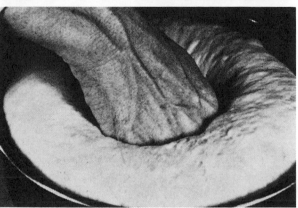

The dough now is ready to be shaped as desired. *Cloverleaf rolls* are shaped by using the thumb and index finger to squeeze small balls of dough from the large dough mass. Three of these balls, each approximately 1/2" in diameter, are placed in each greased cup of a muffin pan. When placing each ball in the cup, be careful to place the rounded, smooth surface upward so that the rough, squeezed region does not show.

Numerous other shapes can be made from roll doughs. *Bread sticks*, *bow knot roll*, and *rosettes* are fashioned by first squeezing off a ball of dough about 1" in diameter. This ball is rolled, either between the hands or by hand on a lightly floured bread board to make a long, uniform strand of dough about 1/4" in diameter. For *bread sticks*, this strand is placed on an ungreased baking sheet. *Bow knots* are made by tying the strand into a rather loose half knot and placing this on an ungreased baking sheet. To make *rosettes*, the strand is tied into a fairly tight half knot with the ends extending an inch beyond the knot. The end coming from under the knot is stretched up and over the knot and forced down through the center of the roll to hide the end. The other loose end is carried from its position on top of the knot of dough, over the knot, and tucked under the roll (shown lower left photo).

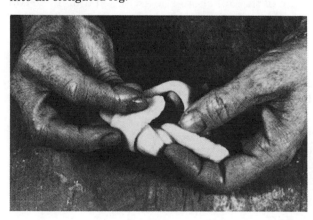

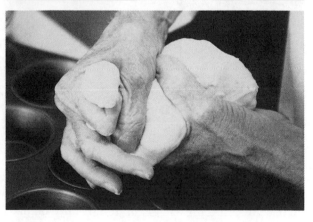

Loaves of bread are made by rolling the dough on a lightly floured board into a rectangle 1/2" thick, with one dimension of the rectangle about 3" greater than the length of the loaf pan in which the bread will be baked. Roll dough into an elongated log.

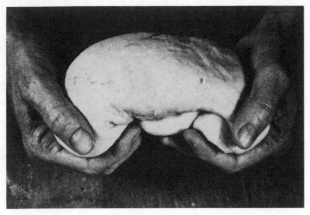

Press the ends of the dough firmly to seal the roll at each end. Tuck the final 1 1/2" of dough under the roll at each end to make a loaf which just fits the greased loaf pan. Gently fit the dough into the pan with the smooth dough surface on top.

Butterflake or *fantan rolls* are made by rolling half the dough into a rectangle about 1/4" thick, 6" wide, and 12" long. Rolling is done on a lightly floured bread board. Melted butter is spread with a pastry brush over the entire surface of the rectangle. A table knife is used to cut the dough into 6 lengthwise strips, each an inch wide. These strips are stacked, and then rolls are made by cutting through this stacked dough at 1" intervals. The rolls are placed in greased muffin cups with the freshly cut surface turned upward. The dough

strips are in a vertical position. Bread sticks, bow knots, cloverleaf rolls and rosettes usually are made with a basic, simple yeast dough. Butterflake, cinnamon rolls, and coffee rings usually are made from richer doughs with more sugar and fat.

Other variations can also be made using the same rectangular, rolled shape that is used for butterflake rolls. Again, this rectangle is brushed lightly with melted butter. *Cinnamon rolls* are created by sprinkling the entire surface of the rectangle very generously with cinnamon. Since the dough will be more than double in volume in the baked roll, the cinnamon will be covering a much greater volume at that point. Unless cinnamon is shaken on until the dough surface is well covered, the cinnamon flavor may be too delicate for many palates.

Chopped nuts or other optional ingredients also may be added before the rectangle is rolled up. Rolling is done by starting lightly at the far edge to make a log. This log is then sliced at regular intervals, usually an inch wide. The pinwheels of dough may be placed on their sides, either in greased muffin cups or on baking pans. If placed on baking pans, the rolls should be spaced at 1/2" intervals to permit some horizontal expansion of the rolls.

The same log just described may be transferred in its entirety onto a baking sheet as the first step in fashioning a *coffee ring*. To keep the ring from unrolling, the seam of the roll should be arranged under the roll

as the ends are being brought together into a ring. The ring shape is assured by squeezing the ends of the dough together to seal them firmly. If the diameter of the dough ring is not uniform, the dough can be manipulated by hand to improve the appearance of the ring. Kitchen shears are used to cut through the log of dough from the edge to within 1/4" of the inner edge.

This cut is repeated at 1" intervals all around the ring. Each of these segments then is twisted carefully to reveal the pinwheel of dough and cinnamon. As each portion is twisted, it is maneuvered to overlap the preceding segment.

Butterhorns provide an example of rolls made with a dough containing a relatively large proportion of whole egg and margarine or butter. A 4" ball of the dough is rolled on a lightly floured board into a circular shape about 1/4" thick. The circle of dough is brushed lightly with melted margarine or butter. A table knife is used to cut the dough into pie-shaped wedges about 2" wide at the perimeter of the circle.

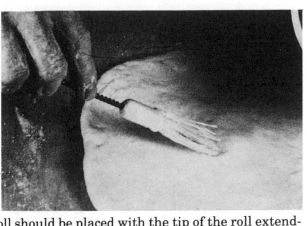

Butterhorns are made by rolling these wedges lightly into their final form. This is done by rolling from the curved edge toward the tip of the dough piece.

These rolls are placed on an ungreased baking sheet at 2" intervals between rolls. Only about an inch distance needs to be maintained between the ends of the rolls. Each roll should be placed with the tip of the roll extending well underneath the roll dough. Unless this is done, butterhorns frequently unroll during baking.

Regardless of the type of dough or the shape of the product, the shaped dough needs to be permitted to rest in a warm place until double in volume. This time the dough is not covered because the slight drying of the surface is not detrimental to the quality of the finished product. In addition, the dough might stick to the covering, and volume would be lost in freeing the roll from the foil. This second rising usually requires about 30 minutes (half as much time as the first rising). For optimum volume and texture in the finished product, it is important to wait until the volume has doubled before baking.

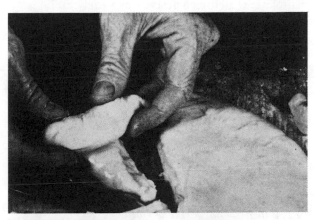

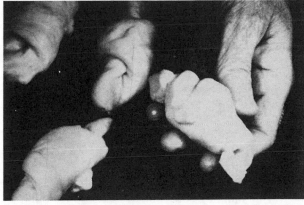

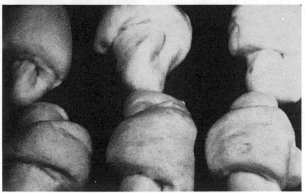

Ten minutes before the shaped rolls have finished doubling their volume again, check to be sure the oven rack is in the center position, and preheat the oven. Plain rolls are baked at 425° F, bread at 400° F, and rich rolls at 375° F. Whenever raisins, currants, sweet syrups, and jams are used, the temperature should be 375° F regardless of the type of dough. Breads containing rich formulas or other additives high in sugar also are baked at 375° F to avoid burning these substances.

When the dough has doubled, the baking pans are placed in the preheated oven. There should be space between the baking pans and the edges of the oven to permit the circulation needed for good browning of the rolls. Pans should not be placed on a lower rack directly under other pans because the crusts will not brown properly. Rolls are baked for 12–15 minutes to a golden brown color if a 425° F oven is used and about 20 minutes if a 375° F oven is used. Bread loaves require about 35 minutes of baking time.

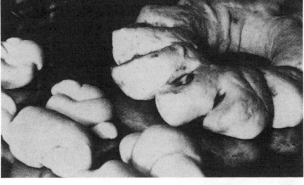

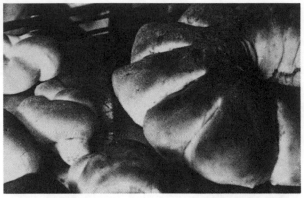 

When yeast breads are done, they are removed from the oven and then transferred from the pan to a cooling rack. It is important to remove products from the pans to avoid steaming the crust and producing a soggy product.

Yeast breads are evaluated on the basis of exterior appearance and interior quality. Volume should be just over twice as large as the original dough. Shapes should be neatly executed and of uniform size. The crust is a pleasing, golden brown and slightly crisp rather than soggy. The interior should reveal uniform, medium-sized cells; the structure does not crumble readily when buttered, but still is tender. Excessive fermentation will cause the structure to be too porous and can even result in a fallen, heavy product. Too little volume is caused by inadequate rising time before baking or by killing the yeast during mixing. A dry, tough product results from incorporating too much flour in the dough. (Note: Quick-rise active dry yeast can be used to save preparation time. Follow package directions. When necessary, dough can be shaped immediately after mixing and allowed to rise only one time before baking.)

RECIPES

ROLLS

Total Time: approximately 2 1/2 hours
Baking: 425° F or 375° F oven for 12–20 minutes

1. Scald the milk until it clings to the sides of the pan.
2. Soften the yeast in the lukewarm water.
3. Meanwhile, put the sugar, salt, and margarine or butter in a mixing bowl, and add the scalded milk.
4. Stir with a wooden spoon to mix the ingredients and melt the margarine or butter.
5. Beat the egg well, and add to the milk mixture.
6. Stir in approximately 1/2 cup flour.
7. Check to be sure the mixture is no warmer than 105° F.
8. Add the flour gradually. When about half has been added, beat the dough vigorously for 3 minutes.
9. Continue adding flour to make a soft dough, yet one that can be handled without too much difficulty.
10. Put the dough out onto a floured bread board.
11. Lightly flour hands, and press dough into a ball.
12. Grasp the far side of the dough, and fold it over to meet the front edge. Push firmly with the heel of the hand.
13. Rotate the dough a quarter of a turn and repeat the kneading operation. Continue rotating the dough and kneading so that a rhythm develops.
14. Knead about 5 minutes until blisters can be seen just under the surface when the dough is stretched.
15. Put dough in a bowl, and oil the surface.
16. Cover the bowl with aluminum foil and put in a warm place. Allow the dough to rise until doubled in volume (about one hour).

(Makes 12 rolls)	
6 tbsp	milk, scalded
1	package active dry yeast
1/4 c	lukewarm water
1 1/2 tbsp	sugar
1/2 tsp	salt
1 1/2 tbsp	margarine or butter
1/2	egg
~2 c	unsifted all purpose flour

(Makes 24 rolls)	
3/4 c	milk, scalded
2	packages active dry yeast
1/2 c	lukewarm water
3 tbsp	sugar
1 tsp	salt
3 tbsp	margarine or butter
1	egg
~4 c	unsifted all purpose flour

17. Punch the dough down with the fist.
18. Pinch the dough in half and shape into rolls.
19. Arrange the rolls on baking pans, and put in a warm place for the second rising. Do not cover the rolls.
20. Let rise until doubled in volume (about 45 minutes).
21. During the last 10 minutes, preheat oven to 425° F for plain rolls or 375° F for sweet mixtures or raisins.
22. Bake about 12 minutes if baking at the higher temperature or 20 minutes at the lower one until golden brown.
23. Remove from pans; cool on rack or serve promptly.

BUTTERHORN ROLLS

Total Time: approximately 2 1/2 hours
Baking: 425° F oven for 12 minutes

1. Use the same procedure as outlined for rolls (see preceding recipe) to make the dough.
2. When dough is ready to be shaped, roll dough into 1/3–1/2" thick circles with diameter of approximately 8 inches.
3. With a table knife, cut dough into wedges about 3" wide on the perimeter.
4. Roll the dough from large end to the tip. Arrange on a baking sheet, allowing a couple of inches between rolls.
5. Let rolls double in volume, uncovered.
6. Preheat oven.
7. Bake at 425° F about 12 minutes.
8. Remove from pan to cool.

(Makes 14 rolls)

6 tbsp	milk, scalded
2 tbsp	lukewarm water
1	package active dry yeast
1/4 c	sugar
1/2 tsp	salt
1/4 c	margarine or butter
1 1/2	eggs
2 1/2–3 c	unsifted all purpose flour

(Makes 28 rolls)

3/4 c	milk, scalded
1/4 c	lukewarm water
2	packages active dry yeast
1/2 c	sugar
1 tsp	salt
1/2 c	margarine or butter
3	eggs
5–6 c	unsifted all purpose flour

SWEDISH RYE BATTER BREAD

Total Time: approximately 3 hours
Baking: 400° F oven for 30 minutes (small),
40 minutes (large)

1. Heat milk, water, and margarine or butter to 125° F.
2. While heating liquids, combine flours. Then put 1/3 of the flour in mixing bowl with sugar, salt, caraway seed, and dry yeast (not hydrated).
3. Gradually stir in the liquids; beat 2 minutes at medium speed on electric mixer.
4. Stir in enough of the flours to make stiff dough. Use additional all pupose flour if the flour mixture is inadequate.
5. Cover and set in warm place to double in volume (approximately 40 minutes).
6. Stir dough down. Transfer to greased 1-quart casserole (small) or 1 1/2-quart casserole (large).
7. Set in warm place to double in volume (approximately 20 minutes). Preheat oven to 400° F during last 10 minutes of rising.
8. Bake 30 minutes (small) or 40 minutes (large). Remove from pan and cool on wire rack.

Note: Dough can be kneaded on a mixer with a dough hook.

(Small loaf)

1/2 c	milk
1/2 c	water
1 tbsp	margarine or butter
1 3/4–2 c	unsifted all purpose flour
3/4 c	unsifted rye flour
2 2/3 tbsp	dark brown sugar
1 tsp	salt
1/2 tsp	caraway seeds
1	package dry yeast

(Large loaf)

1 c	milk
1 c	water
2 tbsp	margarine or butter
3 1/2–4 c	unsifted all purpose flour
1 1/2 c	unsifted rye flour
1/3 c	dark brown sugar
2 tsp	salt
1 tsp	caraway seeds
2	packages dry yeast

RAPID CINNAMON PINWHEELS

Total Time: 2 1/2 hours
Baking: 375° F oven for 20 minutes

1. Heat milk, water, and margarine or butter in saucepan to 125° F.
2. While heating the liquids, mix about 1/3 of the flour, sugar, salt, and dry (not hydrated) yeast in a mixing bowl.
3. Add the hot liquid and mix at medium speed on an electric mixer for 2 minutes.
4. Turn off the mixer to add the eggs and 1/4 c (1/2 c for large recipe) of flour. Beat 2 minutes at high speed. Stop the mixer every 30 seconds to scrape bowl with rubber spatula.
5. Stir in (by hand) enough flour to make a dough stiff enough to be kneaded.
6. Knead for 8 minutes before oiling the top of the ball of dough and placing it in a greased bowl.
7. Cover the bowl and place in a warm spot, out of drafts, until dough doubles in volume (about 40 minutes).
8. Punch the dough down and roll into a rectangle 10" x 12" (for large recipe divide dough in half and make 2 rectangles). Sprinkle with the sugar-cinnamon mixture and roll into a 12" log.
9. Slice log at 1" intervals. On a Teflon-lined baking sheet, arrange on their side to show the pinwheels, leaving a space of approximately 3/4" between rolls.
10. Rub the topping ingredients together in a small bowl until they are crumbly.
11. Sprinkle with the topping and let rise, uncovered, in a warm place until rolls double in volume. Preheat the oven to 375° F about 10 minutes before the dough has doubled.
12. Bake for 20 minutes or until a pleasing, golden brown. Cool on a rack.

Note: Dough may be prepared following the directions for rolls, rather than using Steps 1–7 in this recipe. The dough is then shaped and baked according to Steps 8–12.

(12 rolls)
Dough:

1/2 c	*milk*
6 tbsp	*water*
3 tbsp	*margarine or butter*
~3 1/2 c	*unsifted flour*
3 tbsp	*sugar*
3/4 tsp	*salt*
1	*package active dry yeast*
1 1/2	*eggs*
1 tsp	*ground cinnamon mixed with 2 tbsp sugar*

Topping:

2 2/3 tbsp	*flour*
2 2/3 tbsp	*brown sugar*
1/2 tsp	*cinnamon*
1 1/2 tbsp	*margarine or butter*

(24 rolls)
Dough:

1 c	milk
3/4 c	water
6 tbsp	margarine or butter
~7 c	unsifted flour
6 tbsp	sugar
1 1/2 tsp	salt
2	packages active dry yeast
3	eggs
2 tsp	ground cinnamon mixed with 1/4 c sugar

Topping:

1/3 c	flour
1/3 c	brown sugar
1 tsp	cinnamon
3 tbsp	margarine or butter

WHITE BREAD

Total Time: 2 3/4 hours
Baking: 400° F oven for 35 minutes

1. Scald the milk.
2. Soften the yeast in the lukewarm water while proceeding with the next step.
3. Put the sugar, salt, and margarine or butter in a mixing bowl, and pour the scalded milk in.
4. Stir with wooden spoon to mix the ingredients and melt the margarine or butter.
5. Stir in approximately 1/2 c flour.
6. Check to be sure the mixture is no warmer than 105° F before adding yeast.
7. Add the flour gradually.
8. When about half has been added, beat the dough vigorously about 3 minutes.
9. Continue adding flour to make a soft dough that can be handled without difficulty on the board.
10. Put the dough out onto a floured bread board.
11. Lightly flour the hands and press the dough into a ball.
12. Grasp the far side of the dough and fold it over to meet the fron tedge. Push firmly with the heel of the hand.
13. Rotate the dough and fold it over to meet the front edge. Push firmly with the heel of the hand.
14. Continue rotating the dough and kneading so that a rhythm develops. Knead about 5 minutes until blisters can be seen just under the surface when the dough is stretched.
15. Put the kneaded dough in a bowl, and lightly grease the surface with oil.
16. Cover the bowl with aluminum foil and put in a warm place. Allow the dough to rise until doubled in volume.
17. Punch the dough down with the fist. Pinch the dough in half if making the large recipe.
18. Roll the dough into a rectangle approximately 1/2" thick with one dimension about 3" longer than the length of the loaf pan.
19. Grasping the dough at one edge, roll it into a log.
20. Press both ends of the dough down firmly and then tuck the ends under the loaf and place the dough into a lightly greased loaf pan with the smoothest side of the loaf on top. If making the larger recipe, repeat this process with the other half of the dough.
21. Place the shaped bread dough, uncovered, in a warm place until the dough has again doubled in volume.
22. Preheat the oven to 400° F during the last 10 minutes of rising.
23. Bake for approximately 35 minutes. When the loaf comes from the oven, immediately remove the baked bread from the pans and cool on a wire rack to avoid developing a soggy crust.

(1 loaf)		
1 c	milk	
1	package active dry yeast	
2 tbsp	water, lukewarm	
1 tbsp	sugar	
3/4 tsp	salt	
1/2 tbsp	margarine or butter	
~3 c	unsifted all purpose flour	

(2 loaves)		
2 c	milk	
2	packages active dry yeast	
1/4 c	water, lukewarm	
2 tbsp	sugar	
1 1/2 tsp	salt	
1 tbsp	margarine or butter	
~6 c	unsifted all purpose flour	

FRENCH BREAD

Total Time: 2 1/2 hours
Baking: 375° F oven for 20 minutes

1. Dissolve yeast in lukewarm water.
2. Add remaining water, salt, and 1/3 of the flour.
3. Beat well.
4. Add as much of the remaining flour as can be stirred in with a wooden spoon.
5. Put dough on board, and knead in remaining flour.
6. Let rise until double.
7. Punch down, and divide in half if making large recipe.
8. Roll dough into 12x15" rectangle.
9. Roll into a log, and seal well.
10. Lightly grease cookie sheet over the area to be covered by the bread; sprinkle cornmeal over the greased area.
11. Place bread on cookie sheet. Score (cut slits in) the bread at an angle every 2 1/2".
12. Brush the surface with the mixture made by beating egg white and water.
13. Let rise until double in bulk.
14. Preheat the oven to 375° F during the last 10 minutes of rising.
15. Brush again lightly with egg white mixture and bake 20 minutes until golden brown.

(Makes 1 loaf)	
1	*package active dry yeast*
1/4 c	*lukewarm water*
1 c	*lukewarm water*
3/4 tsp	*salt*
3 1/2 c	*unsifted all purpose flour*
1 1/2 tsp	*cornmeal*
1/2	*egg white*
1 1/2 tsp	*water*

(Makes 2 loaves)	
2	packages active dry yeast
1/2 c	lukewarm water
2 c	lukewarm water
1 1/2 tsp	salt
7 c	unsifted all purpose flour
1 tbsp	cornmeal
1	egg white
1 tbsp	water

WHOLE WHEAT BREAD

Total Time: 3 hours
Baking: 375° F oven for 50 minutes

1. Dissolve yeast in lukewarm water.
2. Scald milk, and pour over sugar, salt, molasses, margarine or butter, and honey.
3. Cool to lukewarm before adding yeast, wheat germ, whole wheat flour, and 1/3 of the all purpose flour.
4. Beat well with a wooden spoon.
5. Add enough of remaining flour to make a stiff dough.
6. Let rest for 10 minutes before kneading thoroughly (approximately 10 minutes) to make a smooth, elastic dough.
7. Place dough in a bowl, grease the surface, and cover tightly.
8. Let rise until double in volume.
9. Punch down. Divide dough in half if making large recipe.
10. Roll into oblong rectangle about 3" wider than the length of a loaf pan.
11. Roll dough into a log, tucking the ends under to fit the loaf pan.
12. Place in lightly greased loaf pan and let rise, uncovered, until dough doubles.
13. Preheat oven to 375° F during the last 10 minutes rising time.
14. Bake for 50 minutes or until done.
15. Remove from pan and cool.

(Makes 1 loaf)	
1	*package active dry yeast*
1/2 c	*lukewarm water*
1/2 c	*milk*
2 tbsp	*brown sugar*
1/2 tsp	*salt*
1 1/2 tsp	*molasses*
2 tbsp	*margarine or butter*
1 1/2 tsp	*honey*
1/4 c	*wheat germ (optional)*
1 c	*sifted whole wheat flour*
~1 1/2 c	*unsifted all purpose flour*

(Makes 2 loaves)	
2	packages active dry yeast
1 c	lukewarm water
1 c	milk
1/4 c	brown sugar
1 tsp	salt
1 tbsp	molasses
1/4 c	margarine or butter
1 tbsp	honey
1/2 c	wheat germ (optional)
2 c	sifted whole wheat flour
~3 c	unsifted all purpose flour

CROISSANTS

Total Time: 3 hours
Baking: 375° F oven for 25 minutes

1. Cream butter or margarine and flour, and refrigerate (tightly covered).
2. Soften yeast in water.
3. Add sugar, salt, milk, and flour. Blend.
4. Knead dough on floured board, adding flour, as needed, to make a stiff dough.
5. Let rise 1 hour in covered bowl.
6. Punch dough down and roll into rectangle 1/4" thick.
7. Pat all of flour-butter mixture all over dough to within an inch of the edge.
8. Fold dough in half and roll into rectangle 1/4" thick.
9. Chill in freezer 15 minutes.
10. Fold each end of dough to center and roll into rectangle 1/4" thick. Repeat folding and rolling twice.
11. Refrigerate overnight, loosely wrapped, or proceed to shape dough.
12. Roll into 1/8" thick rectangle 5x15".
13. Cut into three 5" squares, and cut each square into triangles.
14. Roll triangles, starting from the long end.
15. Place on greased baking sheet.
16. Brush lightly with egg yolk and water mixture.
17. Let rise, uncovered, 1/2 hour; preheat oven to 375° F during last 10 minutes.
18. Bake to golden brown for 20–25 minutes.

(Makes 6 croissants)	
1/2 c	margarine or butter
1 1/4 tbsp	all purpose flour
1	package active dry yeast
1/4 c	lukewarm water
2 tsp	sugar
1/2 tsp	salt
6 tbsp	milk (lukewarm)
1 1/4 c	unsifted all purpose flour
1	egg yolk
1 tsp	water

(Makes 12 croissants)	
1 c	margarine or butter
2 1/2 tbsp	all purpose flour
2	packages active dry yeast
1/2 c	lukewarm water
4 tsp	sugar
1 tsp	salt
3/4 c	milk (lukewarm)
2 1/2 c	unsifted all purpose flour
2	egg yolks
2 tsp	water

PRUNE KOLACHEN

Total Time: 2 hours 15 minutes
Baking: 375° F oven for 15 minutes

1. Remove yeast from hot roll mix, and stir wheat germ into flour.
2. Soften yeast in lukewarm water.
3. Stir in eggs.
4. Beat in flour mixture.
5. With heels of hands, knead dough vigorously on a floured board until smooth and elastic.
6. Place into a greased bowl, cover with foil, and let rise in a warm place until double in bulk (about 1 hour).
7. Meanwhile, combine filling ingredients, and simmer until thick.
8. Cool quickly to room temperature.
9. Punch dough down when it has doubled; cut into 18 pieces.
10. Pat out dough to 3" rounds, and place on greased cookie sheets.
11. Press down center of each round of dough. Fill with cooled filling.
12. Let rise until double in bulk.
13. Bake in a preheated oven for 15 minutes or until richly browned.
14. While buns are baking, mash cream cheese, and beat in honey gradually.
15. Serve buns warm, topped with cream cheese mixture.

(Makes 9 buns)	
Dough:	
1/2	of 13.75 oz package hot roll mix
1/4 c	wheat germ
6 tbsp	lukewarm milk
1	egg, slightly beaten
Filling:	
1 c	pitted and chopped dried prunes
1/2	orange (washed and dried), chopped, rind and pulp
1/4 c	sugar
1/2 c	water
Topping:	
1/2	of 3 oz package cream cheese
2 tbsp	honey

(Makes 18 buns)	
Dough:	
1	13.75 oz package hot roll mix
1/2 c	wheat germ
3/4 c	lukewarm milk
2	eggs, slightly beaten
Filling:	
2 c	pitted and chopped dried prunes
1	orange (washed and dried), chopped, rind and pulp
1/2 c	sugar
1 c	water
Topping:	
1	3 oz package cream cheese
1/4 c	honey

BAGELS

Total Time: 2 hours
Baking: 450° F oven for 15 minutes

1. Soften yeast in the lukewarm water.
2. In a mixing bowl, combine flour, salt, sugar; then stir in the yeast and water mixture and salad oil.
3. Blend in egg, and stir to make soft ball.
4. Knead vigorously on floured board for 10 minutes, adding flour as necessary to make stiff dough.
5. Let rise in covered bowl for an hour.
6. Knead again until smooth and elastic.
7. Pinch off balls of dough 2" in diameter.
8. Roll between palms into ropes 3/4" in diameter and about 6" long.
9. Pinch ends together to form a doughnut-like shape.
10. Preheat oven to 450° F.
11. Drop carefully into boiling mixture of water and sugar.
12. With slotted spoon, turn over each bagel when it surfaces and cook second side 1 minutes.
13. Arrange bagels on greased cookie sheet and bake 12–15 minutes until golden brown.

(Makes 6 bagels)

1	*package active dry yeast*
1/2 c	*lukewarm water*
2 c	*unsifted all purpose flour*
3/4 tsp	*salt*
3/4 tsp	*sugar*
1 tbsp	*salad oil*
1	*egg, slightly beaten*
1 tbsp	*sugar*
1 qt	*boiling water*

(Makes 12 bagels)

2	packages active dry yeast
1 c	lukewarm water
4 c	unsifted all purpose flour
1 1/2 tsp	salt
1 1/2 tsp	sugar
2 tbsp	salad oil
2	eggs, slightly beaten
2 tbsp	sugar
1 qt	boiling water

VOCABULARY

Gluten

Leavening agent

Saccharomyces cerevisiae

Double-acting baking powder

Baking soda

Tartrate baking powder

Quick bread

Biscuit

Roll

Muffins

Carbon dioxide

EVALUATION OF LABORATORY PRODUCTS — YEAST BREADS

RECIPE	NOTES ON COLOR, TEXTURE, FLAVOR, OR OTHER QUALITIES	COMMENTS OR SUGGESTIONS FOR MAKING OR USING THIS PRODUCT IN THE FUTURE

Chapter 10
Cakes

Cakes are more delicate than breads because of their ingredients and their porportions; sugar content is considerably higher in cakes than in breads, and the fat content in cakes also usually is appreciably higher. These two ingredients interfere with the development of the gluten complex during mixing, which results in tender cakes with good volume. You will find that careful measuring of all of the ingredients is critical to success, because deviations from successful recipes can easily result in cakes that have such disappointing results as poor volume or toughness.

Be sure to use the exact ingredient that is specified in your recipe. Cake flour often is listed because it has a lower and more delicate gluten that promotes the desired tenderness sought in cakes. Beware of reaching for baking soda when the recipe says baking powder! Baking soda is an alkaline ingredient that leaves a soapy taste in a cake, a rather yellow color, and poor volume. Baking powder is a formula of an acid ingredient that reacts with the baking

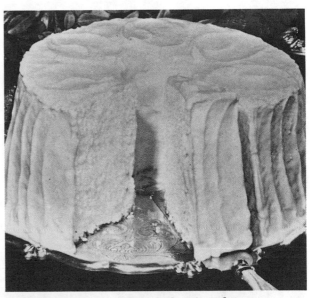

Angel cake is a light and pleasing dessert.

KEY CONCEPTS — CAKES

1) The two basic categories of cakes are: foam cakes and shortened cakes.

   a) The three types of foam cakes are: angel, sponge, and chiffon.

      1. Much of the volume is the result of a well-prepared foam either egg white and/or egg yolk.
      2. Little or no fat is contained in foam cakes.
      3. Foam cakes are cooled inverted to stretch their structure.

   b) Shortened cakes differ from foam cakes in fat content and leavening.

      1. Shortened cakes have a fairly high fat content (usually a solid fat that is creamed in), which results in a tender structure that needs to be cooled in an upright position.
      2. Baking powder or other potential source of carbon dioxide is the principal leavening agent in shortened cakes.

soda in the powder to produce carbon dioxide to leaven your cake. If you are making a cake that specifies baking soda, you will notice that there also is an acid ingredient such as sour cream to react with the soda. In this type of recipe, you will need to work rapidly to get the cake in the oven before all of the carbon dioxide resulting from the reaction of these ingredients escapes from the batter.

FOAM CAKES

TIPS ON PREPARING ANGEL, SPONGE, AND CHIFFON CAKES

Angel and other foam cakes in tube pans are baked with the oven rack in the next position below the center of the oven. In contrast with the baking of sponge and chiffon cakes, which are baked at 325° F, angel cakes are baked at 375° F. The oven is preheated to avoid loss of air from the foam.

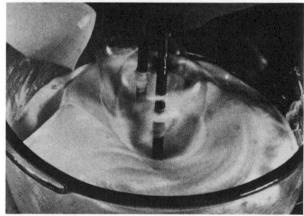

Formation of an excellent egg white foam is essential to preparation of any foam cake. Stability of the foam is enhanced by adding the cream of tartar all at once at the foamy stage (top left). Sugar then is added gradually while beating is continued. Unless a mixer with hypocycloidal action is being used, use a clean rubber spatula to continually scrape the egg white foam away from the edge of the bowl. This will help to promote uniform texture throughout the foam.

After the sugar has been added to the whites, beating of the egg white foam is continued on high speed until the foam reaches the right end point when tested by pulling the foam up into a peak with a rubber spatula. For angel and sponge cakes, the peak should just bend over. A chiffon cake requires a slightly stiffer foam, i.e., the peak stands up straight. Be sure to stop the mixer for this test. If the peak is soft, resume beating until the proper stage is reached. The proper extent of beating helps to stabilize the foam and to produce a cake of good volume and relatively fine texture.

Adequate (but not excessive or rough) folding with a rubber spatula is necessary in foam cakes to blend ingredients. A layer will tend to settle out in chiffon and sponge cakes if folding is inadequate or if baking is delayed.

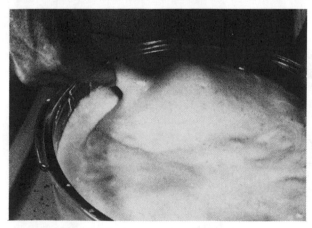

When the baking period has elapsed, foam cakes are tested carefully. Use a hot pad to pull the oven rack out gently. If the cake shakes as the shelf is moved, baking should be resumed immediately by pushing the shelf in and quickly closing the oven door. If the cake appears to be set, pull the rack out so that the surface of the cake can be touched lightly with a finger. When the cake is done, the surface will spring back.

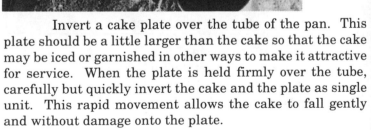

Foam cakes have a rather weak structure when they are hot. By cooling these cakes in an inverted position, the cake hangs suspended in the pan, and the weight of the cake itself pulls the cell walls down in an extended position. This allows the cake structure to be stretched; the cell walls thus are thinner and more tender than they would have been if the cake had been cooled in an upright position. The cake should be cooled to room temperature before being removed from the pan. The structure will then be set sufficiently to withstand the manipulation of the cake.

When the cake has cooled completely, the structure will be strong enough to turn the pan back to its upright position. With a thin, long-bladed knife, such as a slicer, cut carefully around the edges of the cake, being careful to free the cake both at the outer edge and around the tube.

Lift the cake and the tube portion of the pan out of the cake pan. Still using the slicer, slide the knife along the bottom surface of the pan to cut the cake completely free of the pan. Now the cake is ready for removal from the pan.

Invert a cake plate over the tube of the pan. This plate should be a little larger than the cake so that the cake may be iced or garnished in other ways to make it attractive for service. When the plate is held firmly over the tube, carefully but quickly invert the cake and the plate as single unit. This rapid movement allows the cake to fall gently and without damage onto the plate.

RECIPES
ANGEL CAKE

Total Time: 1 hour
Baking: 375° F oven for 25 minutes (loaf) or
35–40 minutes (large tube pan)

1. Preheat oven.
2. Sift the flour and sugar together three times.
3. On an electric mixer, beat the egg whites until foamy.
4. Add the salt, vanilla, and cream of tartar.
5. Continue beating while gradually adding the sugar. Beat the egg whites until the peaks just barely bend over.
6. Sift approximately 1/4 of the flour-sugar mixture over the surface of the egg white meringue.
7. With a rubber spatula, efficiently fold the flour into the egg whites, using two 5-stroke folding cycles for a total of 10 strokes.
8. Sift the second fourth of the flour over the surface of the egg whites and fold 10 more strokes.
9. Similarly, add the third and fourth quarters of the flour. Fold 10 strokes after the third addition. After the fourth addition, continue folding until all the ingredients are thoroughly blended in the cake.
10. Gently push the batter with the spatula into the ungreased baking pan, and bake (about 25 minutes for the loaf and 35–40 minutes for the large cake) in a preheated oven at 375° F until the top springs back when the cake is touched lightly with the finger.
11. Cool inverted, and then remove from pan.

(Use loaf pan)	
1/3 c	sifted cake flour
4 tbsp	sugar
1/2 c	(4) egg whites
	dash salt
1/2 tsp	vanilla
1/2 tsp	cream of tartar
4 tbsp	sugar

(Use 10" tube pan)	
2/3 c	sifted cake flour
3/4 c	sugar
1 c	(8) egg whites
1/8 tsp	salt
1 tsp	vanilla
1 tsp	cream of tartar
3/4 c	sugar

TRUE SPONGE CAKE

Total Time: 1 hour 30 minutes
Baking: 325° F oven for 35–40 minutes (small) or
1 hour (large)

1. Preheat oven.
2. With an electric mixer, beat egg yolks until very thick and lemon colored.
3. Add the water and continue beating until yolks pile.
4. Gradually add the sugar and the two extracts. Continue beating until the yolk mixture is thick enough to pile slightly.
5. Sift the salt with the flour. Sift one-fourth of this flour/salt mixture over the yolk mixture and fold in, using two 5-stroke folding cycles for a total of 10 strokes.
6. Similarly add the second, third, and fourth quarters of flour. Fold 10 strokes after all but the fourth addition. Continue folding after the fourth addition until all the flour is folded in.
7. Wash beater blades well and then use the electric mixer to beat egg whites to the foamy stage.
8. Add the cream of tartar; add sugar gradually while beating.
9. Continue beating until all the sugar is added and the peaks just bend over.
10. Fold the yolk and white mixtures together until completely blended.
11. Use a rubber spatula to push batter gently into ungreased pan.
12. Bake in center of oven preheated to 325° F.

(Use loaf pan)	
2	eggs, separated
2 2/3 tbsp	water
1/4 c	sugar
1/4 tsp	vanilla
1/4 tsp	lemon extract
1/2 c	sifted cake flour
	dash salt
1/4 c	sugar
1/4 tsp	cream of tartar

(Use 10" tube pan)	
6	eggs, separated
1/2 c	water
3/4 c	sugar
1/2 tsp	vanilla
1/2 tsp	lemon extract
1 1/2 c	sifted cake flour
1/4 tsp	salt
3/4 c	sugar
3/4 tsp	cream of tartar

13. Bake until the top springs back when lightly touched with the finger (about 40 minutes for small or 1 hour for large cake).
14. Cool in inverted position; remove from pan.

JELLY ROLL

Total Time: 35 minutes
Baking: 375° F oven for 12–15 minutes

1. Preheat oven.
2. Prepare cake batter, using directions for True Sponge Cake (previous recipe).
3. Bake in a Teflon-lined jelly roll pan or in a jelly roll pan lined with aluminum foil in a preheated oven at 375° F until golden brown and top springs back when touched lightly (about 12 minutes).
4. Immediately cut the cake loose from the sides of the pan and invert onto a dish towel lightly coated with powdered sugar. Remove foil if used.
5. Promptly roll the cake and the towel into a roll, rolling from the short side. Allow to cool in the rolled position.
6. When cool, unroll and spread the cake with the filling. Roll the cake and the filling (being sure to omit the towel).
7. Sprinkle powdered sugar lightly over the top. Refrigerate. (Freeze if filled with ice cream.)
8. Slice into 1" pinwheels and serve with whipped cream, fruit, or other topping.

(1 roll for 10 servings)
Batter:

3	eggs, separated
1/4 c	water
6 tbsp	sugar
1/4 tsp	vanilla
1/4 tsp	lemon extract
3/4 c	sifted cake flour
1/8 tsp	salt
6 tbsp	sugar
1/2 tsp	cream of tartar

Filling Suggestions:
  Ice cream or sherbet
  Sweetened whipped cream with sliced seasonal fruit (e.g., strawberries)
  Jam

HAWAIIAN JELLY ROLL

Total Time: 45 minutes
Baking: 375° F oven for 20 minutes

1. Preheat oven.
2. Prepare 15 1/2x10 1/2x1" jelly roll pan by spreading well-drained pineapple evenly over the pan and sprinkling with brown sugar.
3. Sift cake flour, baking powder, and salt together.
4. Beat yolks 10 minutes on mixer set at high speed.
5. Gradually beat in 1/4 c sugar and lemon flavoring.
6. Gently fold (steps 5 and 6 of True Sponge Cake recipe).
7. Wash beater blades in hot soapy water, rinse, and dry before beginning to beat egg whites in a clean bowl.
8. Beat on high speed to the foamy stage, and add the cream of tartar.
9. Beating at high speed, beat 15 seconds before gradually adding the remaining sugar. Beat until the peaks just fold over.
10. Gently fold the yolk mixture and whites together until no streaks remain.
11. Using a rubber spatula, gently spread over the pineapple.
12. Bake at 375° F 20 minutes (until cake springs back when touched).
13. Follow steps 3 through 7 in Jelly Roll recipe.

OPTIONAL PINEAPPLE SAUCE:

1. Prepare sauce, if desired. Mix sugar and cornstarch in saucepan, stirring thoroughly with wooden spoon.
2. Stir in reserved pineapple syrup until smooth.

(1 roll for 10 servings)

3 1/2 c	crushed pineapple, drained (reserve syrup)
1/2 c	brown sugar
1/4 c	sifted cake flour
1 tsp	baking powder
1/8 tsp	salt
4	eggs, separated
1/4 c	sugar
1/2 tsp	lemon flavoring
1/4 tsp	cream of tartar
1/2 c	sugar

Pineapple sauce (optional):

1 tbsp	sugar
1 tbsp	cornstarch
3/4 c	reserved pineapple syrup
2 tsp	lemon juice

3. Place over direct heat and stir constantly until the sauce thickens and boils in the middle of the pan.
4. Remove from heat, stir in lemon juice, and cool.
5. Spoon over individual slices of jelly roll.

FAVORITE CHIFFON CAKE

Total Time: 1 hour 30 minutes
Baking: 325° F oven for 35 minutes (small); 1 hour (large)

1. Preheat oven.
2. Sift the cake flour, sugar, salt, and baking powder in the smaller mixing bowl; make a well in the center.
3. Add coffee crystals, oil, yolks, vanilla, and water to the dry ingredients.
4. Beat until satin smooth on the electric mixer.
5. Stir in the chocolate. Wash beater blades.
6. On an electric mixer, beat egg whites in the larger bowl to foamy stage; and add cream of tartar.
7. Beat at high speed 15 seconds before gradually adding the sugar.
8. Beat whites until the peaks just stand straight, without bending over at all.
9. Pour the batter over the whites and carefully, but efficiently fold until no fluid remains in the bottom of the bowl and the entire mixture is homogeneous. Use the 5-stroke folding technique.
10. Scrape batter into ungreased baking pan and bake in a 325° F oven until cake springs back when touched lightly (about 35 minutes for the small or 1 hour for the large cake).
11. Cool inverted, and then remove from pan.

(Use loaf pan)

1 1/8 c	sifted cake flour
1/4 c	sugar
1/2 tsp	salt
1 1/2 tsp	baking powder
2 tsp	freeze-dried coffee
1/4 c	salad oil
2	egg yolks
1/2 tsp	vanilla
6 tbsp	water
1 1/2 oz	semisweet chocolate, grated
4	egg whites
1/4 tsp	cream of tartar
1/2 c	sugar

(Use 10" tube pan)

2 1/4 c	sifted cake flour
1/2 c	sugar
1 tsp	salt
1 tbsp	baking powder
4 tsp	freeze-dried coffee
1/2 c	salad oil
4	egg yolks
1 tsp	vanilla
3/4 c	water
3 oz	semisweet chocolate, grated
8	egg whites
1/2 tsp	cream of tartar
1 c	sugar

BURNT-SUGAR PECAN CHIFFON CAKE

Total Time: 1 hour 30 minutes
Baking: 325° F oven for 35 minutes (small); 1 hour (large)

1. Preheat oven.
2. Prepare a burnt-sugar syrup, using the first two ingredients, as follows: melt the sugar in a heavy skillet, while stirring constantly with a wooden spoon; heat and continue stirring until sugar becomes a deep golden brown; immediately carry the skillet to the sink, and add boiling water; dissolve the sugar, reheating, if necessary. Measure 3 tbsp syrup for the loaf or 6 tbsp for the large cake and set aside. Save the rest for the icing.
3. Sift the cake flour, sugar, baking powder, and salt together into the smaller mixing bowl.
4. Make a well and add the oil, yolks, water, vanilla, and 3 tbsp (loaf) or 6 tbsp (tube) of the burnt sugar syrup from Step 1.
5. Beat on an electric mixer until satin smooth. Wash beaters.
6. Beat egg whites in larger bowl to foamy stage, using the electric mixer.

(Use loaf pan)

3 tbsp	sugar
1/4 c	water, boiling
1 1/8 c	sifted cake flour
1/4 c	sugar
1 1/2 tsp	baking powder
1/2 tsp	salt
1/4 c	salad oil
2	egg yolks
3 tbsp	water
1/2 tsp	vanilla
3 tbsp	burnt sugar syrup (from Step 1)
4	egg whites
1/2 c	sugar
1/4 tsp	cream of tartar
1/2 c	chopped pecans

7. Add the cream of tartar and gradually begin adding the sugar.
8. Beat the egg whites until the peaks stand up straight.
9. Pour the batter over the egg whites, and sprinkle the nuts over the surface.
10. Fold with a rubber spatula until no fluid remains in the bottom of the bowl and the entire mixture is homogenous.
11. Transfer to ungreased baking pan and immediately start baking.
12. Bake at 325° F until the cake springs back when the surface is lightly touched (about 35 minutes for small and 1 hour for large cake).
13. Cool inverted, and then remove from pan.

(Use 10" tube pan)

6 tbsp	sugar
1/2 c	water, boiling
2 1/4 c	sifted cake flour
1/2 c	sugar
1 tbsp	baking powder
1 tsp	salt
1/2 c	salad oil
5	egg yolks
6 tbsp	water
1 tsp	vanilla
6 tbsp	burnt sugar syrup (from Step 1)
8	egg whites
1 c	sugar
1/2 tsp	cream of tartar
1 c	chopped pecans

The first step in preparing this cake is to caramelize the sugar by placing it in a small skillet and heating it while stirring constantly with a wooden spoon. As the sugar is heated, it will begin to melt and change color from colorless to a gradually deepening caramel color.

When the sugar is being caramelized, bring the water to an active boil in preparation for adding to the caramelized sugar. The sugar is heated alone until the melted sugar is a deep golden brown color, at which time the skillet is removed from the heat and carried to the sink where the boiling water is added quickly to halt the carmelizing of the sugar. The addition of the water to the extremely hot sugar will cause some splattering. The sugar will solidify, but can be melted in the water with a little stirring and heating. This caramelized sugar syrup is set aside until later, when the amount needed for the recipe is measured and added to the other ingredients. The remaining syrup can be used to make a powdered sugar glaze for the cake.

LEMON CHIFFON CAKE

Total Time: 1 hour 30 minutes
Baking: 325° F oven for 35 minutes (small); 1 hour (large)

1. Preheat oven.
2. Sift cake flour, sugar, salt, and baking powder into smaller mixing bowl; make well in center.
3. Add oil, egg yolks, vanilla, water, and lemon rind. Beat until satin smooth.
4. Wash beater blades. Beat egg whites in the larger mixer bowl to the foamy stage, using electric mixer.
5. Add cream of tartar and begin adding the sugar gradually. Beat until peaks stand up straight.
6. Pour batter over whites. Fold (using 5-stroke method) until mixture is homogeneous and no fluid is in the bottom.
7. Pour into ungreased pan gently. Bake immediately at 325° F until cake springs back when touched lightly (about 35 minutes for small or 1 hour for large cake).
8. Cool inverted; remove from pan.

(Use loaf pan)	
1 1/8 c	*sifted cake flour*
1/4 c	*sugar*
1/2 tsp	*salt*
1 1/2 tsp	*baking powder*
1/4 c	*salad oil*
2	*egg yolks*
1/2 tsp	*vanilla*
6 tbsp	*water*
1 tsp	*grated lemon rind*
1/4 tsp	*cream of tartar*
4	*egg whites*
1/2 c	*sugar*

(Use 10" tube pan)	
2 1/4 c	sifted cake flour
1/2 c	sugar
1 tsp	salt
1 tbsp	baking powder
1/2 c	salad oil
4	egg yolks
1 tsp	vanilla
3/4 c	water
2 tsp	grated lemon rind
1/2 tsp	cream of tartar
8	egg whites
1 c	sugar

ZIPPY COCOA CHIFFON CAKE

Total Time: 1 hour
Baking: 350° F oven for 30–35 minutes

1. Preheat oven.
2. In a bowl, stir boiling water into cocoa; cool.
3. Sift cake flour, 6 tbsp sugar, cinnamon, baking powder, and salt into mixing bowl.
4. Make a well; add salad oil, unbeaten yolks, vanilla, and cooled cocoa mixture.
5. Beat on electric mixer until satin smooth.
6. Wash beater blades. Beat egg whites in clean bowl on electric mixer set at high speed until foamy.
7. Add cream of tartar.
8. Beating at high speed, beat 15 seconds before gradually adding 1/2 c sugar. Beat until peaks stand up straight.
9. Gently pour the yolk mixture over the whites. Fold (using 5-stroke method) until mixture is homogeneous and no fluid is in the bottom.
10. Pour into a 9" square, ungreased cake pan lined with waxed paper on the bottom.
11. Bake immediately at 350° F for 30–35 minutes until cake springs back when touched lightly.
12. Cool inverted; remove from pan while still very slightly warm.

(Serves 9)	
3/8 c	*boiling water*
1/4 c	*cocoa*
7/8 c	*sifted cake flour*
6 tbsp	*sugar*
1/2 tsp	*cinnamon*
1 1/2 tsp	*baking powder*
1/4 tsp	*salt*
1/4 c	*salad oil*
4	*eggs, separated*
1/2 tsp	*vanilla*
1/4 tsp	*cream of tartar*
1/2 c	*sugar*

SHORTENED CAKES

Shortened cakes may be made by various methods, including the conventional, modified conventional, conventional sponge, muffin, and single stage methods. The conventional method and its variations have the advantage of producing cakes with excellent texture and keeping quality, but these methods have the disadvantage of requiring a relatively long mixing period. By comparison, the muffin and single-stage methods are quick to prepare, but the texture will be more porous, and the crumb stales quickly.

The conventional method is used to prepare cakes of high quality. Ingredients for a plain cake prepared by the conventional method are 1/2 c shortening, 1 c sugar, 1 tsp vanilla, 2 eggs, 2 c sifted cake flour, 2 tsp baking powder, 1/2 tsp salt, and 1 c milk.

Check to be sure that the oven rack is in the center position before preheating the oven to 350° F. This moderate oven temperature is appropriate for cakes because there is time for the baking powder in the batter to become activated by oven heat and release carbon dioxide to help stretch out the cell walls and produce a good volume before the protein in the walls coagulates and loses its elasticity.

One way of preparing cake pans for easy removal of the baked cake is to line the bottom of the pan with wax paper. This is done quickly by placing the pan on top of a sheet of wax paper, tracing a pattern around the edge of the pan with the tip of a pair of scissors, and then cutting out the pattern just inside the traced line. Two thicknesses of paper may be cut at one time when a layer cake is being prepared. A single layer of the paper then is fitted into the bottom of the pan. The paper should cover the bottom of the pan, but not curl up the sides. Pans need not be greased. The ungreased sides make it possible for the rising cake to cling to the sides and pull up. The wax paper is sufficient help in releasing the bottom of the cake from the pan so that greasing is not needed on the bottom either.

Cream the shortening and sugar together, adding the vanilla after all the sugar has been incorporated. Creaming may be done using an electric mixer or a wooden spoon. This is a vigorous process designed to produce an air-in-fat foam. The sugar granules help to trap very small pockets of air in the fat, resulting in a rather heavy foam which will be of value in producing a cake with a fine texture. Creaming is continued until the foam is comparatively light.

After being beaten well with a rotary egg beater, the eggs are beaten into the fat foam with the aid of either a wooden spoon or an electric mixer. The emulsifying ability of the egg yolk will be an aid in mixing the egg into the foam. This capability also is used later in helping to form an emulsion with milk.

The dry ingredients are sifted together 3 times as an aid in blending the cake flour, baking powder, and salt together throroughly before the proteins in the flour come into contact with liquid, and gluten development begins. Sifting is of particular importance in helping to distribute the baking powder widely throughout the flour. This is an aid in obtaining uniform leavening in the cake.

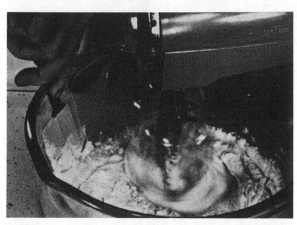

The next addition to the egg-fat foam mixture is approximately a third of the dry ingredients. These ingredients are beaten together just until the batter becomes smooth again. The mixture is quite viscous, but there is enough liquid present from the eggs for some gluten development in the flour to occur. This amount of flour gives a mixture that usually will not curdle when some milk is added.

Half the milk is added and stirred in slowly with either an electric mixer or a wooden spoon. When the excess liquid has been blended with the batter, the mixture is beaten again until smooth. Gluten develops reasonably well at this point because of the increased fluidity of the batter. However, the amounts of shortening and sugar in the batter do retard gluten development. The shortening apparently causes the gluten strands to slide by each other with some ease rather than creating a sticky, stretching environment. Sugar, because of its hygroscopic nature, binds some of the liquid, thus impeding gluten development a little.

The second third of the sifted dry ingredients is added and stirred in slowly until all of the flour is incorporated. Again, the mixture is beaten until smooth. Gluten continues to be developed whenever the batter is mixed. Excessive gluten development will produce a tough cake with some tunnels or passages where gas collects during baking and forces its way upward along strands of very well-developed gluten.

 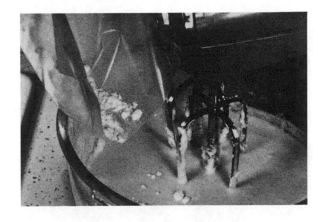

The last half of the milk is added to this viscous batter. The milk is stirred in carefully, and the mixture is beaten again. This is a point in the mixing when gluten develops well. Hence, beating is continued only until the batter is smooth.

The final addition of dry ingredients then is made. Again, the flour is stirred in carefully, and the mixture is beaten until smooth. Although the gluten in cake flour is neither as abundant nor as strong as the gluten in all purpose flour, the mixing described above in this conventional method of making shortened cakes is sufficient to produce a cake that will be tender, yet not be crumbly.

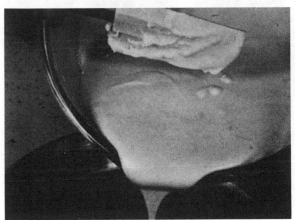

When making a layer cake, pour half the batter into each of the pans which previously were lined with wax paper. Since the cakes will just about double in volume during baking, the pans should be no more than half full. This will produce a cake with a flat surface, one which will not overflow the pan before the structure can set.

Both cake pans are placed on the oven rack at the same time. With the aid of a hot pad, the rack

should be pulled out and the cake pans arranged so that air can circulate freely between the two pans and between the pans and the front, back, and sides of the oven. Free circulation of air is essential for uniform heat distribution to all areas of the cakes. When cake pans block convection currents, the cakes will bake unevenly and will not brown well. With proper placement of pans, a well insulated oven, and a tightly-fitted door, the front and back cakes should bake at the same rate so that they can be removed from the oven at the same time. Layer cakes bake in approximately 30 minutes.

A shortened cake is done when a toothpick can be inserted in the center of the cake and removed without cake clinging to it. This test determines that the protein structure throughout the cake is denatured to the point where the protein structure is rigid enough to hold up the cake even when the hot, expanded gases contract and reduce the pressure holding each cell wall in an extended position. If the cake is pulling away from the sides of the pan when the cake is tested, remove the cake at once. This shrinking actually indicates over-baking.

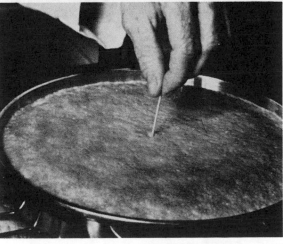

After the cakes have cooled about 5 minutes, they are ready to be removed from the pans. This is done by releasing the cake all the way around the edge with a table knife. Place a cooling rack or plate on top of the layer cake. Invert the cake pan so that the rack is on the bottom, and the cake rests on it. The pan can be removed now while the wax on the paper is still warm and soft. The wax paper layer simply is peeled carefully off the cake.

The *muffin method* for cakes is basically the same as for making muffins although more mixing is required to develop the necessary gluten in cakes. The dry ingredients are sifted together in a mixing bowl, and a well is made in the center. Since the shortening will be considered a liquid in this method, it must be liquified by melting before being combined with the other liquids and beaten eggs. All of the liquid is poured at one time into the dry ingredients, and the batter is beaten for 2 minutes to develop a smooth batter and develop the gluten. The finished batter is baked in the conventional way.

A *single-stage cake* is made with the aid of an electric mixer because the first part of the mixing forms quite a stiff batter which is hard to mix by hand. All the dry ingredients, flavorings, shortening, and 2/3 c milk are put in the mixer's large bowl and beaten at medium speed for 2 minutes.

Preparation of the batter for a cake made by the single-stage method is completed by adding the remaining 1/3 c milk and 4 egg yolks, and then beating for 2 more minutes at medium speed. The batter is poured into two 8" layer cake pans and baked at 350° F for 30 minutes.

ADJUSTMENTS FOR ALTITUDE[1]

INGREDIENT MODIFICATION	3,000 FT	5,000 FT	7,000 FT
For each teaspoon baking powder, *reduce*	*1/8 tsp*	*1/8–1/4 tsp*	*1/4 tsp*
For each cup sugar, *reduce*	*0–1 tbsp*	*0–2 tbsp*	*1–3 tbsp*
For each cup of liquid, *increase*	*1–2 tbsp*	*2–4 tbsp*	*3–4 tbsp*

[1]*Courtesy of Patricia Kendall, Colorado State University.*

PLAIN CAKE (CONVENTIONAL METHOD)

Total Time: 45 minutes
Baking: 350° F oven for 30 minutes

1. Preheat oven.
2. Prepare cake pan(s) by tracing a pattern around the pan onto waxed paper, using a scissors' tip.
3. Cut out the pattern, and fit the wax paper into the pan, being sure that the paper fits the bottom but does not go up the side at all. Do not grease the pan(s).
4. If available, use an electric mixer to cream shortening and sugar until light and fluffy.
5. Add vanilla and well-beaten egg; beat well.
6. Sift the dry ingredients together three times.
7. Add 1/3 of the dry ingredients to the creamed mixture and beat briefly.
8. Add 1/2 of the milk and beat briefly.
9. Add the second third of the dry ingredients, the last half of the milk, and the final third of the dry ingredients, beating after each addition.
10. Pour into pan(s) and bake for 30 minutes at 350° F.
11. Test for doneness by inserting a toothpick in the center of the cake. When it comes out clean, the cake is done. The cake is overbaked if it is pulling away from the sides of the pan.
12. Cool in pan (upright) on rack for 5 minutes.
13. Cut around the edge of the cake with a sharp knife.
14. Invert layer onto a plate, and peel off wax paper.

(Makes one 8" layer)	
1/4 c	shortening
1/2 c	sugar
1/2 tsp	vanilla
1	egg
1 c	sifted cake flour
1 tsp	baking powder
1/4 tsp	salt
1/2 c	milk

(Makes two 8" layers)	
1/2 c	shortening
1 c	sugar
1 tsp	vanilla
2	eggs
2 c	sifted cake flour
2 tsp	baking powder
1/2 tsp	salt
1 c	milk

CHOCOLATE CAKE (MODIFIED CONVENTIONAL METHOD)

Total Time: 45 minutes
Baking: 350° F oven for 30 minutes

1. Preheat oven.
2. Prepare cake pan(s) for plain cake.
3. Melt the chocolate over hot water and set aside to cool.
4. Cream the butter or margarine with the sugar (use an electric mixer, if available).
5. Beat in the vanilla and beaten egg yolks.
6. Stir in the melted chocolate.
7. Sift the cake flour, soda, and salt together.
8. Add 1/3 of the dry ingredients and beat with the electric mixer until completely blended.
9. Add half the water and beat.
10. Add the second third of the dry ingredients, the last half of the water, and the final third of the dry ingredients, beating after each addition.
11. Use a rotary egg beater to beat the egg whites until the peaks just bend over.
12. With the aid of a rubber spatula, gently transfer the foam to the top of the batter. Fold gently and quickly with the spatula just until completely blended, using the 5-stroke folding cycle.
13. Pour into round cake pan(s) and bake for 30 minutes at 350° F until a toothpick inserted in the center comes out clean.
14. Cool 5 minutes upright on the rack.
15. Cut around the edge of the cake with sharp knife.
16. Invert a plate over the pan; quickly flip the cake and plate. Remove pan and wax paper.

(Makes one 9" layer)	
1/3 c	butter or margarine
14 tbsp	sugar
1	egg, separated
1/2 tsp	vanilla
1 oz	unsweetened chocolate
1 1/4 c	sifted cake flour
5/8 tsp	baking powder
1/4 tsp	salt
10 tbsp	water

(Makes two 9" layers)	
2/3 c	butter or margarine
1 3/4 c	sugar
2	eggs, separated
1 tsp	vanilla
2 oz	unsweetened chocolate
2 1/2 c	sifted cake flour
1 1/4 tsp	baking powder
1/2 tsp	salt
1 1/4 c	water

WHITE CAKE (CONVENTIONAL SPONGE OR MERINGUE METHOD)

Total Time: 40 minutes
Baking: 375° F oven for 20 minutes

1. Preheat oven.
2. Prepare cake pan(s) for plain cake.
3. If available, use an electric mixer to cream the short-eining, sugar, and vanilla together until light and fluffy.
4. Sift flour, baking powder, and salt together.
5. Add 1/3 of the dry ingredients to the creamed mixture and beat with an electric mixer.
6. Add 1/2 of the milk and beat.
7. Add the second third of the dry ingredients, the last half of the milk, and the remaining third of the dry ingredients, beating after each addition.
8. Wash the beater blades of the mixer thoroughly before using to beat the egg whites to the foamy stage.
9. Gradually add the sugar while beating the whites until the peaks just bend over.
10. Transfer all of the egg white foam to the cake batter at once; use a rubber spatula to gently fold whites into batter until no traces of whites remain.
11. Pour into 9" round cake pan(s) and bake at 375° F.
12. Place gently on a rack and cool 5 minutes.
13. Cut around the edge of the cake with a sharp knife.
14. Invert a plate over the pan; quickly flip the cake and plate. Remove pan and wax paper.

(Makes one 9" layer)

6 tbsp	shortening
6 tbsp	sugar
3/4 tsp	vanilla
1 1/8 c	sifted cake flour
1 1/2 tsp	baking powder
1/2 tsp	salt
1/2 c	milk
2	egg whites
6 tbsp	sugar

(Makes two 9" layers)

3/4 c	shortening
3/4 c	sugar
1 1/2 tsp	vanilla
2 1/4 c	sifted cake flour
1 tbsp	baking powder
1 tsp	salt
1 c	milk
5	egg whites
3/4 c	sugar

GINGERBREAD (MUFFIN METHOD)

Total Time: 45–55 minutes
Baking: 375° F oven for 35–45 minutes

1. Preheat oven.
2. Prepare cake pan(s) by lightly greasing the bottom, but not the sides.
3. Sift flour, brown sugar, cinnamon, ginger, soda, and salt together into a mixing bowl, and make a well in the center. Set aside.
4. Melt the shortening.
5. Mix the molasses and hot water.
6. Stir in the beaten egg.
7. Pour the liquid ingredients into the dry ingredients, all at once.
8. Mix well to make a smooth batter.
9. Pour the batter into the pan, and bake 35–45 minutes at 375° F, until a toothpick inserted in the center comes out clean.
10. Place pan on rack to cool. Leave gingerbread in pan for easy service and storage.

(Makes one 8" square cake pan)

1 1/2 c	sifted all purpose flour
1/2 c	brown sugar
1 tsp	cinnamon
1 tsp	ginger
1 tsp	soda
1/8 tsp	salt
1/2 c	shortening
1/2 c	molasses
2/3 c	hot water
1	egg, beaten

(Makes one 13x9 1/2" rectangular cake pan)

3 c	sifted all purpose flour
1 c	brown sugar
2 tsp	cinnamon
2 tsp	ginger
2 tsp	soda
1/4 tsp	salt
1 c	shortening
1 c	molasses
1 1/3 c	hot water
2	eggs, beaten

GOLDEN YOLK CAKE (SINGLE-STAGE METHOD)

Total Time: 45 minutes
Baking: 350° F oven for 30 minutes

1. Preheat oven.
2. Prepare cake pan(s) by using scissors' tip to trace a pattern around the pan onto wax paper. Cut out the pattern and fit the wax paper into the pan(s), being sure that the paper fits the bottom of the pan and does not go up the sides at all. Do not grease the pan(s).
3. Sift the flour, sugar, baking powder, and salt into the mixing bowl.
4. Add the shortening, 2/3 of the milk, the extract, and grated rind, and beat at medium speed on an electric mixer for 2 minutes.
5. Add the last third of the milk and the egg yolks, and beat 2 more minutes at medium speed.
6. Pour into cake pan(s) and bake for 30 minutes at 350° F, until a toothpick comes out clean.
7. Place gently on a rack and cool 5 minutes.
8. Cut around the edge of the cake with a sharp knife.
9. Invert a plate over the pan; quickly flip the cake and plate while holding firmly.
10. Remove the pan and wax paper.

(Makes one 8" layer)

1 c	sifted cake flour
2/3 c	sugar
1 1/2 tsp	baking powder
3/8 tsp	salt
2 2/3 tbsp	shortening (room temperature)
1/3 c	milk
1/8 tsp	lemon extract
1/2 tsp	grated lemon rind
2 2/3 tbsp	milk
2	egg yolks

(Makes two 8" layers)

2 c	sifted cake flour
1 1/3 c	sugar
1 tbsp	baking powder
3/4 tsp	salt
1/3 c	shortening (room temperature)
2/3 c	milk
1/4 tsp	lemon extract
1 tsp	grated lemon rind
1/3 c	milk
4	egg yolks

PRUNE BANANA CAKE

Total Time: 1 hour
Baking: 350° F oven for 30 minutes (small);
35–40 minutes (large)

1. Simmer prunes 10 minutes in water to cover.
2. Preheat oven.
3. Grease the bottom of the pan.
4. Sift dry ingredients into large mixing bowl.
5. Add shortening, milk, and vanilla.
6. Mash bananas and add to mixture. Beat at medium speed for 2 minutes.
7. Add eggs; beat 2 minutes.
8. Chop prunes; add prunes and walnuts to batter, stirring in by hand.
9. Pour into baking pan. Bake at 350° F until toothpick inserted in center comes out clean (30 minutes for small and 35–40 minutes for large).

(Makes 8x8" cake)

1/2 c	stewed prunes
1 c	sifted cake flour
3/4 tsp	baking powder
1/2 tsp	soda
1/2 tsp	salt
2/3 c	sugar
1/4 c	shortening
2 tbsp	milk
1/2 tsp	vanilla
1/2 c	mashed bananas
1	egg
1/4 c	chopped walnuts

(Makes 9x13" cake)

1 c	stewed prunes
2 c	sifted cake flour
1 1/2 tsp	baking powder
1 tsp	soda
1 tsp	salt
1 1/3 c	sugar
1/2 c	shortening
1/4 c	milk
1 tsp	vanilla
1 c	mashed bananas
2	eggs
1/2 c	chopped walnuts

SPICE CAKE

Total Time: 40 minutes
Baking: 350° F oven for 20–25 minutes

1. Preheat oven.
2. Prepare pan(s) as for plain cake.
3. Cream fat, spices, and sugars until light.
4. Beat in the eggs.
5. Sift together the flour, baking powder, and salt. Add a fourth of this to the mixing bowl; stir 35 strokes.
6. Add a third of the milk; stir 15 strokes.
7. Continue adding flour by fourths and milk by thirds, stirring 35 strokes after flour additions and 15 strokes after milk additions.
8. Stir 140 strokes after last addition.
9. Pour into pan(s) and bake 20–25 minutes until toothpick inserted in center comes out clean.
10. Cool upright on rack 5 minutes.
11. With a sharp knife, cut around the edge of the cake to loosen it.
12. Place a plate over the cake, invert the cake, and remove the wax paper.

(Makes 8x8" cake)

1/4 c	shortening
1/2 tsp	ground cloves
1/2 tsp	nutmeg
1/2 tsp	cinnamon
1/4 c	brown sugar
1/2 c	granulated sugar
1 1/2	eggs
1 c 2 tbsp	sifted cake flour
1 1/2 tsp	baking powder
1/4 tsp	salt

(Makes 9x13" cake)

1/2 c	shortening
1 tsp	ground cloves
1 tsp	nutmeg
1 tsp	cinnamon
1/2 c	brown sugar
1 c	granulated sugar
3	eggs
2 1/4 c	sifted cake flour
1 tbsp	baking powder
1/2 tsp	salt

POUND CAKE

Total Time: 1 hour 15 minutes (small);
1 hour 35 minutes (large)
Baking: 350° F oven for 1 hour (small);
1 hour 20 minutes (large)

1. Preheat oven.
2. Grease the bottom of the pan.
3. Cream sugar, shortening, margarine or butter, and lemon rind on an electric mixer until fluffy.
4. Slowly beat in the milk, beating until mixture is smooth.
5. Sift the dry ingredients together and add to the mixing bowl.
6. Beat 2 minutes on an electric mixer (use setting for beating cakes).
7. Add 1/3 of the egg and beat for a minute.
8. Add the second and third portions of egg, beating one minute after each addition. Bake in loaf pan at 300° F for about 1 hour for small or 1 hour 20 minutes for large cake (until a toothpick inserted in the center comes out clean).

(Makes 8 1/2x4 1/2x3" loaf pan)

10 tbsp	sugar
2 2/3 tbsp	shortening
2 2/3 tbsp	margarine or butter
1/2 tsp	grated lemon rind
5 tbsp	milk
1 1/8 c	sifted cake flour
1/2 tsp	salt
3/4 tsp	baking powder
1 1/2	eggs

(Makes 9 1/2x5x3" loaf pan)

1 1/4 c	sugar
1/3 c	shortening
1/3 c	margarine or butter
1 tsp	grated lemon rind
2/3 c	milk
2 1/4 c	sifted cake flour
1 tsp	salt
1 1/2 tsp	baking powder
3	eggs

HOMEY GINGERBREAD

Total Time: 1 hour
Baking: 350° F oven for 35–40 minutes

1. Preheat oven.
2. Lightly grease an 8" square pan.
3. Cream shortening and sugar until light and fluffy, using electric mixer.
4. Add egg and molasses.
5. Sift the dry ingredients together before adding 1/3 of the dry ingredients to the molasses mixture. Beat in.
6. Add 1/2 of the boiling water, beating 30 seconds.
7. Add the second third of the dry ingredients; and beat in.
8. Add the last half of the boiling water, beating 30 seconds.
9. Add the final third of the dry ingredients, and beat just until smooth.
10. Pour into cake pan and bake 35–40 minutes (until toothpick inserted in center comes out clean).

(Serves 8)	
1/2 c	shortening
1/2 c	sugar
1	egg
1/2 c	molasses
1 1/2 c	sifted all purpose flour
1/4 tsp	salt
3/4 tsp	baking soda
1/2 tsp	ground ginger
1/2 tsp	cinnamon
1/2 c	boiling water

POPPY SEED BUNDT CAKE

Total Time: 1 hour 15 minutes
Baking: 350° F oven for 1 hour or until done

1. Preheat oven.
2. Spray 3-quart Bundt pan (or tube pan) with no-stick cooking spray.
3. Cream butter and 1 cup sugar on electric mixer until fluffy.
4. Add poppy seed filling and blend.
5. Beat in egg yolks, one at a time with the mixer running.
6. Blend in the sour cream and vanilla.
7. Stir flour, baking soda, and salt together before gradually adding to poppy seed mixture; beat until blended.
8. In clean bowl and with clean beaters, beat egg whites to the foamy stage, using electric mixer. Gradually add 1/2 c sugar while continuing to beat on high speed. Beat until peaks just bend over.
9. Add whites to batter by carefully folding until mixture is homogeneous.
10. Transfer batter to baking pan and bake 1 hour until a toothpick inserted in center comes out clean.
11. Cool upright 10 minutes before removing from pan.

(Serves 16)	
1 c	butter or margarine
1 c	sugar
1	can poppy seed filling (generally found with Kosher foods in grocery store)
4	eggs, separated
1 c	sour cream
1 tsp	vanilla
2 1/2 c	all purpose flour
1 tsp	baking soda
1 tsp	salt
1/2 c	sugar

ICING RECIPES

MARSHMALLOW FROSTING

1. Beat egg whites and salt on electric mixer and gradually add sugar while continuing to beat on high speed.
2. When peaks form, begin adding the corn syrup very slowly while continuing beating on high speed.
3. Beat until firmly peaked before adding vanilla.

(Icing for 2 layers)	
1/4 tsp	salt
2	egg whites
1/4 c	sugar
3/4 c	light corn syrup
1 1/4 tsp	vanilla

NEVER FAIL ICING

1. Cream the butter or margarine until soft.
2. Add the sugar, vanilla, and milk.
3. Beat with an electric mixer, slowly at first, until the mixture is light and creamy.
4. If necessary, gradually add more milk to achieve the desired spreading consistency. Food coloring can be used to vary the color, as desired.

Note: This icing may be varied by adding grated lemon rind, grated orange rind, or 2 oz of melted chocolate chips. Icing may be used between layers; jams, marmalade, or cream pudding also make suitable fillings. If a cream pudding filling is used, the cake must be refrigerated to avoid growth of harmful levels of microorganisms.

(Icing for 1 layer)	
2 tbsp	*butter or margarine*
2 1/4 c	*powdered sugar, sifted*
1/2 tsp	*vanilla*
1 1/2 tbsp	*milk*

(Icing for 2 layers)	
1/4 c	butter or margarine
4 1/2 c	powdered sugar, sifted
1 tsp	vanilla
3 tbsp	milk

SEVEN-MINUTE FROSTING

1. Beat egg white, sugar, cream of tartar, water, and salt in the top of a double boiler, using an electric mixer at top speed.
2. After one minute, cook over boiling water while continuing to beat with the mixer. Continue cooking and beating the mixture until firm enough to hold peaks.
3. Remove from heat, beat in the vanilla, and beat until thick enough to spread well.

Note: Be careful to observe if the mixer motor is overheating. Some mixers, especially the portable electric mixers, are not powerful enough to maintain the prolonged period of maximum operation without overheating.

(Icing for 1 layer)	
1	*egg white*
3/4 c	*sugar*
1/8 tsp	*cream of tartar*
6 tbsp	*water*
3/4 tsp	*vanilla*
	few grains salt

(Icing for 2 layers)	
2	egg whites
1 1/2 c	sugar
1/4 tsp	cream of tartar
1/3 c	water
1 1/2 tsp	vanilla
	dash salt

NUTTY COCONUT FROSTING

1. Stir ingredients together and spread evenly over the surface of the cake.
2. Place cake at lowest position in broiler compartment and broil until the frosting bubbles and coconut begins to brown.
3. Watch carefully to avoid burning the coconut.

(Icing for 2 layers)	
1/3 c	*margarine or butter*
2/3 c	*brown sugar*
1/4 c	*milk*
1 c	*shredded coconut*
1/2 c	*chopped walnuts*

To ice a cake, first dust off the crumbs. Then apply the filling or icing on the top of the bottom layer. Position the second layer, and then swirl the icing on the sides of the cake. Finally, apply the icing artistically to the top surface of the cake.

VOCABULARY

Angel cake

Chiffon cake

Sponge cake

Shortened cake

Conventional method

Modified conventional method

Conventional sponge method

Muffin method

Single-stage method

EVALUATION OF LABORATORY PRODUCTS — CAKES

RECIPE	NOTES ON COLOR, TEXTURE, FLAVOR, OR OTHER QUALITIES	COMMENTS OR SUGGESTIONS FOR MAKING OR USING THIS PRODUCT IN THE FUTURE

Chapter 11
Pies

When you look at the recipe for pastry, you probably will think that it is bound to be simple to put only four ingredients together and end up with a great pie crust. Actually, it is easy to make wonderfully tender and flaky pie crust — after you have learned how to manipulate the fat, flour, and water into a thin crust that you arrange attractively in a pie pan. All it takes is knowledge and practice!

ONE CRUST PIES

PRINCIPLES OF PREPARING ONE-CRUST PIES

Check to be sure that the oven rack is positioned in the center of the oven before beginning to preheat the oven. Then heat the oven to 425° F.

The ingredients for a 9" pie crust are very simple: 1 c sifted all purpose flour, 1/4 tsp salt, 1/3 c hydrogenated vegetable shortening, and 2 2/3 tbsp water. Margarine or butter should not be substituted for shortening in this recipe because both of these fats contain water as well as fat, and the resulting crust will be tough. The substitution of oil is not recommended because oil promotes a mealy rather than a flaky texture in the finished product.

The ingredients are combined by first stirring the salt thoroughly into the flour, using a table fork for mixing. This blends the salt flavoring throughout the crust uniformly. The fat is cut into the flour-salt mixture with the aid of a pastry blender. A light, tossing motion is used to facilitate cutting the shortening into discrete,

---

KEY CONCEPTS — PIES

1) Gluten needs to be developed in pastry by very limited mixing after the water is added.

   a) Too much water and/or too much mixing will develop the gluten too much and result in a tough crust.

   b) With too little water and/or too little mixing, pastry is difficult to handle and will tend to fall apart because of inadequate gluten development.

2) The cutting of fat into particles contributes flakiness to pastry, but reduces the tenderizing effect that could be achieved if the fat were spread thinly throughout.

small flour-coated pieces. The shortening which collects on top of the wires should be scraped off frequently to avoid having large particles of fat remaining when the rest of the fat has reached the correct size. Cutting in of the shortening continues until the pieces are generally about the size of split peas. Some particles will be a bit smaller than this, while others will be a bit larger. This variation in size is appropriate in helping to develop the desired flaky character of the crust.

Water is added in a dropwise fashion at a very slow rate. While the water is being added a drop at a time, the mixture is tossed with a fork. Addition of the drops of water needs to be spread throughout the bowl so that all parts of the dough are moistened equally. The mixing action is done very gently as the water is being added to avoid unnecessary gluten development.

When all of the water has been added, the dough is stirred into a ball. A table fork can be used in a mashing motion to help form a cohesive dough without developing the gluten extensively. Mixing is done only until the dough holds together.

The dough is turned out onto a piece of wax paper. Then the wax paper-wrapped ball of dough is worked very quickly and lightly with the hands until the dough holds together well. This operation needs to be done quickly and lightly to avoid the excessive gluten development that will occur when a warm dough is manipulated. The heat from the hands is sufficient to warm the dough unless the step is done quickly.

Let the dough rest in the wax paper while rubbing a light coating of flour into a pastry cloth. The cloth will feel like suede when the correct amount of flour has been rubbed in. Then the rolling pin covered with its stocking is rolled over the floured cloth to flour the sock. Avoid using more than the minimum amount of flour because the crust will

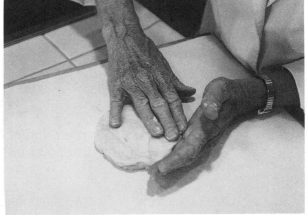

pick up dough from the cloth and sock during rolling. The result will be a less tender crust. Now place half of the large ball of dough on the cloth. Use the left hand as a guide, and flatten the half ball of dough into a flat, circular shape in preparation for rolling. When shaping this disk of dough, strive to develop a circular shape which is free from cracks around the edges. This will make the rolling of the crust quite simple because the dough will already have the basic shape desired.

Roll the flattened disk of dough into a crust large enough to be fitted into the pie plate and extend at least over the lip of the pie plate. The sock-covered rolling pin should be moved with light, gentle strokes over the dough. Quick, long strokes which lift toward the edge of the dough will permit efficient rolling of the crust to a uniform thickness throughout and will not stretch the gluten unduly. Heavy stretching strokes will tend to tear the gluten strands in the dough and will also promote a less tender crust.

Hold the pie plate over the crust when rolling is apparently completed. Be sure that the crust is large enough to fit down into the plate and to extend to the outer edge of the lip of the plate. This requires that the circular crust must be at least 1 1/2" larger at its narrowest dimension than is the pie plate being used.

Quickly test the crust at several points to see if the crust is a uniform thickness throughout. When the crust is touched with a firm thump of the index finger, only a slight impression of the finger should show in the crust. If the crust is too thick in some areas, roll lightly in those regions until the correct thickness has been achieved. Avoid rolling any areas too thin. There is not a satisfactory way of correcting too thin a crust because any rerolling that might be needed to correct the error will cause the crust to become tough.

To aid in transferring the crust from the cloth to the pie plate without stretching or tearing the dough, gently fold the dough in half and then in half again. This gives a small enough package of dough to be able to handle it easily without risk of tearing.

Very carefully unfold the dough into the pie plate, being sure to let the dough rest on the bottom of the plate as much as possible. When the dough is unfolded and resting loosely in the plate, hold the edge of the dough loosely in the left hand and use the right hand to help ease the dough against the edge and bottom of the plate so that the dough conforms precisely to the contour of the pan. Be par-

ticularly careful to have the crust fit into the junction between the side and bottom of the pan. Repeat this operation all around the edge of the crust. The weight of the dough itself should be the main means of getting the crust to fit into the junction. Be sure to let the left hand allow the dough to fit down in the plate. The right hand is used only to ease, not to stretch the dough into place. Unless this operation is done carefully, the crust will shrink and pull away from the plate when it is baking. This makes the pie less attractive and more difficult to serve.

Use a pair of kitchen shears to trim the crust 1/2" beyond the edge of the pie plate. This needs to be done carefully as an aid in achieving a pie with a rim of uniform thickenss. The scraps from trimming the crust are put aside.

On the far side of the pie plate, fold the overhanging crust under and stand the crust upright on the flat rim of the pie plate. This operation is continued all the way around the edge of the pie.

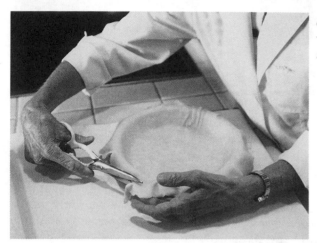

The edge of the pie may be trimmed in a variety of ways to suit individual preference. However, any trim selected needs to be uniform in appearance all the way around the edge of the pie. It also should be executed to give a sharp pattern because the pattern will soften and be much less distinct after the crust is baked.

One attractive, yet simple edging is done by using the thumb and index finger of the right hand as a pattern and the index finger of the left hand as a press. To do this, the right hand thumb and index finger are placed on the rim of the pie plate. The left index finger is placed just opposite these fingers on the inside of the crust. Then the left index finger is pressed firmly toward the pinched pattern made by the right hand. This leaves a sharp point of crust as a design in the edge of the pie. Then the right hand is moved so that the thumb is immediately adjacent to the edge of the point just made. The left index finger is positioned inside the crust opposite the right hand, and a second point is pressed into the rim. This process is repeated

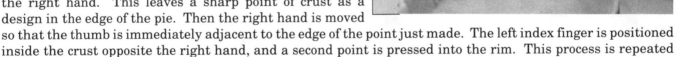

continuously around the edge of the pie to make an even, sharp-point trim which rests on the lip of the pie plate all the way around the pie.

One crust pies, such as meringue pies, are made using a baked, rather than an unbaked pie crust. Pie crusts baked withouth a filling will tend to blister badly and form large air pockets unless they are pricked before being baked. To avoid these problems, unfilled pie crusts can be pricked with a table fork in a number of places. It is important to prick at frequent intervals all the way around the circle where the bottom and sides of the pan are joined.

Be sure to prick all the way through the crust. This will keep the crust from forming large blisters and pulling away from the plate.

In addition, the fork should be used to prick frequent holes all around the side and across the bottom of the crust. These holes, of course, are not pricked if a filling is to be poured into an unbaked crust because the filling will run through the holes and cause the crust to stick to the pan.

The unfilled pie crust is baked in a 425° F oven for about 12 minutes until the crust is a pleasing, golden brown all over. If any portion of the crust begins to get somewhat dark, it will be necessary to stop baking the crust. Uneven browning is an indication of uneven thickness in the pastry itself and suggests the need for more careful rolling techniques when preparing a crust another time. If a meringue pie is being prepared, turn the oven thermostat to 350° F when the baked crust is removed from the oven.

RECIPE

PASTRY

Total Time: 25 minutes
Baking: 425° F oven for 12–15 minutes

1. Preheat oven.
2. With a fork, stir the flour and salt together.
3. Add the shortening all at once, and cut into pieces the size of split peas, using a pastry blender.
4. Toss the dough with a fork, while adding the water slowly in drops all over the dough.
5. Press dough together with a fork to form a ball.
6. Turn dough out onto a piece of wax paper. Pick up the paper and quickly press firmly into a ball with the hands.
7. Flour a pastry cloth and sock until they feel like suede.
8. Put the ball of dough on the cloth and work into a round, flat pancake shape by pressing down with the right hand and using the left hand as a guide to curve the edge of the dough. (If making the tart recipe, divide the dough approximately in half before beginning to handle the dough.)
9. Roll with a rolling pin covered with a lightly-floured pastry sock.
10. Roll the dough into a circle about 1/8" thick and large enough to extend 1/2" beyond the edge of the pie plate.
11. Fold the rolled dough in half and then into quarters.
12. Gently pick up the dough, and fit it into the pie plate.
13. Ease the pastry into the pie plate, being sure that it fits snugly along the bottom and sides.
14. With kitchen shears, trim the pastry 1/3" beyond the edge of the pie plate. Turn the edge under and make a fluted trim that rests on the lip of the pie plate. Puncture holes with a fork all around the side and across the bottom of the crust if the crust is being baked unfilled. Bake at 425° F about 12 minutes until the crust is a pleasing golden brown.

(Makes two tart shells)	
1 c	*flour, sifted*
1/4 tsp	*salt*
1/3 c	*shortening*
2 2/3 tbsp	*water*

(Makes one 9" pie shell)
1 c	flour, sifted
1/4 tsp	salt
1/3 c	shortening
2 2/3 tbsp	water

Custard and custard-type pie fillings are prepared at this point and poured into the baked crust. A pecan pie filling is prepared at this point and poured into the partially baked crust. A pecan pie filling is prepared by slowly beating 3 eggs until well blended and not foamy. Then 3/4 c brown sugar, 1/4 tsp salt, 1 tbsp sugar, 1 c light corn syrup, 1 c pecan halves, and 1 tsp vanilla are blended into the eggs without making any foam. Custard and pumpkin pie fillings are prepared in basically the same way.

These fillings are thickened with the coagulating egg during the baking process, but are very fluid prior to baking. Therefore, the fillings should be poured into the partially-baked crust and then baked immediately for 8 minutes at 425° F to avoid soaking the crust. Then the oven thermostat is turned down to 325° F to finish coagulating the filling. If the edge of the crust begins to get too dark, cover it with aluminum foil.

Custard pies are baked until a table knife can be inserted in the filling half-way between the center and edge of the pie and be removed with its surface showing clean, although slightly moist. The filling will be soft enough to shake just a bit when the pie is moved, but the residual heat in the filling will be just sufficient to finish coagulating the egg proteins in the center of the pie filling. If baking is allowed to continue until the knife comes out clean from the center of the pie, the filling will be overbaked. An overbaked custard filling will be porous and exhibit syneresis (liquid draining from the filling), and the crust will become soggy. A properly baked custard pie will be firm enough to hold its shape when cut after it is allowed to cool. The crust will be flaky and tender, but will not be soggy. Pies with egg in the filling should be stored in the refrigerator as soon as they have cooled to avoid the possibility of food poisoning, such as staphylococcal or salmonella infections.

CUSTARD PIE RECIPES

PECAN PIE

Total Time: 1 hour 10 minutes
Baking: 425° F oven 4 minutes then 325° F 30 min., tarts;
425° F oven 8 minutes then 325° F 25 min., pie

1. Preheat oven.
2. Prepare pastry and bake 5 minutes (see Pastry Recipe, p. 223).
3. Beat the egg(s).
4. Add the sugars, salt, vanilla, and corn syrup.
5. Beat with rotary beater until well blended.
6. Stir in the pecans.
7. Pour in the partially-baked pie shell.
8. Bake for 8 minutes at 425° F.
9. Then reduce heat to 325° F about 30 minutes for tarts and about 45 minutes for pie until a knife inserted halfway between the center and the edge comes out clean.
10. Cool on rack until room temperature; refrigerate promptly until served.

(Makes 2 tarts)

	Pastry for 2 tarts (see p. 223)
1	egg
1/4 c	light brown sugar
	dash salt
1 tsp	sugar
1/3 c	light corn syrup
1/4 tsp	vanilla
1/3 c	pecan halves

(Makes one 9" pie)

	Pastry for 9" pie (see p. 223)
3	eggs
3/4 c	light brown sugar
1/8 tsp	salt
1 tbsp	sugar
1 c	light corn syrup
1 tsp	vanilla
1 c	pecan halves

PUMPKIN PIE

Total Time: 55 minutes
Baking: 425° F oven 4 minutes then 325° F 15 min., tarts;
425° F oven 8 minutes then 325° F 25 min., pie

1. Preheat oven.
2. Prepare pastry and bake 5 minutes (see Pastry Recipe, p. 223).
3. Scald the milk.
4. Beat the egg(s) with a rotary beater.
5. Stir in the pumpkin, salt, sugars, and spices.
6. Quickly stir in the hot milk.
7. Pour into the partially-baked pie shell.
8. Bake for 4 minutes (for tarts) or 8 minutes (for pie) at 425° F.
9. Reduce heat to 325° F for 15 minutes (tarts) or 25 minutes (pie) until knife inserted halfway between the center and the edge comes out clean.
10. Cool on a rack until room temperature; refrigerate immediately until served.

(Makes 2 tarts)	
	Pastry for 2 tarts (see p. 223)
1	*egg*
1/8 tsp	*salt*
10 tbsp	*canned pumpkin*
1/4 c	*sugar*
1 tbsp	*brown sugar*
1/2 tsp	*cinnamon*
1/8 tsp	*ground cloves*
1/8 tsp	*nutmeg*
1/8 tsp	*ginger*
1/8 tsp	*allspice*
10 tbsp	*milk, scalded*

(Makes one 9" pie)	
	Pastry for 9" pie (see p. 223)
2	eggs
1/4 tsp	salt
1 1/4 c	canned pumpkin
1/2 c	sugar
2 tbsp	brown sugar
1 tsp	cinnamon
1/4 tsp	ground cloves
1/4 tsp	nutmeg
1/4 tsp	ginger
1/4 tsp	allspice
1 1/4 c	milk, scalded

CUSTARD PIE

Total Time: 1 hour
Baking: 425° F oven 4 minutes then 325° F 15 min., tarts;
425° F oven 8 minutes then 325° F 25 min., pie

1. Preheat oven.
2. Prepare pastry and bake 5 minutes (see Pastry Recipe, p. 223).
3. Scald the milk.
4. Beat the eggs slowly to completely blend the yolk and white without making a foam.
5. Stir in the other ingredients including the hot milk. Blend completely and then pour into partially-baked pastry shell.
6. Sprinkle with nutmeg.
7. Bake at 425° F for 8 minutes (see note below).
8. Reduce heat to 325° F for about 15 minutes (tarts) or 25 minutes (pie) until knife inserted halfway between the center and the edge comes out clean.
9. Cool on rack until room temperature; refrigerate promptly until served.

Note: This pie filling may be prepared by baking the pastry in a glass pie plate, then pouring in the filling, covering loosely with plastic wrap, and microwaving to coagulate the filling at low setting for 13–15 minutes.

(Makes 2 tarts)	
	Pastry for 2 tarts (see p. 223)
1	*egg*
3 tbsp	*sugar*
	dash salt
2/3 c	*milk, scalded*
1/4 tsp	*vanilla*
2	*drops almond extract*
	nutmeg

(Makes one 9" pie)	
	Pastry for 9" pie (see p. 223)
3	eggs
1/2 c	sugar
1/4 tsp	salt
2 c	milk, scalded
3/4 tsp	vanilla
1/8 tsp	almond extract
	nutmeg

MERINGUE PIE

The filling for meringue pies begins with preparation of a gelatinized starch mixture. A lemon meringue pie filling is made by stirring together 6 tbsp cornstarch, 1 1/2 c sugar, and 1/4 tsp salt until the starch is blended thoroughly with the other dry ingredients.

Then 1 1/2 c water can be added slowly while stirring with a wooden spoon. A smooth slurry should be formed before applying any heat to this mixture.

Place the pan over direct heat and stir continuously with a wooden spoon while bringing the mixture to a boil. Continue heating until the spoon leaves a path across the bottom of the pan and the mixture appears to be relatively translucent. In fillings using flour and/or milk, the translucent appearance will be difficult to detect, so the viscosity will be the guide to use. *Remove the thickened filling from the heat.*

Beat 3 egg yolks with a table fork until blended. Stir approximately a tablespoonful of the hot starch mixture into the yolks, being sure to avoid letting any of the hot mixture come in contact with the yolks without being stirred in thoroughly. This is very imporant if lumps in the yolk are to be avoided. When the first spoonful has been blended completely, repeat the process with a second spoonful. Continue with a third and finally a fourth spoonful of the hot starch paste. This procedure is used to dilute the egg yolk protein and raise the temperature at which coagulation will take place in the total mixture. As a result of the higher coagulation temperature, there will be less likelihood of developing lumps of egg yolk in the pie filling.

Now the diluted egg mixture is ready to be added to the hot starch paste. The hot starch paste should be stirred efficiently with a wooden spoon while the egg yolk mixture is poured slowly into the hot paste. The total mixture should be stirred with a wooden spoon until no streaks of yolk or starch paste remain in the mixture.

The mixture then is returned to the heat by placing either over boiling water or on the simmer setting of a temperature-controlled range unit. The filling must not boil after the egg has been added because the very high temperature of boiling will cause the egg yolk to curdle. The egg yolk-starch mixture is stirred very slowly during a 5-minute heating period. The mixture should become slightly thicker and should become less glossy when the egg yolk thickens. Complete coagulation of the egg yolk at this step is essential. Incomplete coagulation of the yolk will result in a pie filling which is quite thin when the pie is served even though the pie filling appeared to be thick before the egg was added. When the yolk has thickened, the starch-yolk mixture is removed from the heat.

The final step in preparing the filling for a lemon meringue pie is the addition of 6 tbsp lemon juice, 1 tsp grated lemon rind, and 1 1/2 tbsp margarine or butter. The acidic lemon is added after the starch has been gelatinized and the egg yolk protein has been coagulated to avoid the acid hydrolysis which would result in less than optimum thickening of the filling. By adding the lemon after cooking of the filling is completed, hydrolytic breakdown to smaller, more soluble molecules is prevented. All meringue pie fillings except banana cream pie are covered at this point to help keep the filling warm while the meringue is being prepared. Banana cream pie filling is allowed to cool so that it will not be hot enough to cook the bananas when the pie is assembled.

Just as soon as the filling is completed, 3 egg whites are beaten in the small bowl of the electric mixer. When the whites reach the foamy stage, 1/4 tsp cream of tartar and the first of 6 tbsp of sugar is added. The mixer is set at high speed, and the remaining 5 tbsp of sugar are added gradually, a tablespoonful at a time.

Beating is continued until the correct stage is reached. To test the extent of beating, stop the mixer. Use a rubber spatula to pull some of the egg white foam up into a peak. Lift the spatula up slowly so the true character of the foam will show. When tested in this way, the egg white foam will form peaks that just barely bend over.

Assemble the pie by pouring the filling into the baked crust. Gently scrape all of the meringue from the bowl onto the surface of the pie with the aid of a rubber spatula.

Use the spatula to spread the meringue gently clear to the edge of the pie and to seal the meringue into each point of the edging. It is important to seal the meringue to the crust in this way to help avoid having the meringue pull away from the edge during the baking. When the edge is sealed all the way around, swirl an attractive design in the meringue with the aid of the spatula, being careful to prevent any peaks in the meringue. Peaks need to be avoided because they will get too dark before the rest of the meringue bakes enough to coagulate the egg white protein.

Immediately place the pie in the oven which has been set at 350° F. Bake the meringue until the surface is a pleasing golden brown. The valleys in the meringue design will still be rather white when the upper surfaces are appropriately browned. Remove the pie from the oven at this time and cool it at room temperature until the pan can be handled comfortably without hot pads. Store the pie in the refrigerator until serving time.

A meringue pie is evaluated on the basis of the crust, the filling, and the meringue. The crust should be crisp, tender, flaky, and a pleasing golden brown. The filling should be firm enough to be cut easily, but should soften almost imperceptibly along the cut edge when served cold. The texture of the filling should be smooth, and there should be a light, rather than a pasty feeling on the tongue. The meringue is evaluated on its volume, general appearance, cutability, and stability. A good meringue will be a pleasing golden brown on the higher surfaces and only very slightly brown in the valleys; the volume will be excellent. A fresh, properly baked meringue will cut without clinging to the knife. There should be virtually no liquid collecting between the meringue and the filling. The use of a hot filling is an aid in avoiding this problem because the filling helps to coagulate the egg white proteins in the lower part of the meringue, thus minimizing drainage from the meringue.

CREAM PIE RECIPES

LEMON MERINGUE PIE

Total Time: 1 hour
Baking: 425° F oven 12–15 minutes, pastry;
350° F oven 12–15 minutes, meringue

1. Preheat oven.
2. Prepare and bake the pie crust. Then reduce oven to 350° F.
3. With a wooden spoon, mix the cornstarch, sugar, and salt together thoroughly in a 1-quart saucepan.
4. Add the water gradually while stirring.
5. Continue to stir; heat to boiling, being careful to stir all across the bottom and around the sides of the pan.
6. Remove from heat, and stir a spoonful of the hot filling into the beaten egg yolk.
7. Repeat three more times, and then stir the yolk mixture back into the filling.
8. Place mixture over boiling water and cook for 5 minutes or until filling thickens slightly and loses its gloss. (Direct heat may be used if the heat never rises to the point where the filling boils.) Stir slowly while coagulating the egg yolk.
9. Remove from the heat, and stir in the butter, lemon juice, and lemon rind. Cover and set aside.
10. With an electric mixer, beat the egg white to the foamy stage.
11. Add the cream of tartar.

(Makes two tarts)	
	pastry for 2 tarts (see p. 223)
3 tbsp	cornstarch
3/4 c	sugar
1/8 tsp	salt
3/4 c	water
1	egg yolk, beaten
2 tsp	butter or margarine
3 tbsp	lemon juice
1/2 tsp	grated lemon rind
1	egg white
2 tbsp	sugar
1/8 tsp	cream of tartar

LEMON MERINGUE PIE (CONTINUED)

12. Pour the filling into the baked pie shell(s).
13. Top with the meringue; use a rubber spatula to seal the meringue carefully to the edge of the crust all the way around.
14. Swirl the top of the meringue without drawing up peaks.
15. Bake at 350° F 12–15 minutes or until golden brown.
16. Chill at least 2 hours before serving, and keep in refrigerated storage until served to avoid possible growth of microorganisms.

(Makes one 9" pie)

	pastry for 9" pie (see p. 223)
6 tbsp	cornstarch
1 1/2 c	sugar
1/4 tsp	salt
1 1/4 c	water
3	egg yolks, beaten
1 1/2 tbsp	butter or margarine
6 tbsp	lemon juice
1 tsp	grated lemon rind
3	egg whites
6 tbsp	sugar
1/4 tsp	cream of tartar

COCONUT CREAM PIE

Total Time: 1 hour
Baking: 425° F oven 12–15 minutes, pastry;
350° F oven 12–15 minutes, meringue

1. Preheat oven.
2. Prepare and bake the pie crust. Then reduce oven to 350° F.
3. With a wooden spoon, mix the flour, sugar, and salt together in a 1-quart saucepan.
4. Slowly add the milk while stirring. Stir constantly while heating the mixture to a boil.
5. Continue boiling until a spoon leaves a path in the mixture.
6. Remove from the heat, and stir a spoonful of the hot filling into the beaten yolk.
7. Repeat three more times and then stir the yolk mixture back into the filling.
8. Place the mixture over boiling water and cook for five minutes or until the mixture thickens slightly and loses its gloss. (Direct heat may be used if the heat never rises to the point where filling boils.) Stir slowly while coagulating the egg yolk.
9. Add margarine or butter and vanilla. Cover pan to help retain heat while making meringue.
10. With an electric mixer, beat the egg white to the foamy stage and add the cream of tartar.
11. Beating at high speed, beat 15 seconds before gradually adding the sugar. Beat until peaks just fold over.
12. Stir the shredded coconut into the filling.
13. Pour the filling into the baked pie crust.
14. Pile the meringue on the filling and spread it carefully over the surface of the pie. Use a rubber spatula to press the meringue firmly against all edges of the pastry. Then make a circular swirl in the meringue to give some contrast without developing peaks which will burn before other portions are baked.
15. Bake the meringue in a 350° F oven for 12–15 minutes or until a golden brown.
16. Chill at least two hours before serving, and keep pie in refrigerated storage until consumed to avoid possible growth of microorganisms.

(Makes two tarts)	
	pastry for two tarts (p. 223)
2 2/3 tbsp	*flour, sifted*
1/3 c	*sugar*
1/8 tsp	*salt*
1 c	*milk*
1	*egg yolk*
1/2 tsp	*margarine or butter*
1/2 tsp	*vanilla*
1	*egg white*
1/8 tsp	*cream of tartar*
2 tbsp	*sugar*
1/2 c	*shredded coconut*

(Makes one 9" pie)

	pastry for 9" pie (p. 223)
1/3 c	flour, sifted
2/3 c	sugar
1/4 tsp	salt
2 c	milk
3	egg yolks
1 tsp	margarine or butter
1 tsp	vanilla
3	egg whites
1/4 tsp	cream of tartar
6 tbsp	sugar
1 c	shredded coconut

BANANA CREAM PIE

Total Time: 1 hour
Baking: 425° F oven 12–15 minutes, pastry;
350° F oven 12–15 minutes, meringue

1. Preheat oven.
2. Prepare and bake the pie crust. Then reduce oven to 350° F.
3. With a wooden spoon, mix flour, sugar, and salt together in a 1-quart saucepan and gradually stir in the milk.
4. Heat to boiling while stirring constantly.
5. Remove from the heat, and stir a spoonful of the hot filling into the beaten yolk.
6. Repeat 3 more times.
7. Pour the yolk mixture back into the filling as the filling is being stirred.
8. Cook the filling over boiling water for 5 minutes or until the mixture thickens slightly and loses its gloss. (Direct heat may be used if the heat never rises to the point where the filling boils.) Stir slowly while coagulating the yolk.
9. Remove from the heat, stir in the vanilla and margarine or butter, cover, and cool the filling by placing pan in ice.
10. When the filling has cooled to about 100° F, begin to make the meringue.
11. With an electric mixer, beat the egg whites to the foamy stage.
12. Add the cream of tartar.
13. Beating at high speed, beat 15 seconds before gradually adding the sugar. Beat until peaks just fold over.
14. Slice the bananas in the pie crust.
15. Pour in the filling.
16. Spread the meringue on top.
17. Use a rubber spatula to seal the meringue to the crust, and swirl the meringue surface without pulling up high peaks.
18. Bake at 350° F for 12–15 minutes or until the meringue is a golden brown.
19. Chill at least 2 hours before serving, and keep in refrigerated storage until served to avoid possible growth of microorganisms.

Note: Other cream pies may be made by using the recipes from the section "Cream Puddings" as the filling in a baked crust and topping with a meringue. Use the meringue recipe for the bananas cream pie, above.

(Makes two tarts)

	pastry for two tarts (p. 223)
2 2/3 tbsp	flour, sifted
1/3 c	sugar
1/8 tsp	salt
1 c	milk
1	egg yolk, beaten
1/2 tsp	margarine or butter
1/2 tsp	vanilla
1	egg white
2 tbsp	sugar
1/8 tsp	cream of tartar
1	banana

(Makes one 9" pie)

	pastry for 9" pie (p. 223)
1/3 c	flour, sifted
2/3 c	sugar
1/4 tsp	salt
2 c	milk
3	egg yolks, beaten
1 tsp	margarine or butter
1 tsp	vanilla
3	egg whites
6 tbsp	sugar
1/4 tsp	cream of tartar
3	bananas

CHIFFON PIE RECIPES
LEMON CHIFFON PIE

Total Time: 1 hour
Baking: 425° F oven 12–15 minutes

1. Preheat oven.
2. Prepare and bake pastry (see pastry recipe, p. 223).
3. In a double boiler, soften the gelatin in the cold water.
4. Stir in the first measure of sugar, the lemon juice, and the beaten egg yolks.
5. Stir while heating over boiling water until mixture thickens enough to pile.
6. Add the lemon rind.
7. Chill until mixture begins to congeal.
8. With an electric mixer, quickly beat the egg whites to the foamy stage.
9. Gradually add the remaining measure of sugar while continuing beating.
10. Beat until the peaks just bend over when the beater is withdrawn.
11. Fold the gelatin mixture into the beaten whites thoroughly, but gently.
12. Pile into the baked pie shell.
13. Chill in the refrigerator. Garnish with whipped cream.

(Makes two tarts)

	pastry for two tarts (p. 223)
1/2	*envelope unflavored gelatin*
3 tbsp	*cold water*
1/4 c	*sugar*
1/4 c	*lemon juice*
2	*eggs, separated*
1 tsp	*grated lemon rind*
1/4 c	*sugar*
	whipped cream for garnish

(Makes one 9" pie)

	pastry for 9" pie (p. 223)
1	envelope unflavored gelatin
1/3 c	cold water
1/2 c	sugar
1/2 c	lemon juice
4	eggs, separated
2 tsp	grated lemon rind
1/2 c	sugar
	whipped cream for garnish

EGGNOG CHIFFON PIE

Total Time: 1 hour
Baking: 425° F oven 12–15 minutes

1. Preheat oven.
2. Prepare and bake pastry (see pastry recipe, p. 223).
3. Soften the gelatin in cold water.
4. Combine the beaten yolks, hydrated gelatin, first measure of sugar, salt, and warm water in the top of a double boiler.
5. Cook over boiling water, stirring constantly, until mixture thickens.
6. Chill until partially congealed.
7. With an electric mixer, beat the egg whites to the foamy stage, and then gradually add the remaining sugar while beating until the peaks of the whites just bend over.
8. Add the nutmeg and flavorings, and blend.
9. Fold the first mixture into the egg whites gently, but thoroughly, using a rubber spatula.
10. Pile into the pie shell and chill.
11. Garnish with whipped cream and almonds.

Note: Chiffon pies can be made with a variety of pie shells. The fillings should be uniform and should have a light, airy texture with no obvious pieces of gelatin. They should be tender and easy to cut. For best results, chiffon pies should be served the same day they are made.

(Makes two tarts)

	pastry for two tarts (p. 223)
1/2	*envelope unflavored gelatin*
2 tbsp	*cold water*
2	*egg yolks, beaten*
1/4 c	*sugar*
1/8 tsp	*salt*
1/4 c	*warm water*
1/4 c	*sugar*
2	*egg whites*
1/8 tsp	*nutmeg*
1 tsp	*rum flavoring*
1/8 tsp	*almond extract*
1/2 c	*whipping cream*
1/4 c	*slivered almonds, toasted*

(Makes one 9" pie)

	pastry for 9" pie (p. 223)
1	envelope unflavored gelatin
1/4 c	cold water
4	egg yolks, beaten
1/2 c	sugar
1/4 tsp	salt
1/2 c	warm water
1/2 c	sugar
4	egg whites
1/4 tsp	nutmeg
2 tsp	rum flavoring
1/4 tsp	almond extract
1 c	whipping cream
1/2 c	slivered almonds, toasted

TWO-CRUST PIES

PRINCIPLES OF PREPARING TWO-CRUST PIES

Although the dough is prepared the same for one- and two-crust pies, the treatment in the pan is different. Two-crust pies are made by trimming the bottom crust even with the edge of the pan.

The top crust is rolled and folded into quarters, ready for placement on the filling. Then the filling is prepared. This avoids having the filling sitting in the unbaked crust while the second crust is rolled, thus reducing the likelihood of a soggy bottom crust.

Fresh fruits needs to be arranged as compactly as possible to help minimize the shrinkage of the filling during baking. Unless care is taken to do this and also to position the top crust gently, but firmly on the fruit, the fruit filling may shrink during baking and leave the top crust suspended an inch or more above the fruit. This makes the baked pie difficult to serve. If *canned* or *frozen fruits* are used for the filling, there will be essentially no shrinkage of the filling.

The top crust is unfolded to a semicircle and arranged over the nearest half of the pie. Then the other half of the crust is unfolded carefully and positioned over the remainder of the pie. Gently press the top crust to the bottom crust around the lip of the pie plate. Use kitchen shears to trim the top crust 1/2" beyond the lip of the plate. This trimming should be done carefully and uniformly.

Finish assembling the crusts by turning the extension of the upper crust under the portion of the lower crust which is resting on the lip of the plate. This operation, in essence, makes a sandwich, with the bottom crust serving as the sandwich filling which is encased in two layers of the upper crust. This technique effectively seals the pie filling into the pie crusts and reduces the possibility of overflow.

Some people prefer the appearance of the baked crust if the crust has been dusted with a bit of granulated sugar or brushed with a light glaze of milk before baking. If desired, this treatment is applied at this point.

To improve the appearance of the pie and also strengthen the seal of the filling, an edge trim is used. A simple edge trim is done by placing the index finger and thumb of the right hand right next to the crust on the lip of the pie plate and then pressing the crust between the fingers into a sharp point with the aid of the index finger of the left hand. This process is repeated all the way around the edge of the pie, being sure to place the thumb of the right

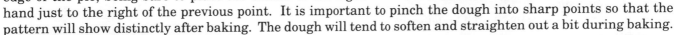

hand just to the right of the previous point. It is important to pinch the dough into sharp points so that the pattern will show distinctly after baking. The dough will tend to soften and straighten out a bit during baking.

Use a sharp knife to cut steam vents in the top crust of the pie. These steam vents can be an attractive design which enhances the appearance of the pie while serving their utilitarian function of releasing steam from the hot filling during baking. These vents should be primarily in the center of the pie and ideally will extend no closer than within 1 1/2" of the edge of the pie. This helps to keep the boiling filling from running over. Be sure that the steam vents are large enough to remain open during the entire baking period. Vents less than 1/4" long tend to seal over while the pie is baking. When steam cannot escape from the filling, the top crust will become soggy.

For a lattice crust, the bottom crust is trimmed 1/2" beyond the edge of the pie plate, using kitchen shears. After the filling is added, the lattice strips are placed in position and trimmed even with the edge of the bottom crust. Then the lower crust is folded up and over the edge of the lattice strips before the edge is fluted.

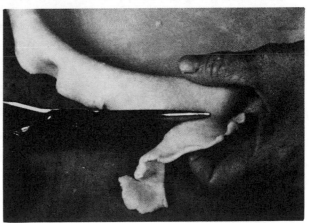

TWO-CRUST PIE RECIPES

PASTRY (FOR TWO-CRUST PIE)

1. Mix the flour and salt with a fork.
2. Cut in the shortening until it is the size of split peas. Use a pastry blender to cut shortening efficiently.
3. Toss the pastry lightly with a fork as the water is added dropwise throughout the pastry.
4. Press together with a fork.
5. Turn dough out onto wax paper and press it firmly into a ball.
6. Divide the dough (in halves for large recipe, in quarters for small).
7. On a lightly floured pastry cloth, shape one of the pieces of dough into a round shape.
8. Press it into a disk.
9. Put a floured stocking on the rolling pin, and roll out the first crust.
10. When it is 1/8" thick and large enough to fit the pan, fold the dough in half and then in quarters.
11. Pick it up and transfer it to the pie plate.
12. Unfold it carefully, and fit it gently into the pie plate.
13. Use a table knife to trim the edge of the crust along the edge of the pie plate.
14. Roll the second crust in the same manner.
15. Fold it in quarters and set aside until the pie is assembled. If tarts are being made, repeat the process for the other tart.

(pastry for 2 two-crust tarts)	
2 c	*flour*
1/2 tsp	*salt*
2/3 c	*shortening*
1/3 c	*water*

(pastry for one 9" two-crust pie)	
2 c	flour
1/2 tsp	salt
2/3 c	shortening
1/3 c	water

OIL PASTRY (FOR TWO-CRUST PIE)

1. Follow directions for Pastry above but substitute 1/2 c salad oil for shortening.
2. Add oil and water all at once and stir in until mixed.
3. Roll out between 2 pieces of wax paper.

(pastry for 2 two-crust tarts)	
2 c	*flour*
1/2 tsp	*salt*
1/2 c	*oil*
1/3 c	*water*

(pastry for one 9" two-crust pie)	
2 c	flour
1/2 tsp	salt
1/2 c	oil
1/3 c	water

APPLE PIE

Total Time: 1 hour
Baking: 400° F oven 25 minutes for tarts; 35 minutes for pie

1. Preheat oven.
2. Prepare crust recipe for two-crust pie (see pastry recipe, p. 234).
3. Pare and core the apples. Slice very thin.
4. In a mixing bowl, mix the sugar, cornstarch, salt, and cinnamon; stir the apples in it so the slices are well coated.
5. Arrange the apples in the bottom pie crust, pressing them down gently to help pack them.
6. Sprinkle the lemon juice over the apples.
7. Dot filling with small pieces of butter or margarine.
8. Unfold the top crust over the filling and center it on the pie.
9. Press the edges so they conform to the lip of the pie plate.
10. With kitchen shears, trim the top crust 1/2" beyond the lip of the plate.
11. Turn the extension of the upper crust under the lower crust on the lip of the plate.
12. Flute the edge of the pie.
13. Use a paring knife to cut an artistic design to serve as a steam vent in the middle of the pie.
14. Sprinkle the top with some sugar. Bake at 400° F until the filling begins to bubble and the crust is a pleasing golden brown (about 25 minutes for tarts or 35 minutes for pie).

(Makes 2 two-crust tarts)	
	pastry for 2 two-crust tarts (p. 235)
2	*pippins or other tart apples*
1/2 c	*sugar*
1 tbsp	*cornstarch*
1/2 tsp	*cinnamon*
	few grains salt
1 tsp	*lemon juice*
1 1/2 tsp	*margarine or butter*

(Makes one 9" two-crust pie)	
	pastry for 1 two-crust pie (p. 235)
5	pippins or other tart apples
1 c	sugar
2 tbsp	cornstarch
1 tsp	cinnamon
	dash salt
2 tsp	lemon juice
1 tbsp	margarine or butter

Note: Fresh peaches or pears may be substituted for apples. One teaspoon (large recipe) grated lemon rind (1/2 tsp for small recipe) may be added with the cinnamon.

RHUBARB PIE (LATTICE TOP)

Total Time: 50 minutes
Baking: 400° F oven 25 minutes for tarts; 35 minutes for pie

1. Preheat oven.
2. Prepare crust recipe for two-crust pie (see pastry recipe, p. 234). When fitting the bottom crust, let the pastry extend 1/2" beyond the lip of the pie plate.
3. Roll out the top crust and use a pastry wheel to cut strips for making a lattice top.
4. In a mixing bowl, mix sugar, flour, salt and grated orange rind together, and stir in the rhubarb.
5. Put in the bottom crust, and dot filling with small pieces of margarine or butter.
6. Weave the strips of lattice across the top of the pie. For a quick lattice, lay all the strips across in one direction and then put the other strips on top of them at right angles without actually weaving the strips.
7. Press the end of the lattice strips firmly to the lower crust along the lip of the pie plate.
8. With kitchen shears, trim the strips even with the lower crust.
9. Fold the lower crust up over the strips, and stand the edge of the crust up along the lip of the pie plate.
10. Flute the edge. Bake at 400° F until the filling is bubbling, and the crust is a golden brown (about 25 minutes for tarts or 35 minutes for pie).

(Makes 2 two-crust tarts)	
	pastry for 2 two-crust tarts (p. 235)
1 1/2 c	*fresh rhubarb, washed and cut in 1/2" pieces*
1/2 c	*sugar*
1/2 tsp	*grated orange rind*
1 1/2 tbsp	*flour*
	few grains salt
1 1/2 tsp	*margarine or butter*

(Makes one 9" two-crust pie)	
	pastry for 1 two-crust pie (p. 235)
3 c	fresh rhubarb, washed and cut in 1/2" pieces
1 c	sugar
1 tsp	grated orange rind
3 tbsp	flour
	dash salt
1 tbsp	margarine or butter

CANNED CHERRY PIE

Total Time: 1 hour
Baking: 400° F oven 30 minutes for tarts; 40 minutes for pie

1. Preheat oven.
2. Prepare crust recipe for two-crust pie (see pastry recipe, p. 234).
3. In a saucepan, mix half of the sugar and cornstarch together, and gradually stir in the cherry juice.
4. Heat to boiling while stirring constantly with a wooden spoon.
5. Cook until thick and clear.
6. Remove from heat.
7. Add the other half of sugar, cherries, margarine or butter, and almond extract. If desired, tint with red food coloring.
8. Put filling in pie crust, and fit the top crust as described in the recipe for apple pie.
9. Bake at 400° F until the filling is bubbling, and the crust is golden brown.

(Makes 2 two-crust tarts)

	pastry for 2 two-crust tarts (p. 235)
1/2 c	sugar
2 tbsp	cornstarch
1/3 c	cherry juice
1 1/2 c	canned cherries, well drained
1 tsp	margarine or butter
2	drops almond extract
	red food coloring (optional)

(Makes one 9" two-crust pie)

	pastry for 1 two-crust pie (p. 235)
1 c	sugar
1/4 c	cornstarch
2/3 c	cherry juice
3 c	canned cherries, well drained
2 tsp	margarine or butter
4	drops almond extract
	red food coloring (optional)

CANNED PEACH PIE

Total Time: 1 hour
Baking: 400° F oven 30 minutes for tarts; 40 minutes for pie

1. Preheat oven.
2. Prepare crust recipe for two-crust pie (see pastry recipe, p. 234).
3. In a saucepan, mix the sugar and cornstarch together; gradually stir in the measured juice.
4. Heat to boiling while stirring constantly with wooden spoon.
5. Cook until thick and clear. Remove from heat.
6. Add the drained peaches, cinnamon, almond extract, and margarine or butter.
7. Pour filling into pie crust, and fit the top crust as described in the recipe for apple pie.
8. Bake at 400° F until the filling is bubbling, and the crust is golden brown.

(Makes 2 two-crust tarts)

	pastry for 2 two-crust tarts (p. 235)
1/4 c	sugar
2 tbsp	cornstarch
1/3 c	peach juice
1	1 lb can sliced peaches, well drained
1/4 tsp	cinnamon
2	drops almond extract
1 tsp	margarine or butter

(Makes one 9" two-crust pie)

	pastry for 1 two-crust pie (p. 235)
1/2 c	sugar
1/4 c	cornstarch
2/3 c	peach juice
2	1 lb cans sliced peaches, well drained
1/2 tsp	cinnamon
1/8 tsp	almond extract
2 tsp	margarine or butter

Note: Canned fruits must be drained thoroughly, with the amount of juice required in the recipe being reserved for use in the filling. Unless this is done, the filling will be too thin because of the extra juice introduced with the fruit.

VOCABULARY

Flakiness

Mealiness

Gel

Shortening power of fats

EVALUATION OF LABORATORY PRODUCTS — PIES

RECIPE	NOTES ON COLOR, TEXTURE, FLAVOR, OR OTHER QUALITIES	COMMENTS OR SUGGESTIONS FOR MAKING OR USING THIS PRODUCT IN THE FUTURE

Chapter 12
Sugar Cookery

Yes, there is no doubt that making candy is a sweet job! However, you may be surprised at how much there is to learn about sugar cookery. There is a lot that is happening right before your eyes while you are cooking it and also while it is cooling. You will notice that the temperature of boiling candies gets ever higher as the concentration of sugar increases due to evaporation of liquid. If you are making caramels or toffee, you will be able to see the color changes that begin to occur as sugar undergoes chemical changes at very high temperatures. The transition from a saturated solution to a supersaturated solution and ultimately to formation of sugar crystals will be evident when you make crystalline candies.

KEY CONCEPTS — SUGAR COOKERY

1) The temperature of a boiling sugar solution rises because water evaporates and causes a decrease in vapor pressure, which means that boiling cannot occur unless more heat energy is added.

2) At very high temperatures, sugar molecules begin to break apart and form smaller compounds that add color and flavor to candies.

3. Crystalline candies are characterized by organized crystalline structures, whereas amorphous candies cannot organize into crystalline areas as they cool because of the high viscosity of these very hot and concentrated sugar solutions.

   a) Careful cooling of a syrup that is to be a crystalline candy results in a highly supersaturated sugar solution that can be beaten when it reaches 100° F to form such fine crystals that the texture of the candy is velvety on the tongue.

   b) Solutions that are to be crystalline candies will form large sugar crystals that feel rough on the tongue if crystallization begins at high temperatures and/or if beating is not vigorous or is not continued until the moment the candy structure sets.

   c) Care must be exercised during boiling of syrups that are to become amorphous candies because sugar syrups scorch and burn easily if they are not stirred adequately at such high temperatures.

CRYSTALLINE CANDY RECIPES
PENUCHE

Total Time: 45 minutes
Final Temperature: 236° F

1. Test the accuracy of the thermometer by boiling water and carefully noting the temperature of the actively boiling water. If thermometer does not show that the "boiling water is at 212° F, correct the final temperature to which candy is cooked to compensate for the error of the thermometer. For example, if the thermometer reads 210° F (2° F below the expected value), subtract 2° F from the temperature in the recipe to obtain the desired final temperature for the thermometer being used.
2. Put the sugars and milk in a 1-quart saucepan (small recipe), 2-quart saucepan (large recipe).
3. Stir slowly while heating to a boil. When the sugar has dissolved, stir only occasionally.
4. Boil the candy to a temperature of 326° F.
5. Remove from the heat and add the margarine, being careful not to stir at all.
6. Cool the candy where it will not be disturbed.
7. While the candy is cooling, grease a shallow pan.
8. Cool until the bottom of the pan feels a bit warm to the hand (110° F). Do not insert a thermometer; the hand test is accurate enough.
9. Add the vanilla and chopped nuts and beat vigorously with a wooden spoon until the thickening candy softens very slightly and loses its gloss.
10. Quickly spread in the pan. Cut into squares.

Note: Penuche typically has a more granular texture than other crystalline candies.

(Small recipe)	
3/4 c	sugar
1/2 c	brown sugar
1/3 c	milk
1 1/2 tbsp	margarine or butter
1/2 tsp	vanilla
1/4 c	chopped nuts

(Large recipe)	
1 1/2 c	sugar
1 c	brown sugar
2/3 c	milk
3 tbsp	margarine or butter
1 tsp	vanilla
1/2 c	chopped nuts

FUDGE

Total Time: 45 minutes
Final Temperature: 234° F

1. Test boiling point of water on the thermometer, as described in Penuche, Step 1.
2. In a 1-quart (small recipe) or 2-quart (large recipe) saucepan, combine chocolate, sugar, salt, corn syrup, and milk.
3. Stir while slowly heating to boiling.
4. When cocholate has melted and the sugar has dissolved, increase the rate of heating to medium and stir occasionally to keep candy from burning.
5. Continue boiling the candy until it reaches 234° F. Remember to correct for the thermometer if necessary. Just as soon as the candy reaches the correct final temperature, add the butter or margarine and vanilla without stirring, and remove candy from the range.
6. Place the candy in a cool place where it will not be disturbed at all. Avoid touching or moving the candy until the temperature has dropped to about 110° F. The bottom of the pan will feel moderately warm to your hand when the candy reaches 110° F. (This temperature need not be checked with the thermometer; inserting thermometer would start crystallization even if the candy had not cooled sufficiently.)
7. While candy is cooling, grease a shallow pan.
8. Beat vigorously with a wooden spoon until the thickening candy loses its gloss.
9. Quickly spread in the pan. Cut into squares.

(Small recipe)	
6 tbsp	milk
1 oz	unsweetened chocolate[1]
1 c	sugar
	few grains salt
1 tsp	light corn syrup
1 tbsp	butter or margarine
1/2 tsp	vanilla

(Large recipe)	
3/4 c	milk
2 oz	unsweetened chocolate
2 c	sugar
	dash salt
2 tsp	light corn syrup
2 tbsp	butter or margarine
1 tsp	vanilla

[1]One square of chocolate is equivalent to approximately 3 1/2 tbsp cocoa plus 1/2 tbsp butter or margarine.

FONDANT

Total Time: 45 minutes
Final Temperature: 238° F

1. Test boiling point of water on thermometer, as described in Penuche Recipe, Step 1.
2. In a 1-quart (small recipe) or 2-quart (large recipe) saucepan, combine the ingredients.
3. Heat at a medium heat, stirring slowly until the sugar dissolves.
4. Continue boiling, until the candy reaches 238° F.
5. Remove from heat, and cool without disturbing it.
6. While candy is cooling, grease a platter or jelly roll pan.
7. Cool until the bottom of the pan feels a bit warm to the touch (110° F). Do not insert a thermometer; the hand test is accurate enough.
8. Pour onto a greased platter, and begin beating immediately with a wooden spoon until candy becomes firm and loses its gloss.
9. Wash hands with soap; rinse and dry thoroughly. Knead fondant with fingers until perfectly smooth.
10. Wrap tightly in foil to ripen 24 hours. Ripened fondant may be kneaded into after dinner mints or may be used as the center for stuffed dried fruits or chocolate-dipped candies.

(Small recipe)	
1 c	sugar
1 tbsp	light corn syrup or dash of cream of tartar
1/2 c	water

(Large recipe)

2 c	sugar
2 tbsp	light corn syrup or 1/8 tsp of cream of tartar
1 c	water

Variations: knead in any of the following:

1/8 tsp	lemon extract and yellow food coloring
1/8 tsp	orange extract, 1 drop yellow and 1 drop red food coloring
1/8 tsp	rum extract

DIVINITY

Total Time: 45 minutes
Final Temperature: 261° F

1. Test boiling point of water on thermometer, as described in Penuche Recipe, Step 1.
2. In a 1-quart (small recipe) or 2-quart (large recipe) saucepan, combine the sugar, corn syrup, water, and salt.
3. Stir slowly while heating the candy to boiling. When the sugar has all dissolved, stir only occasionally.
4. Boil the candy to a temperature of 261° F (263° F in humid or rainy weather). Remove from heat.
5. On electric mixer, beat the egg white until stiff.
6. Add cream of tartar and vanilla, and then gradually pour the hot candy syrup into the beaten white while running the mixer on its fastest speed.
7. Continue beating with the electric mixer until the candy is stiff.
8. Drop by 2 spoons onto a cookie sheet.

(Small recipe)	
1 c	sugar
1/4 c	light corn syrup
1/4 c	water
1/8 tsp	salt
1	egg white
1/8 tsp	cream of tartar
1/2 tsp	vanilla

(Large recipe)

2 c	sugar
1/2 c	light corn syrup
1/2 c	water
1/4 tsp	salt
2	egg whites
1/4 tsp	cream of tartar
1 tsp	vanilla

AMORPHOUS CANDY RECIPES
ALMOND TOFFEE

Total Time: 2 hours
Final Temperature: 300° F

1. Test boiling point of water on thermometer, as described in Penuche Recipe, Step 1.
2. In a 1-quart (small recipe) or 2-quart (large recipe) saucepan, combine the sugar, corn syrup, and water.
3. Stir while melting the margarine or butter and heating the mixture. After the sugar is dissolved, stir continuously to keep the mixture from burning.
4. Boil the candy to a final temperature of 300° F, being careful not to burn any portion of it.
5. Stir in half the almonds, and pour onto a greased or teflon-lined jelly roll pan. Spread into layer 1/3" thick.
6. Place in freezer to chill. Meanwhile melt half the milk chocolate over hot water.
7. Remove toffee from freezer, and spread melted chocolate over the surface of the candy. Sprinkle with half the remaining almonds, finely chopped.
8. Chill in freezer until chocolate is firm. Meanwhile, melt remaining milk chocolate. Remove from freezer. Flex pan to loosen candy, and turn entire sheet of candy over.
9. Spread melted chocolate over the second side and sprinkle with remaining finely chopped almonds.
10. Chill in freezer until chocolate is hard.
11. With a mallet or a knife handle, break the candy into serving-sized pieces.

(Small recipe)	
1/2 c	butter or margarine
2/3 c	sugar
1 1/2 tsp	light corn syrup
2 tbsp	water
3/4 c	blanched almonds, chopped
6 oz	milk chocolate

(Large recipe)	
1 c	butter or margarine
1 1/3 c	sugar
3 tsp	light corn syrup
3 tbsp	water
1 1/2 c	blanched almonds, chopped
1 lb	milk chocolate

CARAMELS

Total Time: 30 minutes
Final Temperature: 260° F, hard caramels;
250° F, chewy caramels

1. Test boiling point of water on thermometer, as described in Penuche Recipe, Step 1.
2. In a 1-quart (small recipe) or 2-quart (large recipe) saucepan, combine the sugar, corn syrup, margarine or butter, and cream.
3. Stir while bringing to a boil.
4. Stir occasionally while heating the candy to its final temperature.
5. Grease an 8" square pan.
6. Just before pouring out the candy into the pan, stir in the pecans and vanilla.
7. Score the pieces when the candy is still warm, and actually cut them when it has cooled.

(Small recipe)	
1/2 c	sugar
7 tbsp	light corn syrup
1/4 c	margarine or butter
1/2 c	light cream
1/4 c	pecans, broken (optional)
1/4 tsp	vanilla

(Large recipe)	
1 c	sugar
7/8 c	light corn syrup
1/2 c	margarine or butter
1 c	light cream
1/2 c	pecans, broken (optional)
1/2 tsp	vanilla

TAFFY

Total Time: 30 minutes
Final Temperature: 260° F, hard caramels;
250° F, chewy caramels

1. Test boiling point of water on thermometer, as described in Penuche Recipe, Step 1.
2. In a 1-quart (small recipe) or 2-quart (large recipe) saucepan, combine all ingredients except the vanilla.
3. Stir slowly while heating the mixture to a boil. Stir occasionally as the candy is boiled to its final temperature of 265° F.

(Small recipe)	
1 c	sugar
1/4 c	light corn syrup
1/4 c	water
1/8 tsp	cream of tartar
1/2 tsp	vanilla

(Large recipe)	
2 c	sugar
1/2 c	light corn syrup
1/2 c	water
1/4 tsp	cream of tartar
1 tsp	vanilla

4. Remove from the heat, stir in the vanilla, and pour onto a large, buttered platter.
5. Allow to cool until the taffy can be handled easily without burning the hands.
6. Grease the hands, and begin to pull some of the taffy. Pull it into long strands, double it back, and pull again.
7. Keep repeating this process until the candy is very light in color and a bit porous.
8. Twist into a rope about 3/4" in diameter.
9. Cut into pieces with kitchen shears.

PEANUT BRITTLE

Total Time: 30 minutes
Final Temperature: 290° F

1. Test boiling point of water on thermometer, as described in Penuche Recipe, Step 1.
2. In a 1-quart (small recipe) or 2-quart (large recipe) saucepan, combine the first three ingredients.
3. Stir slowly while heating the solution to 240° F.
4. Add the blanched, unroasted peanuts (and a dash of salt, if desired).
5. Continue boiling the candy to a temperature of 290° F, stirring slowly to keep candy from burning.
6. Remove from the heat, and stir in butter or margarine and soda.
7. Pour onto a greased or teflon-coated jelly roll pan.
8. Flex pan to loosen candy.
9. Break into pieces when cool.

(Small recipe)

1 c	*sugar*
1/2 c	*light corn syrup*
1/2 c	*water*
1 c	*unroasted peanuts*
1 tsp	*butter or margarine*
1/8 tsp	*baking soda*

(Large recipe)

2 c	sugar
1c	light corn syrup
1 c	water
2 c	unroasted peanuts
2 tsp	butter or margarine
1/4 tsp	baking soda

VOCABULARY

Crystalline

Amorphous

Inversion

Saturated solution

Super-saturated solution

Hygroscopic

Acid hydrolysis

Invert sugar

EVALUATION OF LABORATORY PRODUCTS — CANDIES

RECIPE	TYPE OF CANDY	FLAVOR	CONSISTENCY	TEXTURE
Penuche				
Fudge				
Fondant				
Divinity				
Almond toffee				
Caramels				
Taffy				
Peanut brittle				

Chapter 13
Beverages

Tea and coffee provide the background fabric for many meetings and social occasions. The way in which these two classic and universal beverages is served may differ widely from country to country and even within parts of a country, but they still serve as classic symbols of hospitality. You will find that entertaining is easier if you are able to prepare and serve them. After you master the basics, you can explore the many variations that currently are available to add variety and interest to your meals. You will also learn to make cocoa and hot chocolate in this chapter.

KEY CONCEPTS — BEVERAGES

1) The color, aroma, and flavor of tea are determined by the treatment of the leaves.

 a) Green tea is made from unfermented leaves, resulting in a pale green, somewhat astringent beverage with a light aroma.

 b) Oolong tea leaves have been fermented a bit and yield a moderately golden brown beverage with a mild flavor and pleasing aroma.

 c) Black tea is made from leaves that have been allowed to ferment longer than oolong, producing a beverage that has a fairly deep golden brown color, a full flavor, and a satisfying brisk character.

2) Coffee beans are roasted to varying degrees to suit preferences around the world before they are ground and brewed to make the beverage.

 a) Roasting develops flavors, but grinding leads to gradual loss of aromatic and flavor compounds as well as detrimental oxidation of the oils in the beans over long storage.

 b) Coffee most commonly is made by the drip method today, although percolator coffee also is brewed; drip (dripolator) coffee is usually a bit fuller in flavor and less bitter than percolator coffee.

3) Cocoa and hot chocolate are brewed from cocoa or chocolate made from the nibs obtained from the cacao pods.

 a) Preparation of either cocoa or hot chocolate requires gelatinization of the starch that is present.

 b) Care must be taken when making cocoa or hot chocolate to avoid scorching the milk and to minimize scum formation.

TEA RECIPES
HOT TEA

Total Time: 6 minutes

Note: To compare the characteristics of green, oolong, and black teas and some of their variations, prepare the tea beverages according to the following procedure.

1. Fill teapot with hot water to preheat the pot.
2. Heat water to boiling in a 1-quart covered saucepan.
3. Pour the hot water out of the teapot.
4. Place either the tea leaves enclosed in a tea ball or the tea bags in the empty teapot.
5. Pour the freshly boiled water over the tea leaves and cover the teapot.
6. Steep for 3 minutes, remove the leaves, and serve the beverage.

(Serves two)	
2 tsp	tea leaves or 2 tea bags
1 1/2 c	boiling water

(Serves four)
4 tsp	tea leaves or 4 tea bags
3 c	boiling water

ICED TEA

Total Time: 7 minutes

1. Prepare tea infusion as above.
2. After tea infusion has been steeped 3 minutes, remove the tea leaves and pour the beverage over ice.

(Serves two)	
2 tsp	tea leaves or 2 tea bags
3/4 c	boiling water
8	ice cubes

(Serves four)
4 tsp	tea leaves or 2 tea bags
1 1/2 c	boiling water
16	ice cubes

CRITERIA FOR EVALUATION

Hot and iced teas should be sparkingly clear with no film on the surface. Color, aroma, and flavor should be pleasing and characteristic of the type of tea selected. Black tea will be amber-colored, full-flavored and not bitter, and the aroma will be pleasing. Green tea will be a pale yellow green, and the aroma will be delicate. Oolong is intermediate between these two.

COFFEE RECIPES
DRIPOLATOR

Total Time: 18 minutes

Note: Several variations of dripolators, including electric versions, now are available. Specific directions for the pot should be followed. Electric drip grind coffee should be used in the electric pots.

1. Heat water to boiling in a 1-quart covered saucepan.
2. Measure drip grind coffee into the basket and assemble the dripolator. (If desired, line the bottom of the basket with filter paper before adding the coffee.)
3. Pour the freshly boiled water into the upper container and cover.
4. When all the water has dripped through, remove the upper container and basket of grounds.
5. Place the lid on the lower pot and serve the beverage.

(Serves two)	
4 tbsp	*drip grind coffee*
	(use less, if weaker beverage desired)
1 1/2 c	*water*

(Serves four)	
8 tbsp	drip grind coffee
	(use less, if weaker beverage desired)
3 c	water

PERCOLATOR

Total Time: 6 minutes

Note: To use an automatic percolator, prepare the pot as described and plug it in. When the percolation stops, remove the basket and stem. Leave the pot plugged in to maintain the beverage at serving temperature.

1. Place water in the percolator and put regular grind coffee in the basket. Assemble the basket and its cover on the stem, place in the percolator, and put the lid on.
2. Heat on high temperature setting until the beverage begins to percolate. Adjust the heat somewhat lower to maintain a steady, but not vigorous percolation.
3. Percolate for 3 minutes. (Use longer time if stronger, more bitter beverage is preferred.)
4. Remove from heat and take out the basket containing the grounds and the stem. Serve the beverage.

(Serves two)	
4 tbsp	*regular grind coffee*
	(use less, if weaker beverage
desired)	
1 1/2 c	*water*
	(use cold water for automatic pots)

(Serves four)	
8 tbsp	regular grind coffee
	(use less, if weaker beverage desired)
3 c	water
	(use cold water for automatic pots)

A dripolater is made in three parts: a lower container for collecting the brewed beverage, a basket for the coffee grounds (drip grind), and an upper container to hold the water prior to its passage through the grounds.

A percolator consists of a container for the water, basket for holding the coffee grounds (regular grind), a hollwo stem to support the basket and permit circulation of water up and over the grounds, and a lid to contain the brewing beverage.

CRITERIA FOR EVALUATION

A quality cup of coffee will be flavorful and free of bitterness, dark and clean, relatively free of sediment, and with only a suggestion of a fat film.

EVALUATION OF LABORATORY PRODUCTS — COFFEE

RECIPE	APPEARANCE	AROMA	FLAVOR
Dripolator coffee			
Percolator coffee			

COCOA AND HOT CHOCOLATE RECIPES

COCOA

Total Time: 5 minutes

1. Mix the sugar, cocoa, and salt together.
2. Add the water and heat to boiling while stirring constantly.
3. Add the milk, and heat to simmering while stirring slowly.
4. With a rotary beater, beat briefly.
5. Serve steaming hot.

(Serves two)

1 1/2 tbsp	*sugar*
1 1/2 tbsp	*cocoa*
1/4 c	*water*
	trace salt
1 1/4 c	*milk*

(Serves four)

3 tbsp	sugar
3 tbsp	cocoa
1/2 c	water
	dash salt
2 1/2 c	milk

HOT CHOCOLATE

Total Time: 5 minutes

1. Melt chocolate in water to which sugar and salt have been added.
2. Heat to boiling.
3. Add milk gradually and heat to serving temperature.
4. Beat the hot chocolate briefly with a rotary beater.
5. Serve steaming hot.

(Serves two)

1	*square unsweetened chocolate*
1/2 c	*water*
2 tbsp	*sugar*
	trace salt
1 1/2 c	*milk*

(Serves four)

2	squares unsweetened chocolate
1 c	water
4 tbsp	sugar
	dash salt
3 c	milk

CRITERIA FOR EVALUATION

Hot chocolate or cocoa should be a pleasing, delicate chocolate flavor, with no trace of scorching. There should not be a scum nor a sediment.

RECIPE	APPEARANCE	AROMA	FLAVOR
Hot chocolate			
Cocoa			

VOCABULARY

Oolong tea

Green tea

Black tea

Polyphenols

Astringent

Caffeine

Caffeol

Theine

Tannins

Scum formation

Chapter 14
Gelatin

Gelatin is used in gelling some salads and desserts. Flavored gelatin can be used, or you may prefer to select a recipe such as tomato aspic or lemon chiffon pie that will utilize unflavored gelatin. Either type of gelatin needs to be made with care to assure that the gelatin is dissolved completely; rubbery or chewy areas result when gelatin is not totally dissolved. Flavored gelatin has been ground to a fairly fine powder and is dispersed with sugar or a sweetener to make dispersion of the gelatin quite easy. However, unflavored gelatin should be hydrated in cold water (1/4 c cold water to 1 envelope of unflavored gelatin) until no dry particles of gelatin remain before the hot liquid is added to dissolve the gelatin. Failure to do this initial step makes it much harder to dissolve the gelatin in the hot liquid.

KEY CONCEPTS — GELATIN

1) Gelatin and water form a sol when hot, but the sol transforms into a gel when the concentration of gelatin is adequate and the temperature is cold enough.

   a) Complete solution of gelatin in the correct amount of liquid is necessary to form the sol; adequate chilling time to establish a gel structure and refrigerated storage until serving time then will yield a high quality gelatin product.

   b) Gelatin sols that are chilled to the point that they are just beginning to thicken can be beaten into stable foams with excellent volume if the foam is refrigerated after whipping is finished.

RECIPES
APRICOT SALAD

Total Time: 1 hour

1. In the appropriate pan, dissolve the gelatin in the boiling water. Stir continuously across all portions of the container until no granules of gelatin can be seen.
2. Add ice cubes and stir until gelatin begins to congeal. Remove pieces of ice.
3. Add the salad marshmallows and the drained fruits.
4. Chill in refrigerator while preparing the topping.
5. Blend the sugar, flour, egg, and apricot juice together, and cook over boiling water until mixture thickens.
6. Remove from heat and add margarine or butter.
7. Cool in freezer.
8. Beat the whipping cream until stiff.
9. Fold the cooked mixture into the whipped cream, and then spread on the congealed gelatin.
10. Garnish with pecans.

Note: Pieces of fruit and other ingredients to be incorporated in gelatin salads are added when the gelatin begins to congeal. If they are added earlier, they will float to the top of the salad rather than being distributed uniformly.

(Use loaf pan)
- 1 small package orange-flavored gelatin
- 1 c water, boiling
- 1/2 tray of ice cubes
- 1/3 c salad marshmallows
- 1 3/4 c canned apricot halves, drained
- 1 c canned pineapple chunks, drained

Topping:
- 1/4 c sugar
- 1 1/2 tsp flour
- 1/2 egg, beaten
- 1/4 c apricot juice
- 1 tbsp margarine or butter
- 1/2 c whipping cream
- pecans for garnishing

(Use 8x8" pan)

1		large package orange-flavored gelatin
2	c	water, boiling
1		tray of ice cubes
2/3	c	salad marshmallows
3 1/2	c	canned apricot halves, drained
2	c	canned pineapple chunks, drained

Topping:

1/2	c	sugar
1	tbsp	flour
1		egg, beaten
1/2	c	apricot juice
2	tbsp	margarine or butter
1	c	whipping cream
		pecans for garnishing

TRI-COLOR SALAD

Total Time: 1 1/2 hour

1. Mix the lime-flavored gelatin and boiling water carefully until gelatin is completely dissolved.
2. Add the ice and stir until gelatin begins to congeal. Remove any ice.
3. Stir in the celery.
4. Place in mold or pan, and chill while preparing the next layer.
5. Blend together the cream cheese, salad dressing, and sugar.
6. Whip the cream until stiff and blend in cream cheese mixture.
7. In a bowl, dissolve the lemon-flavored gelatin completely in the water.
8. Stir in the marshmallows.
9. When marshmallows have melted, add ice and stir until gelatin begins to congeal. Remove any ice.
10. Add the crushed pineapple and cream cheese mixture.
11. Spread over the lime layer, and return to refrigerator.
12. Thoroughly dissolve the cherry-flavored gelatin in the boiling water.
13. Add the ice cubes, and stir slowly.
14. When the gelatin begins to congeal, quickly remove the remaining ice.

(Use loaf pan or 1-quart mold)

Lime layer:
- 1/2 small package lime-flavored gelatin
- 1/2 c boiling water
- 1/4 tray of ice cubes
- 1/4 c celery, chopped

Lemon layer:
- 1 1/2 oz cream cheese
- 1/4 c salad dressing
- 1/4 c sugar
- 1/2 c whipping cream
- 1/2 small package lemon-flavored gelatin
- 1/2 c boiling water
- 8 marshmallows
- 1/4 tray of ice cubes
- 1/2 c crushed pineapple, drained[1]

Cherry layer:
- 1/2 small package cherry-flavored gelatin
- 1/2 c boiling water
- 1/2 tray ice cubes
- 1/4 c chopped walnuts

TRI-COLOR SALAD (CONTINUED)

15. Stir in the nuts.
16. Pour over the lemon layer, and return to refrigerator. Refrigerate until set firmly before serving.

(Use 8x8" pan or 2-quart mold)

Lime layer:

1	small package lime-flavored gelatin
1 c	boiling water
1/2	tray of ice cubes
1/2 c	celery, chopped

Lemon layer:

3 oz	cream cheese
1/2 c	salad dressing
1/2 c	sugar
1 c	whipping cream
1	small package lemon-flavored gelatin
1 c	boiling water
16	marshmallows
1/2	tray of ice cubes
1 c	crushed pineapple, drained[1]

Cherry layer:

1	small package cherry-flavored gelatin
1 c	boiling water
1	tray ice cubes
1/2 c	chopped walnuts

[1]Use canned pineapple. Frozen or fresh pineapple will cause gelatin to be fluid due to the action of the enzyme, bromelin, in the products.

CRAB-TOMATO ASPIC SALAD

Total Time: 3 hour

1. Hydrate gelatin in cold water.
2. Simmer tomato juice, celery salt, bay leaf, lemon juice, and onion 15 minutes.
3. Strain tomato mixture before stirring in the gelatin. Stir until all traces of gelatin particles are gone.
4. Chill until starting to thicken; immediately stir in celery and crab.
5. Pour into individual molds or one large ring or other shaped mold.
6. Chill until ready to unmold and serve.

(Serves 3)	
1	*envelope unflavored gelatin*
1/4 c	*cold water*
1 c	*tomato juice*
1/4 tsp	*celery salt*
1/2	*bay leaf*
1 tbsp	*lemon juice*
1/2	*medium onion, sliced*
1/4 c	*diced celery*
3 oz	*canned or fresh crab*

(Serves 6)	
2	envelopes unflavored gelatin
1/2 c	cold water
2 c	tomato juice
1/2 tsp	celery salt
1	bay leaf
2 tbsp	lemon juice
1	medium onion, sliced
1/2 c	diced celery
6 oz	canned or fresh crab

SPARKLING SALAD

Total Time: ~3 hour

1. Dissolve the gelatin completely in the boiling water.
2. Cool to room temperature.
3. Stir in the gingerale, drained fruits, and banana.
4. Pour into molds and chill until firm.

Note: Additional gelatin recipes appear in Chapter 4 (Salads) and Chapter 11 (Pies).

(Makes 4 individual molds)		
1	*small package lemon-flavored gelatin*	
1 c	*boiling water*	
1 c	*gingerale*	
1 1/4 c	*pineapple chunks*[1]	
1/2 c	*mandarin oranges, canned*	
1	*sliced banana*	

(Makes 8 individual molds)	
1	large package lemon-flavored gelatin
2 c	boiling water
2 c	gingerale
2 1/2 c	pineapple chunks[1]
1 c	mandarin oranges, canned
2	sliced bananas

[1]Use canned pineapple. frozen or fresh pineapple will cause gelatin to be fluid due to the action of the enzyme, bromelin, in these products.

STRAWBERRY BAVARIAN CREAM

Total Time: 1 hour

1. Soften the gelatin in cold water.
2. Drain the juice from the strawberries and heat just to a boil.
3. Dissolve the gelatin completely in the hot juice.
4. Stir in the berries, sugar, and lemon juice.
5. Chill until the mixture begins to thicken just a little.
6. Beat with a rotary beater until foamy.
7. Fold in the stiffly beaten whipped cream.
8. Chill in either a mold or pile into sherbet glasses or individual molds.

(Serves 4)		
1	*envelope unflavored gelatin*	
1/4 c	*cold water*	
1	*package frozen strawberries*	
2 tbsp	*sugar*	
1 tsp	*lemon juice*	
1 c	*whipping cream*	

(Serves 8)	
2	envelopes unflavored gelatin
1/2 c	cold water
2	packages frozen strawberries
1/4 c	sugar
2 tsp	lemon juice
2 c	whipping cream

UNMOLDING GELATIN PRODUCTS

1) Be sure gelatin is set firmly.
2) Remove from refrigerator immediately before unmolding the gelatin.
3) Unmold by a fleeting dip in hot water, quickly followed by a sharp shake to loosen the gelatin. Be careful to avoid letting water actually come in contact with the gelatin.
4) Place a plate inverted on the top of the mold.
5) Quickly flip the plate and gelatin over together. The gelatin should slip easily onto the plate. Be careful not to overheat the gelatin. This causes the pattern of the mold to be indistinct in the unmolded product.
6) Return unmolded gelatin to the refrigerator until ready to serve.

VOCABULARY

Gelatin

Gelation

Collagen

Foam

Gel

Bromelin

Proteolytic enzyme

EVALUATION OF LABORATORY PRODUCTS — GELATIN

RECIPE	NOTES ON COLOR, TEXTURE, FLAVOR, OR OTHER QUALITIES	COMMENTS OR SUGGESTIONS FOR MAKING OR USING THIS PRODUCT IN THE FUTURE

Chapter 15
Meal Management

Now that you have completed the preceding chapters, you have the basic knowledge necessary to prepare all parts of a meal. The trick is to plan the entire meal so that it meets nutritional needs while also being pleasing to eat without leaving you exhausted or financially pained. There really is a great deal to coordinate when you are planning and preparing meals.

This chapter provides you the chance to begin to put your growing knowledge of food preparation to good use. Accept the challenge and see how satisfying and rewarding meal management can be. The recipes in previous chapters can serve as your springboard to adventures in the kitchen. There are many other resources you may also wish to explore as you stretch your adventures in meal planning.

ASPECTS OF PLANNING

A good meal requires sound planning of time and budget as well as a knowledge of preparing specific foods. The successful cook has mastered the management of resources, the science and practical skills of food preparation, basic knowledge of nutrition, and the ability to apply aesthetic and psychological principles. The following laboratory experiences provide the format needed to illustrate all aspects of good meal management.

NUTRITION

The total plan of the day's menu should be developed carefully to provide the daily servings recommended in the Food Guide Pyramid:

> Breads, cereals, rice, and pasta at 6–11 servings
> Fruits at 2–4 servings
> Milk and dairy products at 2–3 servings
> Meat and meat substitutes at 2 or more servings

For most people it is important to include a good source of ascorbic acid at breakfast. To insure good nutrition to start the day right, include an egg or other good protein source along with a glass of milk and some cereal or toast. Lunch and dinner should be planned to round out the recommended servings in all the groups of the Food Guide Pyramid plus enough additional food for satisfaction and energy.

KEY CONCEPTS — MEAL MANAGEMENT

1) Meals need to be planned to provide the recommended intake of nutrients in a way that is pleasing to eat and that fits your lifestyle.

2) Menus can be evaluated on the basis of the nutritive value, sensory satisfaction (flavor, color, aroma, and texture), and cost (time, energy, and money).

AESTHETICS

Plan the foods in the menu for optimum color, texture appearance, and flavor appeal. With the menu and the occasion in mind, select the table setting and service to fit the situation. Think carefully about the total setting for the meal so that it is pleasing to the eye, mind, and palate.

TIME

A well-planned time schedule is essential when first learning to coordinate an entire meal. Be sure to plan the time needed for setting the table, preparing foods for cooking, and serving the food. This takes careful thought if all the details are arranged so that the meal is served on time.

COST

Money management can be learned by planning meals using grocery ads to meet the cost limitations. For the most experience, plan a meal and then see what variations might be made to adjust the basic plan to a low, medium, or high cost meal. If possible, do the actual purchasing of food at the grocery store.

Efficient and economical food buying and preparation are boons to everyone with responsibilities for meal preparation. Many types of information are available to today's consumers to aid them in these tasks. The following listings are provided for convenience when shopping for and preparing food.

EQUIVALENT MEASURES

1 tbsp	=	3 tsp
1 fl oz	=	2 tbsp
1/4 c	=	4 tbsp
1 c	=	16 tbsp or 8 fl oz
1 pt	=	2 c
1 qt	=	2 pt or 4 c
1 gal	=	4 qt or 8 pt or 16c

EQUIVALENT WEIGHTS

1 oz	=	38.35 g
1 lb	=	16 oz or 453.6 g
1 kg	=	2.21 lb

SUBSTITUTIONS

1 c nonfat milk	=	1 c minus 1 tbsp of water + 1/3 c instant nonfat dry milk
1 c buttermilk	=	1 c yogurt
1 c milk	=	1 c buttermilk + 1/2 tsp soda + 1 tsp butter; reduce baking powder by 1 tsp in batters and doughs
1 c sour milk or buttermilk	=	1 tbsp lemon juice or vinegar + milk to equal 1 c
1 tbsp cornstarch	=	2 tbsp flour
1 c cake flour	=	1 c – 2 tbsp all purpose flour
1 package active dry yeast (1 oz)	=	1 tbsp active dry yeast
1 package active dry yeast (1 oz)	=	1 cake compressed yeast
1 tsp baking powder	=	1/4 tsp baking soda + 3/4 tsp cream of tartar
1 tsp baking powder	=	1/4 tsp baking soda + 1/3 c molasses
1 tsp baking powder	=	1/4 tsp baking soda + 1/2 c sour milk
1 oz unsweetened chocolate	=	3 tbps cocoa (unsweetened) + 1 tbsp margarine or butter

APPROXIMATE YIELD EQUIVALENTS

1 c whipping cream	=	2 c whipped
1 lb butter or margarine	=	2 c
1 lb cheese	=	4 c grated cheese
1 lb all purpose flour	=	4 c
1 c rice	=	1 2/3 c cooked rice
1 c bulghur	=	2 3/4 c cooked bulghur
1 c macaroni or spaghetti	=	2 1/4 c cooked pasta
1 c noodles	=	1 1/4 c cooked noodles
1 yolk	=	1 tbsp
1 white	=	2 1/2 tbsp
1 lb granulated sugar	=	3 c
1 lb brown sugar	=	2 1/4 c
1 lb nuts	=	3–4 c, depending on type of nuts
1 lb coffee	=	5 c
1 lb coffee	=	40–50 c prepared beverage
1 lb soda crackers	=	5 c medium fine crumbs
1 lb graham crackers	=	4 1/3 c crumbs

COMMON CONTAINER SIZES

CONTAINER (INDUSTRY TERM)	CONSUMER DESCRIPTION		PRINCIPAL PRODUCTS
	~ NET WT./FL. OZ. (CHECK LABEL)	~ CUPS	
8 oz	8 oz	1	Fruits, vegetables, specialties for small families. (2 servings)
Picnic	10 1/2 to 12 oz	1 1/4	Mainly condensed soups. Some fruits, vegetables, meat, fish, specialties. (2–3 servings)
12 oz (vac)	12 oz	1 1/2	Principally for vacuum pack corn. (3–4 servings)
No. 300	14–16 oz (14 oz to 1 lb)	1 3/4	Pork and beans, baked beans, meat products, cranberry sauce, blueberries, specialties (3–4 servings)
No. 303	16–17 oz (1 lb to 1 lb 1 oz	2	Principal size for fruits and vegetables. Some meat products, ready-to-serve soups, specialties. (4 servings)
No. 2	20 oz or 18 fl oz (1 lb 4 oz or 1 pt 2 fl oz)	2 1/2	Juices, ready-to-serve soups, some specialties, pineapple, apple slices. No longer in popular use for most fruits and vegetables. (5 servings)
No. 2 1/2	27–29 oz (1 lb 11 oz to 1 lb 13 oz)	3 1/2	Fruits, some vegetables (pumpkin, sauerkraut, spinach and other greens, tomatoes). (5–7 servings)
No. 3 cyl or 46 fl oz	51 oz or 46 fl oz (3 lb 3 oz or 1 qt 14 fl oz)	5 3/4	Fruit and vegetable juices, pork and beans. Institutional size for condensed soups, some vegetables. (10–12 servings)
No. 10	6 1/2 lb to 7 lb 5 oz	12–13	Institutional size for fruits, vegetables and some other foods. (25 servings)
Other			Meats, poultry, fish, and seafood are advertised and sold almost entirely under weight terminology.

SUGGESTED ACTIVITIES

1) Using the forms which follow, plan the meals for a day for a family of four.

2) Prepare one of the meals planned and evaluate the following:
   a) time plan,
   b) the cost of the meal,
   c) the accuracy of the market order,
   d) the quality of the prepared food,
   e) the table setting,
   f) the service.

BREAKFAST MENU

TIME SCHEDULE

Pre-preparation:

Day of Meal:

Type of Service:

Serving time:

TABLE SETTING

Cloth or mats:

Dishes:

Silverware:

Glassware:

Accessories:

Sketch of place setting:

MARKET ORDER – BREAKFAST

FOOD	QUANTITY	UNIT PRICE	TOTAL COST
Dairy Products			
Meat, fish, poultry, eggs			
Fresh produce			
Canned and frozen foods			
Bread and cereals			
Fats and oils			
Miscellaneous			

Total cost of meal: _____

Cost per person: _____

LUNCH MENU

TIME SCHEDULE

Pre-preparation:

Day of Meal:

Type of Service:

Serving time:

TABLE SETTING

Cloth or mats:

Dishes:

Silverware:

Glassware:

Accessories:

Sketch of place setting:

MARKET ORDER – LUNCH

FOOD	QUANTITY	UNIT PRICE	TOTAL COST
Dairy Products			
Meat, fish, poultry, eggs			
Fresh produce			
Canned and frozen foods			
Bread and cereals			
Fats and oils			
Miscellaneous			

Total cost of meal: _____

Cost per person: _____

DINNER MENU

TIME SCHEDULE

Pre-preparation:

Day of Meal:

Type of Service:

Serving time:

TABLE SETTING

Cloth or mats:

Dishes:

Silverware:

Glassware:

Accessories:

Sketch of place setting:

MARKET ORDER – DINNER

FOOD	QUANTITY	UNIT PRICE	TOTAL COST
Dairy Products			
Meat, fish, poultry, eggs			
Fresh produce			
Canned and frozen foods			
Bread and cereals			
Fats and oils			
Miscellaneous			

Total cost of meal: _____

Cost per person: _____

Complete the following chart with the menus used for breakfast, lunch, and dinner and evaluate the nutritional adequacy of the menus. If shortages exist in particular categories, suggest ways in which the menus could be improved.

SUMMARY CHART OF SAMPLE DAY'S MENUS

FOOD GROUP	MENU ITEM	SERVINGS		ADEQUACY
		RECOMMENDED	ACTUAL	
Bread, cereal, rice, pasta		6–11		
Vegetables		3–5		
Fruits		2–4		
Milk, yogurt, cheese		2–3		
Meat, poultry, fish, dry beans, eggs, nuts		5–7 oz		
Fats, oils, sweets		Sparingly		

Recommendations:

Chapter 16
Food Preservation

Food can be preserved at home by canning, freezing, drying, pickling with acid, and preserving with sugar or salt. The method used most commonly today is freezing because of its speed and convenience (especially for preserving leftovers). Commercial food companies include these techniques as well as irradiation or other techniques that require more sophisticated equipment than is available in the home. In this chapter, you will find a few recipes for preserving food at home. If you happen to live in an area where you have access to produce at good prices when the various crops are in season, you may find that food preservation is a task that you will enjoy and that will be cost effective. However, many people today have limited free time and little access to economical produce buys; for them, food preservation at home probably is not feasible.

KEY CONCEPTS — FOOD PRESERVATION

1) Food to be preserved should be of high quality so that the end product can be of sufficient quality to justify the time and energy spent in preserving it.

2) Food preservation requires use of some method for stopping or greatly retarding growth of microorganisms and chemical reactions within the food. For example, high temperatures or very low ones effectively preserve food by killing or greatly retarding microorganisms and halting biochemical processes.

3) Preservation makes it possible to carry excess food supplies through to times when a particular food may be scarce or less abundant.

CANNING RECIPES
APPLES

Water bath time: 20 minutes

1. Wash jars in hot, soapy water, and rinse thoroughly in very hot water. Be sure to use only glass canning jars in good condition.
2. Combine the water and sugar, and heat to simmering.
3. Keep warm and covered while paring, coring, and slicing apples.
4. Hold sliced apples in water containing a small amount of lemon juice until the apples are ready for canning.
5. Place the apple slices in the hot syrup, and boil gently for 5 minutes.
6. Fill jars with hot apples; be sure to leave 1/2" headspace.
7. Pour the boiling syrup over the fruit until the jar is filled to 1/2" from the top of the jar.
8. Run a rubber spatula around the inside of the jar to release all air bubbles that may be trapped by the fruit. Put on the lid, following the directions for the type of cap being used. (Dome caps are prepared by tightening the metal band, and zinc caps are tightened with a new rubber ring and then loosened slightly.)
9. Place the jars on a rack in a boiling water bath and boil for 20 minutes.
10. The water level should be maintained at 1–2" above the tops of the jars throughout the processing period.
11. Remove the canner, and cool slowly for half a day. Be sure to tighten zinc caps slowly as soon as the jars are removed from the water bath.
12. After the jars are cooled completely, check the seal. The center of the cap is pulled downward if the seal is good. Remove metal bands if using dome caps.

(Makes 1 quart)

1 1/2 lb	Rome Beauty, Winesap, or Jonathan apples
1 1/2 c	sugar
2 c	water
1/2 tsp	ascorbic acid

(Makes 16 quarts)

1	bushel Rome Beauty, Winesap, or Jonathan apples
9 c	sugar
12 c	water
4 tsp	ascorbic acid

PEACHES

Water bath time: 30 minutes

1. Wash jars in hot soapy water, and rinse thoroughly in very hot water. Be sure to use only glass canning jars in good condition.
2. Combine the water and sugar and heat to simmering.
3. Keep warm in a covered saucepan while preparing the peaches.
4. Wash the peaches before blanching them in boiling water for 30 seconds to loosen their skins.
5. Immediately after blanching, dip peaches in cold water.
6. Quickly peel the peaches, cut them in half, and remove the pit and red fibers surrounding the seed.
7. Place peaches in water containing lemon juice or ascorbic acid to prevent discoloration.
8. Pack each peach half, pit side down.
9. Pour hot syrup over peaches. Fruit and syrup should be at least 1/2" below the top of the jar.
10. Use a rubber spatula to release bubbles of air from the jar.
11. Cap as described in the procedure for canning apples and process for 30 minutes, as described above.

(Makes 1 quart)

2 lb	peaches, freestone
1 c	sugar
1 c	water
1/4 tsp	ascorbic acid or lemon juice

(Makes 10 quarts)

1	lug peaches, freestone
8 c	sugar
8 c	water
2 1/2 tsp	ascorbic acid or lemon juice

PEARS

Water bath time: 25 minutes

1. Wash jars in hot, soapy water, and rinse thoroughly in very hot water. Be sure to use only glass canning jars in good condition.
2. Prepare the syrup as described for peaches.
3. Wash, pare, and quarter the pears.
4. Hold in water containing lemon juice.
5. Add pear quarters to the syrup, and boil gently 5 minutes.
6. Pack immediately.
7. Pour hot syrup over the fruit, being sure to leave 1/2" head-space for both the fruit and the syrup.
8. Put the jars on a rack in the water bath, which is half filled with boiling water.
9. Maintain the water level 1–2" above the top of the jars during the 25 minutes boiling period.
10. Cool and check the seal as described above.

(Makes 1 quart)

2 lb	pears
2/3 c	sugar
1 1/2 c	water
1/4 tsp	lemon juice

(Makes 15 quarts)

1	box pears
6 c	sugar
12 c	water
3 3/4 tsp	lemon juice

GREEN BEANS

Pressure cooker time: 20 minutes at 10 pounds for pints
25 minutes at 10 pounds for quarts

1. Wash jars in hot, soapy water, and rinse thoroughly in very hot water. Be sure to use only glass canning jars in good condition.
2. Wash beans, break off ends, and cut or leave whole.
3. Boil in salted water for 5 minutes.
4. Pack jar loosely, leaving 1" headspace for vegetable and liquid.
5. Process according to pressure cooker information. Add 20 additional minutes if using a pressure saucepan.
6. Place jars on rack, leaving space between.
7. Exhaust air from cooker (about 10 minutes).
8. Regulate heat to maintain pressure. Gauge will jiggle several times each minute. (Read directions for pressure device.)
9. Process the length of time indicated.
10. Let cooker return to room temperature before starting to remove jars.
11. Let cool, as above, and check seals.

(Makes 1 pint)

1 lb	green beans
2 c	water
1/2 tsp	salt

(Makes 2 pints)

2 lb	green beans
4 c	water
1 tsp	salt

BEET PICKLES

Water bath time: 30 minutes

1. Wash jars in hot, soapy water, and rinse thoroughly in very hot water. Be sure to use only glass canning jars in good condition.
2. Wash beets and cut off tops, but leave stems and tap root.
3. Put beets in pan of boiling water to just cover the vegetable; boil until tender.
4. Peel and slice the beets into slices about 1/4" thick.
5. Meanwhile, simmer all of the other ingredients in a covered saucepan for 10 minutes.
6. Pack beets and add hot, spiced liquid after the cinnamon and cloves have been removed.
7. Leave 1/2" headspace for the beets and the juice. Process as described above for 30 minutes.

(Makes 1 pint)

1/3 c	sugar
7/8 c	distilled vinegar
1/4 c	water
1/4 tsp	salt
1/2 tsp	pickling spices
2	whole cloves
1/3	stick cinnamon
2 c	sliced, cooked beets

(Makes 3 pints)

1 c	sugar
2 3/4 c	distilled vinegar
3/4 c	water
3/4 tsp	salt
1 1/2 tsp	pickling spices
6	whole cloves
1	stick cinnamon
6 c	sliced, cooked beets

DILL PICKLES

Water bath time: 15 minutes

1. Wash jars in hot, soapy water, and rinse thoroughly in very hot water. Be sure to use only glass canning jars in good condition.
2. Tie the spices in cheesecloth and simmer in a covered saucepan with the sugar, salt, water, and vinegar for 15 minutes.
3. Cut the cucumbers in halves or spears and pack into jars.
4. Remove spices from the salt brine.
5. Heat the brine to boiling, and pour over the cucumbers.
6. Put a sprig of dill weed in each jar.
7. Leave 1/4" headspace in each jar.
8. Heat for 15 minutes in a boiling water bath as described above.

(Makes 1 pint)

6	medium cucumbers
3 1/2 tsp	salt
1/2 c	vinegar
1/2 c	water
1 1/2 tsp	mixed pickling spices
1 1/2 tbsp	sugar
	sprig dry dill

(Makes 4 pints)

24	medium cucumbers
4 1/3 tbsp	salt
2 1/4 c	vinegar
1 1/4 c	water
2 tbsp	mixed pickling spices
6 tbsp	sugar
4	sprigs dry dill

PEACH PICKLES

Water bath time: 10 minutes

1. Wash jars in hot, soapy water, and rinse thoroughly in very hot water. Be sure to use only glass canning jars in good condition.
2. Wash the peaches, and place in boiling water for 30 seconds to loosen skin.
3. Peel the peaches and place them in water containing lemon juice.
4. Combine the vinegar, water, sugar, and cinnamon; bring to boiling.
5. Place a clove in each peach, and put the peaches in the boiling liquid.
6. Continue boiling until the peaches are heated through.
7. Put the peaches in glass jars.
8. Pour the boiling syrup over the peaches, leaving 1/4" headspace.
9. Process as described above for 10 minutes.

(Makes 1 pint)

1 c	white vinegar
1 c	water
1/4 tsp	lemon juice
1 c	granulated sugar
1 1/2	sticks cinnamon
4	whole cloves
4	small peaches

(Makes 6 pints)

2 c	white vinegar
2 c	water
1 tsp	lemon juice
2 c	granulated sugar
3	sticks cinnamon
24	whole cloves
24	small peaches

FREEZING

BROCCOLI

Thoroughly wash fresh broccoli to remove all dirt and possible insects. Trim the leaves from the stalk and cut the stalk where it begins to be slightly woody. If stalks are large, split in quarters lengthwise. Place in a perforated basket and immerse in a large kettle of rapidly boiling water for 3 minutes (blanch 4 minutes if preparation is being done at 4,000 feet elevation or higher). Immediately transfer the blanched broccoli into a large kettle of ice water for 3–4 minutes. Package the drained broccoli in plastic or other relatively air-tight containers. Pack tightly with an absolute minimum of air space. Label the container with the contents and the date of processing. Put in freezer immediately.

ASPARAGUS

Wash asparagus very carefully to remove all traces of sand and dirt. Trim asparagus stalks to remove woody portion of the stlk. Leave in spears or cut into 1" segments. Blanch in a large kettle of rapidly boiling water for 2–4 minutes, depending upon the thickness of the stalk. Chill a comparable length of time in a large kettle of ice water. Package, label, and store as suggested for broccoli.

SPINACH

Wash spinach thoroughly in a sinkful of cold water to remove all sand. Break off the ends of the stems and any bruised leaves. Blanch the spinach in a large kettle of rapidly boiling water for 2 minutes. Immediately plunge into a large kettle of ice water for 2 minutes. Package, label, and store as suggested for broccoli.

CORN

Remove the husk, being careful to clean away the silks. Wash well. Blanch 4 minutes if corn is to be frozen off the cob and 8 minutes if it is to be left on the cob. Chill in ice water for the same length of time as the blanching period. Cut corn from cob, if desired. Package, label, and store as suggested for broccoli.

GREEN BEANS

Wash thoroughly. Cut off the ends and cut as desired or leave whole. Blanch 3 minutes in a large kettle of rapidly boiling water and chill 3 minutes in ice water. Package, label, and store as suggested for broccoli.

STRAWBERRIES

Wash berries well and look them over carefully. Cut away any soft or bruised spots. Pull off the caps. If desired, slice strawberries. Spread 2 c of fruit in a shallow pan and sprinkle 6 tbsp of sugar over the fruit. Stir very carefully until all of the fruit is coated with sugar and the sugar has dissolved to make a syrup over the fruit. Pack carefully into a plastic container or other relatively air-tight package. Label with the contents and the date of processing. Freeze at once.

PEACHES

Wash peaches well. Dip peaches in boiling water for 30 seconds to loosen the skin. Peel the peaches and cut away any bruised or spoiled portions. Cut in half, remove pit, and slice, if desired. Put 1/2 c of sugar syrup in a plastic container. Fill the container with the sliced fruit and pour enough sugar syrup over the fruit to completely cover the fruit. The sugar syrup is made by heating together 1 1/2 c of sugar and 2 c of water until the sugar is completely dissolved. Stir in 1/4 tsp ascorbic acid and thoroughly chill the syrup before using it with fruits. Avoid any delay from the time the fruit is peeled until the peaches are covered with the syrup so that discoloration of the peaches will not occur. The syrup prevents the browning that occurs as a result of oxidation. Seal the fruit tightly, label, and freeze immediately.

PEARS

Wash and peel pears. Prepare syrup as outlined for freezing peaches. Cut pears into halves, quarters, or slices and package as indicated for peaches.

Cut pineapple into slices, spears, or cubes, as desired. Put fruit carefully into plastic container. Seal, label, and freeze promptly.

JAMS AND JELLIES

Before beginning to make jams and jellies, wash the jars carefully in soapy water and rinse them well with scalding water. Melt paraffin carefully in a double boiler. Keep the heat relatively low, but be sure the paraffin is fluid when needed. Be very careful to avoid splashing hot paraffin. Paraffin, when carelessly handled, presents a serious fire and burn hazard.

JAM AND JELLY RECIPES

FREEZER STRAWBERRY JAM

Total time: 25 minutes

1. Wash jars well and rinse thoroughly in very hot water.
2. Wash the strawberries well. Remove the caps and cut away any spoiled or bruised areas.
3. Crush the fruit well.
4. Combine the fruit, sugar, and lemon juice, and let sit 20 minutes.
5. Heat the powdered pectin and water together until it boils and continue to boil 1 minute. If liquid pectin is used, omit water, and do not heat the pectin.
6. Combine the liquid pectin or the rehydrated powdered pectin with the fruit-sugar mixture and stir for 3 minutes.
7. Pour into jars and cover tightly. Store in refrigerator for a maximum of 3 weeks or in the freezer for longer storage.

(Makes 3 jelly jars)
2 c	fresh strawberries
2 c	sugar
1 tbsp	lemon juice
1/4	bottle liquid pectin
or	
1/2	package powdered pectin
6 tbsp	water (omit if using liquid pectin)

(Makes 6 jelly jars)
4 c	fresh strawberries
4 c	sugar
2 tbsp	lemon juice
1/2	bottle liquid pectin
or	
1	package powdered pectin
3/4 c	water (omit if using liquid pectin)

FROZEN STRAWBERRY JAM

Total time: 10 minutes

1. Wash jars well and rinse thoroughly in very hot water.
2. Thaw berries to room temperature.
3. Stir in the sugar completely. Be sure there is no gritty feeling remaining. If necessary to dissolve all the sugar, warm the berries slightly.
4. Stir in the pectin very thoroughly.
5. Pour into jars.
6. Store in the refrigerator in tightly covered jars for a maximum of 6 weeks.

(Makes 3 jelly jars)
1	package frozen strawberries
1 2/3 c	sugar
1/4	bottle liquid pectin
1 tsp	lemon juice

(Makes 6 jelly jars)
2	packages frozen strawberries
3 1/3 c	sugar
1/2	bottle liquid pectin
2 tsp	lemon juice

BLUEBERRY JAM

Total time: 10 minutes

1. Wash jars well and rinse thoroughly in very hot water.
2. Crush the berries, and stir in the pectin.
3. Add the lemon juice, and heat quickly to a boil while stirring slowly.
4. Stir in the sugar, and continue stirring the mixture while it boils actively for 1 minutes.
5. Remove from the heat. Skim off the foam.
6. Alternately stir and skim off the foam for 5 minutes before pouring into jars.
7. Seal immediately with melted paraffin about 1/4" thick.

(Makes 5 jelly jars)
2 c	blueberries, fresh or frozen
1 tbsp	lemon juice
2 c	sugar
1/2	box powdered pectin
	paraffin

(Makes 9 jelly jars)
4 c	blueberries, fresh or frozen
2 tbsp	lemon juice
4 c	sugar
1	box powdered pectin
	paraffin

ORANGE MARMALADE

Total time: 45 minutes

1. Wash jars well and rinse thoroughly in very hot water.
2. With a sharp knife, cut the skin on the oranges and lemons into quarters and peel the fruit. Remove about half of the albedo (white portion of the skin).
3. Slice the remaining rind into very thin slices or shavings.
4. Add the water and soda.
5. Simmer in a covered saucepan for 20 minutes, stirring occasionally.
6. Meanwhile, remove the seeds from the fruit and cut the pulp into small pieces.
7. Add the pulp to the cooked rind, and continue simmering for 10 minutes.
8. Place 3 c of this mixture (6 c for large recipe) in a very large saucepan, and stir in the sugar.
9. Heat over high heat to a rolling boil and boil 1 minute, stirring constantly.
10. Remove from the heat and immediately stir in the liquid pectin thoroughly.
11. Alternately skim off the foam and stir the mixture for 7 minutes.
12. Put in jelly glasses.
13. Cover immediately with 1/4" of melted paraffin.

(Makes 6 jelly jars)	
3	navel oranges
2	lemons
1/8 tsp	baking soda
1 1/2 c	water
5 c	sugar
1/2	bottle liquid pectin
	paraffin

(Makes 12 jelly jars)	
6	navel oranges
4	lemons
1/4 tsp	baking soda
3 c	water
10 c	sugar
1	bottle liquid pectin
	paraffin

RHUBARB MARMALADE

Total time: 10 minutes

1. Wash jars well and rinse thoroughly in very hot water.
2. Thinly slice the well-washed rhubarb, leaving it unpeeled.
3. Heat water and rhubarb to simmering in a covered saucepan; simmer until tender (about 1 minutes).
4. Put 3 c of fruit (6 c for the large recipe) into large saucepan.
5. Stir in the sugar.
6. Bring quickly to a boil and boil hard for 1 minute.
7. Remove from heat.
8. Stir in the liquid pectin thoroughly so that it is well mixed with the fruit.
9. Stir and skim the mixture for 5 minutes to remove all traces of foam.
10. Put into jelly glasses and cover immediately with about 1/4" of melted paraffin.

(Makes 5 jelly jars)	
1 1/2 lb	rhubarb
2 tbsp	shredded orange rind
3/4 c	water
1/2	bottle liquid pectin
5 1/2 c	sugar
	paraffin

(Makes 10 jelly jars)	
3 lb	rhubarb
4 tbsp	shredded orange rind
1 1/2 c	water
1	bottle liquid pectin
11 c	sugar
	paraffin

GRAPE JELLY

Total time: 8 minutes

1. Wash jars well and rinse thoroughly in very hot water.
2. Heat the juice and sugar to a boil.
3. Stir in the liquid pectin and boil 1 minute, stirring continuously.
4. Remove from heat.
5. While cooling for 2 minutes, skim off the foam.
6. Pour into jelly glasses.
7. Immediately pour 1/4" melted paraffin over the jars of jelly.

(Makes 6 jelly jars)	
2 c	bottled grape juice
3 2/3 c	sugar
1/2	bottle liquid pectin

(Makes 12 jelly jars)	
4 c	bottled grape juice
7 c	sugar
1	bottle liquid pectin

APPLE JELLY

Total time: 25 minutes

1. Wash jars well and rinse thoroughly in very hot water.
2. Quarter unpeeled apples, and remove the stem and flower ends of each piece. Chop the quarters into small pieces. Be sure to leave in the core.
3. Put the apple pieces and the water into a kettle and quickly bring to a boil.
4. Simmer fruit 10 minutes.
5. Use a potato masher to crush the fruit and continue simmering.
6. Line a colander with two layers of cheese cloth.
7. Pour the fruit into the colander; catch the juice.
8. Measure 5 c of the juice and combine with the sugar in a large saucepan.
9. Stir constantly while heating to a boil.
10. Stir in the pectin.
11. Heat again to boiling.
12. Boil for 1 minute while stirring.
13. Remove from heat, skim off the foam, and pour into jelly glasses.
14. Cover with a layer of melted paraffin 1/4" thick.

(Makes 4 jelly jars)

4 lb	tart, ripe apples
6 1/2 c	water
7 1/2 c	sugar
1/2	bottle liquid pectin
	paraffin

(Makes 9 jelly jars)

8 lb	tart, ripe apples
13 c	water
15 c	sugar
1	bottle liquid pectin
	paraffin

RASPBERRY-PEAR JAM (WITH FRESH BERRIES)

Total time: 15 minutes

1. Wash jars well and rinse thoroughly in very hot water.
2. Quarter, core and finely chop pears; mash on the cutting board with fork and *pack* to measure.
3. Wash and pick over raspberries and *pack* into measuring cup.
4. Combine fruits, lemon juice and pectin in the kettle; bring to a boil.
5. Boil 1 minute, stirring.
6. Add sugar all at once, and cook, stirring, until it returns to a boil.
7. Boil vigorously 1 minute.
8. Remove from heat; stir and skim for about 5 minutes to cool slightly and remove foam on top.
9. Pour into hot sterilized jars; seal at once with melted paraffin.

(Makes 3 jars)

3	*fresh Bartlett pears (2 c mashed)*
2/3 c	*fresh raspberries (packed firmly)*
1 1/2 tbsp	*lemon or lime juice*
1/2	*package powdered fruit pectin*
1 3/4 c	*sugar*
	paraffin

(Makes 7 jars)

6–8	fresh Bartlett pears (2 c mashed)
1 1/4 c	fresh raspberries (packed firmly)
3 tbsp	lemon or lime juice
1	package powdered fruit pectin
3 3/4 c	sugar
	paraffin

RASPBERRY-PEAR JAM (WITH FROZEN BERRIES)

Total time: 15 minutes

1. Wash jars well and rinse thoroughly in very hot water.
2. Halve, core, and chop pears to measure about 6 c.
3. Combine all ingredients except pectin in kettle; bring to boil and boil vigorously 1 minute.
4. Remove from heat, stir in pectin and stir, skimming off foam, for 5 minutes.
5. Pour into hot sterilized jars; seal at once with melted paraffin.

(Makes 4 jars)

1 1/2 lb	*fresh Bartlett pears (3 c mashed)*
1/2	*package (5 oz) frozen raspberries thawed, undrained*
3 3/4 c	*sugar*
	dash salt
2 tbsp	*lemon juice*
1 1/2 tsp	*grated orange rind*
1/4	*bottle liquid pectin*
	paraffin

(Makes 9 jars)

3 lb	fresh Bartlett pears (3 c mashed)
1	package (10 oz) frozen raspberries thawed, undrained
7 1/2 c	sugar
1/8 tsp	salt
1/4 c	lemon juice
1 tbsp	grated orange rind
1/2	bottle liquid pectin
	paraffin

FRUIT LEATHER

Total time: 9 hours
Baking: 150° F

1. Grind fruits together until very fine.
2. Sprinkle a circle of powdered sugar (about 13" in diameter) on a bread board.
3. Place 1/3 of the fruit (1/6 for the large recipe) on the powdered sugar.
4. Coat with the sugar, and roll into a circle about 1/8" thick.
5. Place on baking sheet and bake until leather-like (8–9 hours).
6. Roll in plastic wrap when cool.
7. Store in refrigerator in a plastic bag.

Note: Fruit leathers are interesting novelty items. They are of particular interest when planning food for camping trips.

(Makes 3 sheets)

1/4 lb	dried prunes, pitted
1/4 lb	dried peaches
1/2 lb	dried apricots
1 c	powdered sugar

(Makes 6 sheets)

1/2 lb	dried prunes, pitted
1/2 lb	dried peaches
1 lb	dried apricots
2 c	powdered sugar

VOCABULARY

Pectin

Pectic acid

Pectinic acid

Protopectin

Botulism

Salmonella

Molds

Jams

Jelly

Freezer burn

EVALUATION OF LABORATORY PRODUCTS — PRESERVED FOODS

RECIPE	NOTES ON COLOR, TEXTURE, FLAVOR, OR OTHER QUALITIES	COMMENTS OR SUGGESTIONS FOR MAKING OR USING THIS PRODUCT IN THE FUTURE

Index